Empires of Dust

Empires of Dust

A Society in Regression

LAYNE WALLACE

WIPF & STOCK · Eugene, Oregon

EMPIRES OF DUST
A Society in Regression

Wipf & Stock
An Imprint of Wipf and Stock Publishers
199 W. 8th Ave., Suite 3
Eugene, OR 97401

www.wipfandstock.com

PAPERBACK ISBN: 979-8-3852-0712-1
HARDCOVER ISBN: 979-8-3852-0713-8
EBOOK ISBN: 979-8-3852-0714-5

VERSION NUMBER 07/08/25

To my wife, Molly, and my daughters.
To Marie S. Wallace.
To George H. Wallace.

Beauty will save the world

—Fyodor Dostoyevsky

Excellence is not a gift but a skill that takes practice. We do not act rightly because we are excellent,
in fact, we achieve excellence by acting rightly

—Plato

Blessed are those who hunger and thirst after righteousness for they shall be filled

—Jesus Christ of Nazareth

Contents

Preface

HE IS A HAWK, I believe. Brown-feathered with a white chest, and he is about as tall as a football standing on its end. He usually makes his appearance with his talons clutching the metal support for the streetlight just across the street from my office. With his yellow eyes, he stares at the ground below. From time to time, he will change his perch just to get a better view of the grassy patch below. Scanning for his next meal, he watches and waits. On occasion, he will soar above using rising currents of air to lift him toward the sun. Most of the time when I see him though, he is on his perch and seems quite happy to be there.

In postmodern thought, there can be no objective truth because no person can be objective. Humans have biases and cultural blinders. They have a perspective, a view. While not giving in to the first part of the postmodern claim, I readily acknowledge I have a view, a perspective. I have come to think of it as my perch.

I am a pastor, a theologian, an instructor of philosophy and religion, a writer, a husband, and a father. These form the perch from which I observe American institutions. As Edwin Freidman notes, an artist works with the medium he or she knows. So, I work with the kinds of analysis I understand. In these pages, I apply philosophical analysis, Bowen theory, and my theological training to look at US institutions. I will cite Plato or Dostoyevsky. I have even mentioned Machiavelli. Just as often, I cite sociological thinkers like Bellah or Eberstadt. My goal in mentioning these thinkers is not to get lost in minutia or gobbledygook. Abstruse philosophical debates are foreign to this text. My first goal is to see US institutions as they are, not as I wish them to be, and not as I fear them to be.

I expect some readers might disagree with me on particular examples I cite, but I hope that, even in disagreement, they will notice what I am arguing: US institutions are in a state of regression. After describing the state of regression, I point out the causes and move to reasons for hope.

Ultimately, hope is the aim of this text. It is not a hope born of delusional thinking or a hope to return to a previous, better time. Hope here is not a wish: it is a determination to make a better world for our citizens and our children.

Special thanks here to my friend Jim Lord whose last-minute help was invaluable.

Introduction

As a pastor, I have long noticed the regression of the church. The church in the US is in a significant, long-term decline. For those who love the church, the regression is both heartbreaking and terrifying. It is heartbreaking because we love the church. We believe in its mission and message. We want nothing more than for people to accept the message and join the mission. It is terrifying because we fear the future of our congregations, denominations, and people who do not have our hope.

Every year, it seems, someone is pitching a new worship plan, evangelism strategy, doctrinal correction, or reorganization to stop the regression in the church. None of them has been effective. The consistent regression has been enough to make many give in to gloom and others to fall prey to magical thinking.

At some point I noticed, however, that the church was not the only institution in regression. I looked at the family, work, and other institutions, and I concluded that something was happening across society that affected the church and all other societal institutions.

When I was younger, I would not have cared as much about institutions. They were insufferable, cumbersome, tedious, useless, and feckless, at least I thought. Despite my previous bleak outlook on institutions, I have learned that society lives because of institutions. Societies cannot function without institutions, and human life is diminished if institutions do not function well. Regressing institutions, then, are a problem for society at large. Cities collapse with ignorance and want when educational systems regress. Generations get locked into poverty. When institutions fail, life is imperiled and impoverished. Institutions matter.

The first part of this book is, then, to lay out the case of institutional regression across society. I could have written about other institutions like the legal system or the political system, but the ones I focus on here are enough, I think, to make the case that the regression of institutions is across all societal institutions. While there may be some exceptions, they are few.

Afterward, I describe some of the causes of the regression. Just as with a medical doctor, no treatment plan is effective when it treats the wrong disorder. Getting a firm grasp of the causes of the regression is central.

That, however, is not enough. The book is a book about hope. What can transform US institutions? I argue that there are resources within Western civilization that can transform and sustain our institutions and lead to societal health. It is in reconnecting to these resources that US institutions can thrive again. The solution, however, is ethical and spiritual. It is magical thinking to conclude the causes of regression are technical. If they were technical, then a technical solution from Congress or another source could provide the answer. Regression in US institutions is not the result of a series of technical mistakes across society. The regression is primarily an ethical and moral problem. Any real solution will be found in an ethical and spiritual renewal.

1

Saint Joseph's Cathedral and a Society in Regression

Beauty will save the world.

—Fyodor Dostoevsky

BEAUTY ABANDONED

St. Joseph's Cathedral towers over Broeck Street in Albany. Completed in 1860, the cathedral was built with blue limestone and trimmed creamy yellow French Caen.[1] Inside its cavernous edifice stand fourteen marble columns, ten of which are monoliths. Majestic stained-glass windows surround the three marble altars while wordlessly telling the biblical story.

The church imported the stations of the cross from Munich. Famed organ builder Wilcox and Simmons of Boston constructed the pipe organ, and it was the second largest in the nation at the time of completion.[2] At least for this organ, the moniker "king of the instruments" is appropriate. A walk in the facility upon its completion might lead one to wonder

1. Abandoned, "St. Joseph's Church."
2. Abandoned, "St. Joseph's Church."

just how much one would have to love God to build a cathedral like this. The sacrifice required to build St. Joseph's was enormous.

Evangelical Protestants seldom build facilities like St. Joseph's. Protestant sanctuaries contemporaneous with St. Joseph's typically feature Greco-Roman-style columns on the front porch and a sea of red carpet on the inside. At the center of the chancel would be a pulpit so that everyone would know the purpose of the sanctuary: listening to the word. Many would employ stained-glass windows and a mural in the baptistry. Other than those few features, evangelicals usually build sanctuaries for the ear, not the eye. Even the most ornate of them would appear spartan compared to St. Joseph's.

More modern evangelical facilities are often renovated grocery stores, repurposed strip malls, and even the occasional renovated hotel. Their interior design is more like a theater than anything else. Their preferred setting is a large stage on which the praise band can bellow out their passionate praise choruses while basking in the glow of professional stage lighting. Shiplap for the background, smoke machines to set the mood, and excellent audio/video equipment for a concert-venue-quality experience is ubiquitous enough to seem as if the congregations were following a manual of some sort. Not likely are they to spend precious resources on an altarpiece from Europe or devote tithe dollars for fine marble to be hewn into a baptistry. Evangelicals usually build sanctuaries on the power of pragmatism. The beauty of the facility is a secondary consideration, and maybe not even secondary.

Not so for the builders of St. Joseph's. The builders believed in the power of beauty to communicate the presence of God. St. Joseph's massive Gothic columns and arches give its guests a sense of the sacred as they tower above them reaching to the heavens, the abode of God. Each Gothic arch is capped with an opening for three stained-glass window-panes, one for each Person of the Trinity. The light beaming into the sanctuary from the stained glass illuminates not only the building but points the way toward the enlightenment of the soul.

Looking up from the floor, one can get lost in the hammerbeam roof and ceiling "diapers," the repeated square tiles adorning the ceiling. The diapers have a sky-blue background with a red center emblazoned with five golden fleurs-de-lis arranged in a cruciform pattern. On the sides of each diaper is a red stripe. Guarding the end of both sides of each stripe is a gold cross fleury on a circular black background.

Hand-carved angels built into the corbels gaze down on the worshipers, each bearing a shield. The angels are not scowling as if a divine tormentor had been invoked to punish the wicked. No, the faces are soft. One could say they are comforting. The impression is far from foreboding; it is almost cheerful.

All is not cheerful in St. Joseph's Cathedral, though. Beams of light shine through the stained-glass window above each Gothic arch illuminating the floor below. In the flow of the light, dust particles are illuminated and trace a path to the nearly vacant floor beneath. Assorted papers are scattered around the floor as if a giant windstorm chased the worshipers out of the building and blew their bulletins out of their hands like autumn leaves. The dust collecting on the vast stone floors and the scattered pews and papers are reminders that St. Joseph's is no longer a center of worship. Its pews, the few that remain which are not piled in the corner, are empty. No musicians are clamoring for a chance to play the stentorian pipe organ, no ministers are vying for the opportunity to preach from the ornate pulpit, no priests are politicking for the chance to lead the sacred liturgy. St. Joseph's is closed. St. Joseph's is abandoned. It has become the haunt of YouTube voyeurs who gawk at the condemned facility, blow through detached pipes from the once-great organ, and frolic in its belfry. It has become the victim of trespassers making their mark on the cathedral in graffiti because they are unlikely to be able to make a mark in society in any other way. A photographer who works with abandoned sanctuaries, C. M. Goodenberry, has called St. Joseph's "The Watcher's Temple." One of the titles of his work on St. Joseph's says it well. He calls it "The Empire of Dust."

Still, the experience of entering St. Joseph's, even as it sits abandoned, instills a holy hush. One can almost feel a gathered congregation for midnight mass on Christmas Eve rise to its feet as the massive pipe organ thunders the first chord of the *Hallelujah* chorus with a power strong enough to rattle their chests and resound in their very souls. One can almost hear them gasp in awestruck wonder as a hundred-voice choir expertly sings Handel's masterpiece as they bask in the light of one thousand flickering candles. One can imagine the wonder of Handel's hallelujahs ascending to the hammerbeam ceiling and reverberating there as the white-robed choir added another and another and another. Even without the privilege of being present at St. Joseph's for such an occasion, one can still somehow know the shivers on the spine, the chills on the arms, the stirring of the soul that occasioned worship on great holy days.

Beyond extraordinary experiences of worship, one can sense the millions of prayers offered in this place by thousands of worshipers in the liturgy of ordinary Sundays. Whether it is correct theology or not, people come to cathedrals and sanctuaries seeking the presence of the Holy and Wholly Other. Yes, God is omnipresent. Yes, God can be found in the silence of the green forest, in the austere beauty of windswept mountains, and in the crashing waves by sea. One can experience God's presence beside a trickling brook, or by seeing the orange leaves on a crisp autumn night. God is in the sacred ordinary. There is something transcendent, however, about seeking God's presence in a place designed explicitly for worship.

Some have found being alone in a house of worship a little frightening. Perhaps that is good, for when one attempts to approach God, one is approaching a Wonder beyond imagining whose holiness is beyond terrifying. Most people, though, sense not fear in a great cathedral, but something sacred, something holy, something awe inspiring. They sense something beyond themselves. Prayers offered here are no more or less powerful than prayers offered elsewhere, but the fact that millions upon millions of prayers were offered in this place makes it extraordinary. The prayers are as real as the stones—and perhaps weightier.

One can see where the pews once sat. The pews offered a place for the devout who had gathered to experience the liturgy as the normal part of their spiritual pilgrimage. No doubt these pews hosted desperate souls who were clinging to some faint hope that God would speak to their situation, to rescue them from the gravity of their crisis. Surely some came in great faith wanting God to nurture their spirit. Some came in great doubt, hoping something would dispel the gloom of disbelief that was stalking their souls. No doubt some came out of habit, some because their parents made them, some because of a spouse's incessant pestering, and some for no reason at all. For a century they came. In a place masterfully built for the glory of God, they worshiped God as best they could, and that history of meeting God develops a sense of wonder that has been engraved in the very stones.

Weddings were performed here. No doubt thousands of couples stood underneath the stained-glass windows high above the marble altar and made their vows to God and each other. No doubt many of them flinched from the resplendent light bearing down on them through stained glass above and from the weight of the vows they were taking.

Countless baptisms were celebrated here. As a place of worship for Catholics, the baptisms were of infants. Many infants had the words of initiation spoken over them as the priest sprinkled their heads with water and their parents and godparents swore off the works of the devil.

No doubt St. Joseph's hosted frequent funerals as well. When a member of the congregation passed, the faithful would gather to hear the promise of eternal life, to celebrate the Eucharist, to share the liturgy, and to mourn their beloved. The presence of God communicated at St. Joseph's helped them begin healing.

Now, though, the cathedral is empty. Owned by the city of Albany, it awaits enough money to be raised for its repair. If repaired, though, then what? Will it become a tourist center, an architectural showpiece for a city bent on keeping its cultural heritage, a museum, a wedding venue, or a dance hall? In the future, will a bearded tenor belt out Gesù Bambino for the uplifting of a gathered congregation? Will an expertly trained alto with gleaming eyes and a galvanized spine stride to the chancel to sing "Ave Maria" and soothe the souls of harried worshipers? Will a modern worship ensemble lift "In Christ Alone" to the rafters? The building's future is unknown, but what is known is that the institution that created the building has perished. Beauty may indeed save the world, as Fyodor Dostoevsky argues, but beauty did not save St. Joseph's.

LOSING A CHURCH

On the surface, the abandonment of St. Joseph's is not of any great significance to society. After all, between 3,000–4,500 congregations close in the United States every year.[3] Like many of those congregations, the most pressing cause of St. Joseph's demise was demographics. As the community around the church shrank and became largely African American, the congregation could not reach it. Eventually, the upkeep of the facility was too costly, and the church closed.[4]

The story is repeated for many congregations in the United States every year. Reports of closing churches often come with startling data about the decrease in religiosity in the US. In 1992, 92 percent of Americans identified as Christian.[5] In 2020 that number was down to 64 percent.[6] Local congregations often face a toxic stew of shifting demographics,

3. Earls, "Protestant Church Closures."
4. Abandoned, "St. Joseph's Church."
5. Gabbat, "Losing Their Religion."
6. Gabbat, "Losing Their Religion."

smaller numbers of believers around the church, and a society with an ever-shrinking number of Christians. While the death of a congregation is a loss to society and an event to be mourned by its members, losing one of them is not extraordinary. Leaders in the church, across most denominations, have long noted the decline in attendance and participation in congregational life. There are many articles and books written about the decline of the church every year.

What if, however, something more is going on? What if St. Joseph's demise can be seen as symbolic of what is going on in the entire society, not just in the church? What if St. Joseph's sacredness became unapproachability? What if its magnificence became rigidity? What if its beauty yielded inflexibility? What if St. Joseph's did not have the determination and skill to address the changing demographics precisely because of what made it beautiful? What if the causes of St. Joseph's demise were widespread and existed both within and without the church?

If the church were alone in its regression, then the secularization thesis could hold.[7] The theory holds that as societies advance, they become more secular and religion becomes less important. The rapid secularization of Europe demonstrates how the thesis works. As Europe has modernized, the role of faith has diminished significantly. Many of the large cathedrals of Europe enjoy few parishioners on Sunday morning and others are closing as the decrease in the worshiping population accelerates. To avoid closure, some of England's cathedrals have resorted to extreme methods. England's Rochester Cathedral installed a putt-putt course to generate traffic, and Norwich Cathedral installed a fifty-foot sliding board known as "helter-skelter."[8]

The indignity these two cathedrals suffered is probably worse than death. A good death is better than a trivial life. The death of an institution is better than the mockery these institutions endure. The secularization thesis holds that most religious institutions will follow St. Joseph's or Rochester Cathedral. As society modernizes, fewer people are religious, and eventually, churches decline and die. What is happening in Europe will eventually happen in the United States. Eventually, religion will become the relic of a world gone by with few modern adherents. It would be a topic for historians, a subject for PhD theses, a subject for dusty tomes

---

7. Scruton, *Fools, Frauds and Firebrands*, 33.

8. Specia, "God Save the Cathedral?"

located in the back of the library, but not a living manifestation of the beliefs of great swaths of people.

What if, however, the church were not alone in its regression? What would that mean for the church, the society, and the institutions under-girding Western civilization? What if the church faced pressures shared among most societal institutions? It would mean that the analysis of secularization would be helpful, but only to a point. It would mean that any analysis of the situation that only studied one institution would be unable to provide a solution because most of the pertinent data would not be analyzed. If the church is alone in its regression, then other institu-tions could rest safe knowing they will be spared the onslaught of societal upheaval.

It is comfortable for those outside the church to believe the church is alone in its regression. It might even be comfortable for the church to believe it is alone. Then it could focus on technique or theology. If, however, the church is not alone, the problem is much bigger than what can be faced by repairing bad techniques or theology.

SHARED REGRESSION

The church is not alone. Social institutions across the United States are in serious decline. Normally, when discussing societal decline, research-ers focus on individual behaviors at large. Consider the work of Roberta Gilbert in *The Eight Concepts of Bowen Theory*:

> Between 1963 and 1993 the crime rate went up 360%, youth crime is up 200%, teen pregnancy is up 600% and teen suicide is up 300% (now the second most important cause of death in teens, after accidents). One in five teens attempt suicide, single parents increased by 300%, SAT scores are down 7% and drug use is up over 1000%.
>
> In 1991, less than 60% of children were living with their biological, married parents. Around 50% of children were living in single-parent homes. There has been little or no change since then. Dissolution of the family is more the rule rather than the exception. 30% of US babies are born out of wedlock.[9]

While there is much information to be gleaned from Gilbert's analy-sis, there is another way of looking at society: through its institutions.

---

9. Gilbert, *Eight Concepts of Bowen Theory*, 93.

While the data have demonstrated the regression of congregations, particularly those that are part of established denominations, most other major institutions are under significant pressure as well. What does it mean that educational systems are under pressure, and the military no longer carries the respect of the citizenry it once did? What societal pressures have contributed to the regression of the institution of the family, the decline of trust in the press, the replication crisis in science, and the recruiting crisis in the military? Since these major societal institutions are under pressure, it does little good to examine only one institution and look for causes for its decline in an isolated sense. Even if analyzing one institution isolated from all the others could yield some solutions for it, the analysis would miss major cross-contaminating factors. Analyzing institutions together and seeing what pressures are common to them will yield analysis less prone to groupthink, more open to unconventional solutions, and less likely to reach for anxiety-delaying yet ineffective solutions to the matter at hand.

"Regression" for this study is not just poorly functioning. It is devolving. Famed therapist and Bowen theory evangelist Rabbi Edwin Freidman defines regression as "more of a 'going down' than a 'going back.'"[10] Regression is not just a loss of progress; in "a societal regression . . . evolutionary principles of life become distorted, perverted, or actually reversed."[11]

WHAT IS AN INSTITUTION?

To begin such a study, one must come to some understanding of what an institution is exactly. While that task seems simple enough, the term is not clear. Even for sociologists who study institutions, the term itself is slippery and difficult to define. Part of the difficulty is in colloquial language. Authors and speakers use the term in a variety of ways. A food critic can refer to a restaurant as an institution, a sports reporter can refer to a long-tenured announcer as an institution, and a politician can refer to election day as an institution.

From the outside, it would be easy to think that the academic study of institutions would lead to clarity of their nature and purpose. Unfortunately, clarity about institutions is missing even among those who

10. Friedman, *Failure of Nerve*, 88.
11. Friedman, *Failure of Nerve*, 88.

study them most frequently. Florida State University sociologist Patricia Yancey Martin notes even social scientists have applied the term "institution" in very unclear ways. Social scientists use "institution" and "social institution" to refer to taxation, handshakes, schools, socialism, mental hospitals, dating, property, sports, courts, religion, and marriage.[12] Her research even notes the vague nature of the definition of institutions in authoritative sources in the field.[13] If "institution" can refer to a customary greeting like a handshake and an organization with the purpose of educating young adults, the term has been stretched so far as to make it almost meaningless.

Here "institutions" and "social institutions" refer to two concepts. The first is social agreement. These institutions are institutions like marriage and work. They predate complex societies and form the foundation for them. The second sense of an institution is an organization. These organizations are what people in complex societies need to maintain the society itself. Included in these organizations are education, science, media, hospitals, the military, and the police, among others.

Gary Lafree, distinguished university professor at the University of Maryland, states, "Institutions are arguably the most important of human creations."[14] When one considers the vast number of human creations, Lafree's suggestion seems a bit hyperbolic. Humans have invented the wheel, harnessed electricity, created farming, and domesticated dogs and farm animals. Surely the plow and the cart were more important than institutions. Surely discovering the germ concept of disease and developing antibiotic treatments were more significant for humanity than institutions. Each of those human creations, however, is subsequent and dependent on functioning institutions.

Consider the state of humanity in an undifferentiated nature. Seventeenth-century philosopher Thomas Hobbes describes it this way:

> There is no place for industry; because the fruit thereof is uncertain; and consequently, no cultivating the earth; no navigation, nor use of the comfortable buildings; no instruments of moving and removing, such things as require much force; no knowledge of the face of the earth; no account of time; no arts; no literature; no society; and which is worst of all, continual fear, and danger

---

12. Martin, "Gender as Social Institution," 1249–50.
13. Martin, "Gender as Social Institution," 1251.
14. Lafree, "Social Institutions," 1349.

of violent death; and the life of man solitary poor, nasty, brutish, and short.[15]

This disastrous state of affairs is predicated on each human being doing exactly what their instincts dictate. They fight for goods, for reproduction, for survival.

Hobbes's outlook on human behavior is famously bleak. Humans, according to Hobbes, would live in a constant state of war were it not for a power over them creating obedience to the law through fear. One does not have to accept Hobbes's thinking in full to concur with at least one aspect of his thinking: agreements among people are required for society to exist.

Humans, by definition, are social creatures. If stranded on an island alone, one person could exist without institutions—although survival is greatly imperiled. The moment a group of people emerge—as is necessary for the human condition—institutions emerge. Perhaps the oldest human institution is marriage, predating recorded history, law, and possibly even religion.[16] The reasons marriage emerged so early in human history are revealed in some of its functions. Marriage exists to ensure the paternity of children, ensure they have provision, and socialize them, among other reasons.

Once there is a group beyond the family to consider, the logic requiring other institutions emerges quite naturally. If there is a group beyond just one family unit, someone has to make decisions for the group. The need for decision-making for the whole would be the birth of politics and governance. If there is a large group, someone has to protect the weak in the group from those who would harm them. This need is met through the birth of law and law enforcement.

Once there are multiple groups, each group needs to defend itself from outsiders. This is the birth of defense. Competition for scarce resources would naturally yield violence among disparate groups. The need to protect one's tribe from outside harm would have developed long before human inventions like the wheel.

Institutions predate the invention of modern society and make modern society possible. Without institutions, society is impossible. Since it is in the very nature of human existence to be a social species,

15. Hobbes, *Leviathan*, loc. 1628 of 9076.
16. Bala, "Debates About Same-Sex Marriage," 195.

without institutions, our nature as humans would be thwarted. In the most basic sense, institutions are necessary for human flourishing.

INSTITUTIONS ARE CUMBERSOME

Being an apologist for institutions is a lonely venture. Institutions can become insufferably inflexible and destructive to themselves and their participants. Institutions can get bogged down in minutia and endure endless, useless turf wars. It is common in leadership literature to start with the understanding that the institutions of Western civilization are not serving the public very well. In his classic book, *Servant Leadership*, Robert Greenleaf recalls a lecture he was attending:

> There is a new problem in our country. We are becoming a nation that is dominated by our large institutions—churches, businesses, governments, labor unions, universities—and these big institutions are not serving us well. I hope that all of you are concerned about this. Now you can do as I do, stand outside and criticize, bring pressure if you can, write and argue about it. All of this may do some good. But nothing of substance will happen unless there are people inside these institutions who can (and want to) lead them to better performance for the public good.[17]

While Greenleaf did not mention the date of the lecture he attended, judging by the dates of his first employment with American Telephone and Telegraph in the mid-1920s, the lecture must have been somewhere in the late 1910s to the early 1920s.[18] In other words, he was observing the regression of institutions over a century ago. It would be difficult to find observers who conclude institutions as a whole have improved in the subsequent century.

If institutions are difficult and frustrating, and if they are not working as well as they should, why care about them at all? Why not just accept their inevitable decline? Why not just think of them as constructs that die when they outlive their usefulness? The best reason to preserve them is that institutions are not valuable for what they are in themselves. Institutions are instrumental. Common life depends on institutions.[19] The continued breakdown of foundational societal institutions is an

17. Greenleaf, *Servant Leadership*, 15–16.
18. Greenleaf, *Servant Leadership*, 16.
19. Bellah, *Good Society*, 4.

ominous trend for Western civilization.[20] Civilization itself is imperiled if all its institutions are imperiled.

While institutions are under significant pressure, at their best, they are powerful and good. Institutions have the power to shape individuals for the good. Families, schools, and churches help to create well-socialized individuals who have a moral compass and who can provide for themselves and their families. When these basic institutions are functioning well, they have salutatory effects on society.

Lafree notes crime surged during the 1960s when distrust in political institutions was high, economic institutions were producing stresses on society, and family institutions were declining in strength.[21] In short, his thesis is, "Weak institutions yield high crime." He argues the reason for the crime "bust" in the 1990s was the stabilization in the legitimacy of political, economic, and family institutions coupled with increased investment in criminal justice, education, and welfare, producing downward pressure on crime rates.[22]

FUNCTIONS

Institutions have other functions as well. Institutions have the power to transform agents.[23] They allow societies to endure over time as individuals join or are replaced by new members,[24] create collective memory,[25] and help form the identity of the nation-state.[26]

Institutions transmit societal rules and norms, but they also transmit the unutterable. There is always a layer of knowledge that can never be articulated.[27] So, these norms are transferred by experience, observation, and participation. Much like children learn much from observing their parents' behavior, societies teach by example. How does one know not to wear a tuxedo to a monster truck rally or to avoid using Shakespearean English at an Eminem concert? One learns by observing what is acceptable in society.

20. Bellah, *Good Society*, 4.
21. Lafree, "Social Institutions," 1325.
22. Lafree, "Social Institutions," 1326.
23. Hodgson, "What Are Institutions?," 2.
24. Lafree, "Social Institutions," 1349.
25. Ocasio et al., "History, Society, and Institutions," 676.
26. Scruton, *Fools, Frauds, and Firebrands*, 22.
27. Hodgson, "What Are Institutions?," 4.

While it is true that institutions pass down the norms and values at the heart of society,[28] they often do so without even a word.

Institutions have another important function: they transfer ownership of the institution's story.[29] Imagine a drill sergeant standing close enough to a private to instill terror in his soul and for the brim of the sergeant's hat to make contact with the private's eyebrows. The veins on the sergeant's neck are enlarged and pulsating. His eyes are bulging like balloons being squeezed by an overzealous toddler. Even with no audio, it is obvious the sergeant is berating the private, most likely with foul invective and profanities galore. The private is motionless, looking straight ahead, partially out of protocol and partially because terror has petrified his legs. He is "scared stiff." The goal of the sergeant's tirade is more than just correcting behavior or instilling unit discipline. What the sergeant is doing is forging the recruit into a Marine, an intense and painful process. Once successful, the newly minted Marine is now an owner of the United State Marine Corps's story. The new Marine's actions now speak for the whole. If he is courageous, it speaks well of the Marines. If he is corrupt, he disgraces the Marines. While the sergeant's methods make no sense outside of basic training, the goal is very familiar to those who are part of institutions. When persons are formed by a process in an institution, they become owners of the institution's story.

Institutions do not just grant information; they are important in human formation.[30] Consider the role of the educational system. On the surface, the educational system has a role in creating a thriving populace by teaching the essentials. Just beneath the surface, though, the educational system provides something else. The educational system also plays a vital role in socialization. Individuals who attend school are with a large collection of their peers divided by age. In this peer group, they learn to understand human relationships in a monitored environment. Because of the complexity of human relationships, learning this skill may be as important as any other skill developed during the educational process. Having multiple relationships among one's peers requires learning the skills needed to cultivate friendships, learning to monitor one's appearance and speech, and understanding the need for cooperation with authority and each other. By the use of artistic and athletic opportunities,

28. Scruton, *Fools, Frauds and Firebrands*, 3.

29. Dr. Terry York of Baylor University first introduced me to this concept in a doctoral seminar, and the image of the drill sergeant is his.

30. Scruton, *Modern philosophy*, 436.

the educational system helps provide a sense of identity and belonging to students. While education is not the only institution that socializes individuals, its power to socialize is almost without peer.

Institutions are responsible for teaching moral behavior.[31] Of course, this responsibility is obvious when it comes to religion and family. Both of these institutions teach morality by course. There are a large number of institutions that teach morality as a by-product of their work, however. When enforcing the law, the police teach morality by insisting on consequences for bad behavior. When enforcing an honor code, a college or university teaches what is acceptable behavior. These honor codes not only function to teach what is fitting behavior in the school but foreshadow what would be expected of a person outside educational confines.

Although neo-Marxist thinkers assert that institutions are complicit in the subjugation of the poor and oppressed minorities, institutions have the effect of calling for societal transformation. It was William Wilberforce who brought the end to the slave trade in England. It was President Abraham Lincoln who ended human slavery in the United States. It was Martin Luther King Jr. who helped to bring an end to segregation in the United States. Dr. King's "I Have a Dream" speech is instructive. Rather than averring that the US was corrupt from the beginning and needed to tear down all institutions, he called on the US to "live out the true meaning of its creed." The creed to which he referred was the Declaration of Independence: "We hold these truths to be self-evident, that all men are created equal, that they are endowed by their Creator with certain unalienable rights." Far from concluding the Declaration of Independence was a racist document, he used Jefferson's rhetoric to argue for the fundamental incompatibility of the Declaration with segregation.

In a time when institutions are under intense pressure, it is vital to realize deconstruction is easier than construction. While it may be easy to destroy the institutions that are clinging to life, it is not easy to replace them. The society that will emerge after the destruction and rebuilding of institutions is uncertain, and the nations that have tried to replace all of their institutions usually have ended up in tyranny and terror.

---

31. Lafree, "Social Institutions," 1350.

2

Church in Regression

There is no surer sign of decay in a society than to see the rites of religion held in contempt.

—NICCOLÒ MACHIAVELLI

Without God, anything is possible.

—FYODOR DOSTOEVSKY

RELIGION IN DECLINE

TO THE DELIGHT OF militant secularists and the dismay of believers, religion in society is in a state of decline. That decline accelerated until the last two years when the percentage of people who report no particular religion stopped growing. Even if the number with no religion has plateaued, religious communities worry over declining attendance and smaller budgets. While Christianity is still the largest religion in the US, the decline in overall membership and participation is worrisome. Also lost is the respectability religion once had.

It is not just the statistical data that are problematic. The way many individuals practice their faith is fundamentally different in contemporary culture. Notre Dame philosopher of religion David Bentley Hart writes:

> We certainly . . . do not draw near the "mystery of God" with anything like the fear and trembling of our ancestors, and when we tire of our devotions and drift away we do not expect to be pursued, either by the furies or by the hounds of conscience.
>
> This is especially obvious at modern Western religion's pastel-tinged margins, in those realms where the gods of the boutique hold uncontested sway. Here one may cultivate a private atmosphere of "spirituality" as undemanding and therapeutically comforting as one likes by purchasing a dream catcher, a few pretty crystals . . . until this mounting congeries of string, worthless quartz . . . and fraudulent scholarship reaches that mysterious point of saturation at which religion has become indistinguishable from interior decorating.[1]

One does not have to accept Hart's jeremiad against religious practice in the modern West to concur that congregational life is declining. Worship attendance and church membership are in decline. The decline is across denominations and demographic identifiers. It is easier to count the denominations that are growing than the ones that are not. Charismatic denominations like the Assemblies of God are growing along with the Roman Catholic Church. Also growing are nondenominational congregations. With a few outliers, the remaining denominations are shrinking, and many are shrinking rapidly.

A generation ago, conservative denominations could point to liberal mainline denominations with some relief. The conservative denominations were growing, while mainline denominations began shrinking in the 1970s. The conservative advantage on this issue, however, is gone.

A LOOK AT THE SOUTHERN BAPTIST CONVENTION

Perhaps the best way to look at the shrinking of conservative evangelicalism is to look at the Southern Baptist Convention (SBC). At their origin, Baptists had an ethos and spirit that lent itself well to the American experience. Unlike Methodism and other more structured traditions, Baptists had no particular requirements for their clergy. Each congregation

1. Hart, *Atheist Delusions*, 23–24.

could find and ordain its own leadership. Further, each congregation was governed democratically. No authority outside the congregation could compel the congregation to act against its wishes.

This democratic spirit and ability to mint its new pastors gave Baptists an advantage. While Methodist churches would have a circuit rider who had other congregations under his charge, a Baptist congregation, once it had the means, could find someone to serve it without going through a long approval and ordination process.

The other advantage Baptists had was flexibility. Because of their self-governing practice, a Baptist congregation could address issues and seize opportunities quickly. For a Baptist church, a majority vote was all it took to make most decisions. Baptist churches were flexible and could be fast if they chose to be.

RAPID GROWTH AND THE CONSERVATIVE RESURGENCE

By the twentieth century, the SBC became an evangelical success story. It was fueled by rapid growth and missionary zeal. By 1979, the SBC had 13.3 million members.[2] There were undercurrents of discontent, however. In a now-infamous meeting in New Orleans, SBC stalwarts Paige Patterson and Paul Pressler met and developed the strategy that would become known as the "conservative resurgence" in the SBC. The meeting now is an embarrassment to the SBC. Patterson is nearly a pariah among many in the SBC because he mishandled rape accusations, publicly gawked at a young woman during a sermon, and mismanaged Southwestern Baptist Theological Seminary while he was President.

Pressler is thoroughly discredited. If press reports and settled lawsuits are to be believed, Pressler has been a serial abuser of underage boys and young men at his law firm for decades. He was forced to leave his Presbyterian church in the 1970s for his behavior and failed an FBI background check in the late 1980s, and rumors of his abuse go back decades.

When Pressler and Patterson met in New Orleans, however, none of their issues were known to the SBC at large and perhaps not to each other. The meeting became a sort of legend, a mythological tale of two titans facing down the forces of evil. The story was that the SBC was beginning a leftward drift in its seminaries and agencies. Liberal professors and

2. Johnston, "SBC Organization."

administrators were poisoning the minds of ministerial students. These liberals were going to turn the SBC seminaries into indoctrination centers for theological liberalism. The seminaries would push the SBC left, leaving it to become like the liberal mainline denominations. Without drastic intervention the SBC would enter a death spiral, they believed.

Patterson and Pressler began a strategy of electing conservatives to the SBC presidency. After the victory, the president would use his appointed power to place conservatives on boards and agencies. Eventually, all the boards and agencies would come under conservative control. The strategy would take years to complete, but by patient political maneuvering, it would lead to a conservative-dominated SBC.

THE TARGETS

Two groups caught the ire of the conservatives in the SBC, moderates and liberals. To be fair to the conservative resurgence, there were liberals in the SBC, and some of them taught in the SBC's six seminaries. Most of them, however, left in 1987 to form the Alliance of Baptists. The nonconservatives who remained in the SBC referred to themselves as "moderates."

As a clarification, an SBC moderate was not a moderate in any sense outside the SBC. SBC moderates would be more conservative than most Methodists and Presbyterians and much more conservative than the average Lutheran in the Evangelical Lutheran Church in America. In the grand scope of the Protestant life, they were conservative. Their conservative nature becomes much more obvious when compared to those in nonreligious circles. The moderates tended to be socially and politically center-right. Understanding they were being castigated as spineless leftists by the use of the term "moderate," moderate leaders tried to use the term "moderate-conservative" as an alternative. The name would not stick. They became the moderates, and for many congregants in SBC churches, they might as well have been descendants of Beelzebub.

When the conservative resurgence began, moderates were a strong part of the SBC. While seldom winning they would often garner over 40 percent of the vote in presidential elections. They were not strong enough to win, but they were an important faction.

The moderates remained a force in the SBC even after conservatives started winning elections and excluding them from denominational leadership. Finally, many moderates left the SBC and created the Cooperative Baptist Fellowship (CBF) in 1991. Because of the SBC's governance, a church could contribute to both the SBC and the CBF and be a member of both organizations at the same time. Most CBF congregations were dually aligned at the time of the CBF's founding and remain so now.

By the early 1990s, the conservative victory was complete. They controlled all of the seminaries and boards of the SBC. Liberals were largely gone, and the conservatives purged moderates from denominational life and seminaries. The conservative victory in the SBC had its genesis in the meeting in New Orleans.

The story, often told, lionized a probable pedophile and his friend whose poor treatment of women followed him. The SBC has not reckoned with the fact that the conservative resurgence was their creation as of yet.

THE LEFTWARD FLIGHT OF THE CBF

As the conservative leadership predicted, once unmoored by connection to the SBC, the moderates in the CBF began an inexorable leftward drift. The CBF had been a supporter of women in ordained congregational leadership from its inception, but leaders of the movement denied the accusation that the organization was supportive of gay clergy and gay marriage. Resistance melted quickly, however. As of 2024, some CBF congregations and most CBF leaders are open to gay clergy. Further, some of its seminaries feature LGBTQ+-affirming professors and leaders. To have a denomination shift on a theological and cultural issue as quickly as the CBF has is stunning. The CBF did not drift left, it leaped left.

The SBC has not liberalized, at least on the congregational level. On matters of biblical interpretation, the inspiration of Scripture, the role of women, LGBTQ+ issues, abortion, and social issues, the SBC is strongly conservative even if there are some dissenters and some missteps.

THE RESULTS OF THE CONSERVATIVE RESURGENCE

What the leaders of the conservative resurgence promised was rapid denominational growth after the completion of the process. Once the

Convention drove out the moderates and liberals, growth would ensue because it was liberal theology that prevented church growth.

The numbers did not bear out their prediction. The SBC peaked in 2006 with 16.3 million members. The decline since then has been precipitous. As a percentage, the numbers are shocking: it is a 19 percent decrease. Because of the size of the SBC, the numbers are very large. In 2023, the SBC had 12.9 members,[3] a decrease from its peak of 3.4 million members. Worse, the SBC lost 457,000 members in 2022 alone.[4] To put these numbers in perspective, when the two largest Presbyterian denominations merged in 1983 to form the Presbyterian Church USA (PCUSA), the new denomination had 3.1 million members.[5] The SBC lost a denomination-sized group of members in seventeen years.

Part of the SBC's problem is its success. The SBC has convinced many in the broader religious public of congregational governance and individualism in matters of faith. These parts of the theology and ethos of the SBC are prominent in the nondenominational movement. Many nondenominational congregations are functionally Baptist. Baptist polity without denominational affiliation is how they function.

Of course, that is also a little embarrassing. Since the SBC has no direct control over its congregations, affiliation with the group can be as small as donating. Why would a church of like faith not get the benefits of inclusion in the SBC like employee benefits, access to seminaries, the ability to fund missionaries, and national advocacy if the cost is so small? Part of the answer could be the same reason new SBC church plants often do not use the word "Baptist" in their name. The SBC's public perception is fairly toxic.

Although these are some of the reasons the SBC is in decline, they hardly account for the size of the decline. The numbers are very large. It is a decline that does not seem to be slowing. If the goal of the conservative resurgence was to prevent denominational decline, it failed.

The denomination has other significant issues. The Executive Committee, the committee that runs the daily operations of the SBC when it is not in session, is on a path to financial ruin.[6] Further, it has forfeited trust among its churches by defying the votes of the Annual Meeting.

---

3. Shellnutt, "SBC Membership Falls."
4. Gryboski, "Southern Baptist Convention."
5. Hyer, "Newly Merged Presbyterian Church."
6. Wingfield, "SBC Executive Committee."

The SBC also finds itself in significant controversy over its handling of sexual abuse and harassment. In 2019, the Houston Chronicle reported over seven hundred cases of sexual abuse in the denomination. Many of those are cases of clergy who abused children. In 2024, the leading candidates for SBC president all denied that the SBC had a sexual abuse crisis. They believed individual congregations and individual SBC members had committed abuse but that the denomination itself had not covered up or enabled abuse.

This is even though an independent investigation funded by the SBC found that a former SBC president had assaulted the spouse of a ministerial colleague while on vacation with them, a founder of the conservative resurgence had been a serial abuser of boys, a seminary president publicly gawked at the appearance of a young woman in a sermon, and repeated abuses by large church clergy.

Once the largest and fastest-growing denomination in the US, the SBC is mired in controversy, and its denial of its sexual abuse problem is disturbing. In its 2024 Annual Meeting, the SBC focused on the Law Amendment which requires the SBC to remove churches from membership if they have a woman pastor. Messengers hotly debated this amendment even though fewer than 1 percent of SBC churches have a woman as a senior pastor.

For those outside the SBC, SBC congregations often use the term "pastor" to refer not just to the senior pastor who preaches every Sunday but to those who have the title but never preach. In other words, a woman might be a children's pastor and not be outside SBC's theological commitments. Because, however, she has the title, the congregation may be voted out of the convention. Simple nomenclature, not job description, would be cause for disfellowshipping a church. In a denomination of 47,000 churches, there are about two hundred women who have that title, although estimates vary. Getting rid of them was on the agenda of the 2024 SBC Annual Meeting. What was not on the agenda was repentance for partnering with a probable pedophile.

A decline in membership, inability to face and resolve sexual abuse issues, unwillingness to address the issues surrounding Pressler, and focusing on issues affecting a few participants are textbook examples of how regression works.

It is not as if Baptist theology and practice have failed, though. Nondenominational Christianity is among the largest and fastest-growing segments of Christianity.[7] If nondenominational churches were a denomination, they would be the largest Protestant denomination in the United States.[8] Looking at nondenominational churches' theology and practice, they are largely of the Free Church tradition and largely evangelical in theology. Many of them, then, function like Baptists.

The SBC has lost much of its distinctive push and purpose. It is shrinking despite being theologically and ideologically similar to a large group of growing believers. It remains an open question as to whether the SBC can solve its woes.

HARDLY ALONE

Of course, the SBC is hardly alone. The mainline churches are in catastrophic decline. In 2017, Ed Stetzer, author and dean of Talbot School of Theology, wrote that if the declines were not reversed, the mainline denominations had twenty-three Easters to celebrate before collapse.[9] Stetzer was optimistic that the decline will slow, but there has been scant evidence of that. Stetzer was writing in 2017, before the pandemic. After COVID hit and the shutdowns that followed, the losses for most denominations accelerated. Now, nearly seven years after his article, it is likely that the end is much closer than Stetzer expected. His addendum that toward the end the numbers might stabilize may have the ring of truth. Churches are harder to kill than kudzu in the summer sun. Life for the members of a dying denomination, like a dying church, is a dirge.

The trend regression in the mainline traditions is not new. Mainline denominations have been in a steep decline for more than a generation. Most of their members are older, and with fewer younger adults—and with younger adults having fewer children—any hope of recapturing the past is largely a fantasy.

PRESBYTERIAN CHURCH USA (PCUSA)

At its formation in 1983, the PCUSA had high hopes. Those hopes are merely charred embers now. The denomination is down to 1.1 million

---

7. Leonard, "Nondenominationalizing of American Christianity."
8. Leonard, "Nondenominationalizing of American Christianity."
9. Stetzer, "If It Doesn't."

members.[10] In 2022, the PCUSA lost an additional 53,000 members and 108 churches. More striking, the number of new professions of faith continues to fall. In 2016, the PCUSA had 20,000 professions of faith and reaffirmations. In 2022, that number was 15,000. According to the data, the PCUSA has 8,705 congregations. That means there were fewer than two professions and reaffirmations per church on average.

There is no other way to describe the PCUSA's condition than a death spiral. In fact, there are more pagans than PCUSA members in the US.[11] While other Presbyterian groups are emerging, it will be some time, if ever, before they gain the size the PCUSA had at its founding. They are also unlikely to gain the prominence the PCUSA had in informing religious culture.

THE UNITED METHODIST CHURCH

The largest of the mainline traditions, the United Methodist Church (UMC), was formed by a merger between the Evangelical United Brethren Church and the Methodist Church in 1968. The peak membership of the UMC was 11 million members.[12] As of October 2022 that number had fallen to 5.4 million members.[13]

Worse for the UMC is their controversy. The UMC has suffered from a long-running controversy over LGBTQ+ issues. Those issues came to the forefront with the election of the UMC's first openly LGBTQ+ bishop. The controversy was significant and heated as Methodists from Africa and others defended the denomination's historical teachings. The controversy became intractable and the UMC offered congregations who held to the church's teachings on issues of sexuality a path to leave. As of January 2024, 7,600 congregations have voted to leave the UMC, with many of them joining the newly minted Global Methodist Church.[14]

10. Presbyterian Church (U.S.A.), "Church Membership Still in Decline."
11. Pew Research Center, "US Muslims."
12. Smith, "United Methodists."
13. United Methodist Communications, "United Methodists."
14. Adams and Nguyen, "Most United Methodist Church Disaffiliations."

SEMINARY ATTENDANCE

Another way to measure the decline of churches is the number of clergy in training. For congregations to have a viable future, there must be leaders for them. A downward trend in the number of future clergy attending seminary is, therefore, very concerning. In its report on the 2022 school year, the Association of Theological Schools (ATS) reports that students enrolled in member schools working toward their Master of Divinity, the standard degree for ministers, had dropped below 28,000 for the first time in nearly thirty years. Further, there are sixty fewer MDiv-granting institutions partnering with ATS.[15]

LOSS OF TRUST

While the loss of trust among Americans in institutions is unsurprising, the loss of trust in its clergy is problematic for the church. Thirty-two percent of Americans trust the ethics of the clergy.[16] While that is above used-car salesmen and US representatives, those facts are hardly encouraging. The loss of trust in clergy is deeply problematic for the church.

While there have been many high-profile scandals involving clergy, the vast majority of clergy are doing their best to remain faithful to their calling and the teachings of their faith. Very few of them generate wealth, and most of them work long hours. Clergy are, as a rule, good and morally upright. Their reputation among the populace is as tragic as it is unwarranted. The perception of clergy is destructive to the faith.

THE PERSISTENCE OF RELIGIOUS BELIEF

While the data are rather bleak, the interesting point is that belief in God remains high. People in the US still believe in God, angels, and in the afterlife. What has happened is that the institutions created to transmit belief in God from one generation to the next are in serious decline.

Sometimes institutional regression is the fault of the institution, and sometimes it is the fault of the public. Yes, religious institutions have been rigid and insufferable. They, in many cases, have violated the tenets of the

15. Wingfield, "BSK and Wake Forest Divinity."
16. Earls, "Public Trust of Pastors."

faith they are charged with transmitting. While that remains true, one of the most notable failures of churches is a demographic one.

Although it is directly contradictory to conventional wisdom, those with graduate degrees are the most likely to be religious.[17] For generations, believers worried about sending their children to public colleges and universities where their faith might be under assault. While the atmosphere in many universities can be toxic to people of faith, particularly if they are conservative, the largest pool of those who attend worship regularly are those with graduate degrees. Consider also that people with graduate degrees are the most likely to have higher incomes. Weekly religious practice, then, is becoming the habit of the well educated and the upper-middle class.[18]

The group most likely to not attend regular worship services are those who have not completed high school.[19] Not many of those are among the highest earners in society. What has happened is that the church has lost its ability to engage the poor and less educated. Of course, this is a great reversal. The church was born among the poor and less educated, and for generations, it was made up largely of the poor. Ted Turner once famously said that Christianity was for losers.[20] If by "losers" he meant "largely made up of the poor and working poor," he had a point. Now, though, worship has become the pastime of the affluent, and Christian traditions have a very difficult time attracting the working class.

Something of the ministerial training process has to be part of the reason. Although this is changing, most ministers have earned the MDiv. For most of its history, the MDiv has been a ninety-hour degree, an extremely long master's degree. While many seminaries and divinity schools have made significant changes, the degree is still supposed to take three years to complete. That means that the average minister has spent four years earning a bachelor's degree and three years working on a master's degree. That amount of time in the educational process alone can lead to cultural distance. So much time in the educational process leads ministers to have a different vocabulary, different priorities, and different cultural norms than those who only completed high school or less. While an educated clergy is good for the church, one should note that denominations with the most educated clergy are struggling the most

17. Burge, "Religion Has Become."
18. Burge, "Religion Has Become."
19. Burge, "Dropping Out of Everything."
20. *Chicago Tribune*, "Turner Backtracks."

and the denominations with the least educated clergy are growing the fastest. This fact cannot be an accident.

SYSTEMIC FAILURE

It has become a business adage that "your systems are precisely aimed to get the results you are now achieving." Denominational decline, fewer students in MDiv programs, declining congregations, and church regression are the results. The systems of congregational life are producing these results. That, however, is not the most striking failure of congregational life.

One of the most telling failures of congregational life is the disconnect between people's experience of God or spiritual realities and the connection to their congregation.[21] In a recent Pew study, 45 percent of Americans have had an experience of something transcendent,[22] and a 2012 poll reports an astonishing 81 percent of Americans say they have experienced God's love.[23]

The disconnect comes in that people do not connect those experiences with their congregation.[24] Congregations are where such experiences are to be encouraged, interpreted, and shared. It is as though "ordinary people who have extraordinary spiritual experiences often do not think that their congregations or clergy would be interested or able to help interpret those experiences."[25]

If congregations and clergy are not interested or able to help interpret those experiences, then people are left to their own devices. Lurching for explanations and often finding nostrums, spiritual experiences can get lost over time—or worse, denied: "Maybe it was just nothing."

This divorce between experience and congregation cannot be accidental. It is a result of the structure and function of congregational life. Little wonder, then, that the fastest-growing edges of Christianity are charismatic and Roman Catholic.

In charismatic Christianity, spiritual experiences are normative. Congregations cultivate them and would be quite disappointed if a

---

21. Mead, *Transforming Congregations*, 53.
22. Kallo et al., "4. Spiritual Experiences."
23. Religion News, "Majority of Americans."
24. Mead, *Transforming Congregations*, 53.
25. Mead, *Transforming Congregations*, 53.

member did not have them. In the Roman Catholic Church, mystery and wonder are in the fabric of the faith. The architecture and liturgy are designed to create awe. Confession is a means of helping interpret that awe.

Without spiritual experiences and awe, congregations have only information to share. They become educational enterprises with a humanistic mission. Allowing a perception to exist where the people believe their congregation is not interested in their spiritual experiences necessarily leads to people thinking the congregation is unnecessary.

RELIGION AS AN INSTITUTION

Although it will raise the hackles of Baptists and other Free Church Christians, sociologists consider religion an institution. Baptists are insistent that churches are not institutions but have institutions. In other words, the collection of people is the church, not the institution, in much of Free Church theology. There is another sense of the word "institution," however. An institution can be a social agreement. Looking at the term that way, religion is a social institution, and a foundational one at that.

Religion is foundational to society because it provides ethical norms. If one were to look carefully at the legal and moral system of the ancient Romans, it would become quite obvious that the mores and legal norms were altered significantly by the emergence of Christianity. Against incendiary charges in much of the modern "New Atheist" movement, religion has provided significant social and political change for the good.

Believing that all people are created in the image of God led to the ending of concubinage and gladiator games in ancient Rome. While many may want to discredit Christianity over slavery, it was Christians William Wilberforce and Abraham Lincoln who brought an end to slavery in their nations. Yes, slaveholders in the Southern United States used the Bible to justify slavery; however, it was a misuse of the text. Since the Bible teaches that the image of God is in every person, then one cannot own another. The Bible, taken as a whole, is the enemy of all who would subjugate others. The same religious concept, the image of God, was foundational to the development of human liberty, limited government, an individual rights.

Further, at every point where there has been advancement of human life, liberty, education, and health, religious people have been at the forefront of advancement. Religiously motivated people have built hospitals and orphanages. They built universities and organized public education. They have funded billions of dollars in science and health research.

In the US, significant public charity arises from religious believers. Religious institutions are an important part of the US social safety net, providing 40 percent of all social safety net dollars.[26] Religious people are more likely to give to charitable causes.[27]

More than that, they act with compassion. A group of evangelicals, North Carolina Baptists are effective in disaster relief. When natural disasters strike, North Carolina Baptists have a team of trained volunteers ready to serve the needs of the victims. They have buses equipped to provide hundreds of warm showers per day and to provide thousands of meals per day. After the immediate needs are met, teams of North Carolina Baptists assist with debris removal, removal of damaged parts of homes, and reconstruction. To meet the emotional and spiritual needs of the victims, North Carolina Baptists send in trained chaplains to serve. North Carolina Baptists are not alone in their ventures. Virginia Baptists and Texas Baptists, among others, lead similar efforts. At its highest, religion creates compassion in its adherents and motivates them to act.

THE SINS OF RELIGION

Religion is not without its crimes, however. There have been many atrocities committed in God's name. Militant atheists often note horrors like the Inquisition, religious persecution, and conquest in the name of evangelism among them. Religious-minded people and leaders of religious institutions need to hear that critique. Doing evil in God's name discredits the very notion of religious faith. Institutions should be extremely careful to monitor their behavior so that this blight on religious faith is relegated to the dustbin of history.

While there is some merit to the critique, it is not true to say, as Christopher Hitchens might, that religion poisons everything.[28] Hitchens is quite capable of describing bad behavior among believers, but any college sophomore could do that. To point to particular sins and generalize to the whole is poor argumentation at best. As David Bentley Hart notes,

26. Bridgespan Group, "Faith-Inspired Nonprofits."
27. Richardson, "Religious People."
28. See Hitchens, *God Is Not Great.*

the charge is similar to noting that governments have done many terrible things and concluding that there should be no government.[29]

Missed also by those who would denigrate religion is that not all religions are created equal. Some religions condone mutilation, stoning of adulterers, banning music, and forcibly converting others. Religion wrongly construed and wrongly practiced can be a malignancy. Good religious traditions seek the highest good of humanity in general and individual persons.

A WORLD WITHOUT RELIGION

Religion rightly construed and practiced gives social interactions their limit and promotes ethics. The great Russian writer Fyodor Dostoevsky is often paraphrased, "Without God, everything is permissible." Dostoevsky does not mean that as a positive.[30] Without God, at least as a concept, it is very difficult to have the kinds of moral agreements among persons that make a thriving society possible. One does not have to believe in divine command theory ethics to conclude God is an important concept for ethics and morality.

In *All Art is Propaganda*, George Orwell writes about a person who had started having an affair. At first, the person was very concerned about spiritual matters. The person gradually gave in to his temptation, however. Orwell argues that someone who truly believed in God and that God would send them to hell for such behavior would not have had an affair. His observation seems rather banal, yet it is potent. His loss of religion and religious conviction allowed him to feel comfortable with flagrantly unethical behavior.[31]

For society, the regression of religion has consequences. Young people do not receive the training in morals and ethics that were once the norm, and as a result, they can give themselves license to behave as they want. Without thriving religious institutions, society is less effective at caring for the poor and victims of natural disasters, less creative with educational ventures, and less generous. Society needs healthy religious institutions.

29. Hart, *Atheist Delusions*, 14.

30. The actual quote is, "Without God and immortal life? All things are lawful then." Dostoevsky, *Brothers Karamazov*, loc. 453 of 15308.

31. Orwell, *All Art Is Propaganda*, 350.

3

Education in Regression

If there were a new religion of education, universities would be its cathedrals.

—Daniel Boorstin

The object of education is to teach us to love the beautiful.

—Plato

ON TOBACCO ROAD

Nestled on one end of "Tobacco Road," the University of North Carolina at Chapel Hill (UNC) has rightly earned the moniker "blue heaven." Even partisans from rival universities concede UNC's tree-lined campus is breathtaking.

An over 300-year-old poplar tree, the Davie Poplar, towers over campus and silently observes the formation of young minds. The Davie Poplar is not alone. Numerous old-growth trees bear witness to the educational enterprise. Near the middle of the fall semester, the green leaves on the countless trees turn, and the falling foliage blankets the campus with yellow, orange, and red leaves. Dogwoods bloom in the spring and azaleas along UNC's walkways bloom in the early summer. UNC's majestic campus is a feast for the eye and the soul in all four seasons.

Founded in 1789, UNC is the oldest public university in the United States.[1] As such, the university has developed many traditions. A student favorite takes place at the Old Well. As the most recognizable symbol of the university, the Old Well has been a campus landmark since its construction in 1897. Modeled after the Temple of Love at Versailles, the Old Well boasts a marble base, white columns, and a copper roof.[2] It is a UNC tradition for students to drink from the Old Well at the beginning of the semester for good luck.

UNC alumni and supporters are very proud of the university, its campus, and its traditions. Alumnus Charles Kuralt addressed the university on the celebration of its bicentennial and beautifully expressed the sentiments of the gathered throng. He said:

> What is it that binds us to this place as no other? It is not the well, or the bell, or the stone walls, or the crisp October nights, or the memory of dogwoods blooming. . . . No, our love for this place is based on the fact that it is, as it was meant to be, the university of the people.[3]

A walk along the budding dogwoods in the warm North Carolina spring would lead a person to think all was well in the world of university education. That would be a mistake. The regression seen in the church is present in university education as well. Elite universities like UNC may not be experiencing the struggles prevalent in other universities, but the regression of the university system is significant.

According to the National Center for Educational Statistics, 2,267 United States institutions offered bachelor's degrees in 2021–22.[4] With the thousands of universities in the United States, the millions of students, and the billions of dollars invested in the system, it is hard to imagine the university system itself is experiencing significant distress. Facts, however, disrupt illusions. The university system in the United States is facing significant pressures. While those pressures have not disrupted many elite universities as of yet, they are present even in them.

1. University of North Carolina at Chapel Hill, "History and Traditions."
2. The Carolina Story, "The Old Well."
3. Baucom, "What Is It."
4. National Center for Educational Statistics, "Characteristics."

PERCEPTION

Since the end of World War II, Americans have seen a university degree as an entrance into the middle class. College education became part of the American dream, and most parents wanted it for their children as evidenced by the public support of the expansion of funding for education.[5]

2023 data, however, point to a new reality. Americans do not trust college education at the level of the historical norm. According to Gallup, American confidence in university education has fallen to 36 percent. Notably, the fall has accelerated in the last decade. In 2015, 57 percent of Americans had a great deal of confidence in university education, and in 2018, 48 percent expressed such confidence.[6] Dropping 21 percent in eight years is a fall from grace that could make Adam and Eve blush. Of course, there are ideological sources of the problem as Republicans' confidence in higher education has fallen further and faster. The loss of trust in higher education, however, takes place across political parties, educational levels, gender, and age. Society as a whole has lost confidence.

Zack Hrynowski, an education researcher at Gallup, said that while the results were "eye-popping," higher education officials need not be concerned. They only needed to be paying attention.[7] His response is simply mind-boggling. Consider that 53.7 percent of Americans have a college degree or a postsecondary certification.[8] That means that a significant portion of those with college degrees view colleges negatively. To read the data without seeing cause for alarm is denial. In fact, there should be more than concern: higher education officials should be distressed about this data. The data have a cause, and it is not just the politically polarizing times. Something has gone wrong in higher education. In fact, 66 percent of Americans believe college education does not meet the needs of students, and only 49 percent of Americans believe a college education is worth the cost.[9]

---

5. Weir, "American Middle Class," 179.
6. Brenan, "Americans' Confidence."
7. Blake, "American Confidence."
8. Nietzel, "Percentage Of U.S. Adults."
9. Public Agenda, "America's Hidden Common Ground."

ATTENDANCE

From 2019–22, undergraduate enrollment in the United States fell 8 percent.[10] From 2010–21, undergraduate admission in the United States fell by more than 15 percent.[11] At the peak of college attendance in 2010, there were 18.1 million undergraduates, and by the fall of 2021, there were 15.4 million.[12] While experts anticipate a rise in college attendance in the coming years, even optimistic numbers project only 16.8 million college students by 2031.[13] If that estimate is correct, even after two decades, the number of college students will not have rebounded to the 2010 level.

Startling as that number is, it does not tell the full story. Included in the number of college students are dually enrolled students. Dually enrolled students are high school students taking college courses, usually at a community college, to earn both high school and college credit.

Twenty percent of all community college students are now high schoolers getting college credit for their classes.[14] Education reporter Jill Barshay reports that there were an estimated 1.4 million students in dual enrollment programs in the 2022–23 academic year, and some scholars were suggesting a much higher number closer to 2 million.[15] Even the upper estimates were wrong, however. By the time the data were analyzed a whopping 2.5 million students were dually enrolled.[16] In fact, there is some evidence that the decline in college attendance may have stopped, but the cause is an increasing number of dually enrolled students, not increasing college attendance among the population of high school graduates.[17]

There are significant benefits for the student for dual enrollment. The student gets both high school and college credit for classes. Students can begin college with significant college credit and reduce the number of hours they need to take to complete their degree. There is a cost

10. Blinkley and Associated Press, "Labor Shortage."
11. Meyer, "Case for College."
12. Irwin et al., "Report," 4.
13. National Center For Education Statistics, "Undergraduate Enrollment."
14. Mehl, "Twenty Percent."
15. Barshay, "Dual Enrollment Has Exploded."
16. Barshay, "How Dual Enrollment."
17. Knox, "Can High Schoolers."

reduction; dually enrolled students can take classes for free or at a substantially reduced rate.

Whatever benefits dual enrollment has for the student, however, do
not get passed along to the college or university. Dually enrolled students
do not pay full tuition, so the cost has to be paid by the institution or
the state. When the students become undergraduates, they need fewer
classes to graduate. That means the universities will have fewer opportunities to charge the student tuition. In other words, more students have to
pay less money for a college degree, reducing the cash flow of the institution. Since about 95 percent of universities are reliant on tuition dollars
to operate,[18] being able to charge individual students for fewer semester
hours is a drain on the system.

The popularity of dual enrollment programs also inflates the number of college students. Dual enrollment has existed for decades, but participation has increased significantly since 2010. If estimates are correct
that 2 million students were in the program in 2023, then the number
of college students in 2023 includes students who would not likely have
been counted in 2000.

The situation will not likely improve anytime soon. Colleges and
universities are facing an "enrollment cliff." Beginning with the class of
2025, the size of the high school population in the United States will
shrink significantly. Most estimates are that the size of the class of high
schoolers is 15 percent below demographic expectations.[19] To maintain
the level of college students currently enrolled, colleges and universities
will have to increase the percentage of high school students who will attend college.

The data are difficult for colleges. They present a picture of a difficult
present and an uncertain future. As the number of students declines, colleges and universities will be under increased financial pressure. Since
2016, ninety-one private colleges have closed.[20] One study estimates
20 percent of US four-year institutions are at risk.[21]

18. Burris, "Why More and More Colleges."
19. Burris, "Why More and More Colleges."
20. Burris, "Why More and More Colleges."
21. Buchanan, "Universities Facing."

FINANCIAL DATA

The largest Catholic university in the United States, DePaul University, is facing significant financial woes.[22] For the 2023–24 fiscal year, DePaul has a shortfall of $56 million.[23] To meet this shortfall, DePaul is offering voluntary separation to 15 percent of its staff and administration.[24] DePaul notes the pressures it is facing: decreased graduate school enrollment, ending of COVID support, inflation, and increases in financial aid.[25]

DePaul has managed to keep its number of undergraduates at a steady level; it has, however, admitted more students from lower-income families. While this is a noteworthy goal, it results in more students who need significant financial aid. That financial aid has strained DePaul's financial reserves.

DePaul has also had a decrease in attendance in its graduate programs. That shortfall, while significant, cannot explain DePaul's financial straits. Inflation and the end of COVID support are likely causes, but they cannot explain the totality of the picture either.

DePaul is not alone in facing significant financial pressures. Many universities are responding to the financial pressure by cutting programs. Chancellor Frank Gilliam of UNC Greensboro recommends the university cut nineteen "cost prohibitive" programs, including religious studies, physics, and anthropology. Clarkson University in Potsdam, New York, plans to phase out all of its humanities and social sciences majors and close its Department of Communication.[26] Miami University of Ohio informed members of seventeen departments they must merge, reorganize, or close.[27] Even the venerable University of Chicago has implemented a hiring freeze. Despite having a $10 billion endowment, the university has a budget shortfall of $239 million and has $5.8 billion in debt.[28]

Nearly 30 percent of all colleges took in less revenue per student in 2017–18 than in 2009–10.[29] Birmingham Southern College was unable to stem the financial onslaught. After eighteen months of seeking help, the

22. Querolo, "Largest Catholic University."
23. Moody, "What Do DePaul's Budget Woes."
24. Querolo, "Largest Catholic University."
25. Moody, "What Do DePaul's Budget Woes."
26. Grindon, "Clarkson Announces Plan."
27. Lederman, "Citing Significant Budget Deficits."
28. Moody, "2024 Begins."
29. Butrymowicz, "Crisis Is Looming."

College Board of Trustees voted to close the venerable 168-year-old institution.[30] Marietta College in Ohio is laying off twenty-two faculty members, fourteen administrators, and leaving thirteen positions unfilled.[31]

One university where financial pressures are most acute is West Virginia University (WVA). As a flagship institution, WVA's struggles are unusual. That, however, does not make them less difficult. The university faces projected budget deficits to climb as high as $75 million over the next five years. WVA faces intense pressure from decreasing enrollment, as it has fallen 10 percent since 2015.[32] To compensate for the reduction in revenue, WVA's administrators have proposed cuts to thirty-two programs, including the entire program of world language, literature, and linguistics.[33]

Another flagship institution, the University of Kansas (KU), is facing budget woes as well. As early as 2020, KU had a budget deficit of $120 million, more than one-fourth of its operating budget.[34] Much of that financial collapse had to do with COVID. Because KU's campus was closed during the pandemic, the university lost major revenue streams, including housing, dining, event fees, and research funding.[35] Unfortunately, KU did not recover financially after COVID-19. In 2022, the university still faced a budget shortfall of $75 million and proposed cutting forty-two academic programs.[36]

LESS PUBLIC SUPPORT

Often in cases of declining financial situations, public institutions will blame state legislatures for lack of support. Indeed, the overall spending for two- and four-year institutions fell $9 billion from 2008 to 2017.[37] Since 2017, the situation has changed dramatically. States have increased spending on higher education by 27.5 percent over the last five years, and devote now over $100 billion to it.[38]

30. Mitchell, "Another Small Liberal Arts College."
31. Burke, "Marietta College."
32. Knox, "Shrinking Pains."
33. Associated Press, "Financial Crisis."
34. AP Wire, "University of Kansas."
35. AP Wire, "University of Kansas."
36. Moody, "University of Kansas."
37. Mitchell et al., "A Lost Decade in Higher Education Funding."
38. Nietzel, "State Support."

There are other causes than a reduction in the size of the student population. Consider the case of Yale University. While Yale has never been known as a lower-price option in university education, it has developed a problem with administrative bloat, creating financial pressure on the institution. In 2021, Yale had more administrators than faculty members.[39] The growth in administrators led to a 5 percent cost increase in personnel to $2.7 billion.[40] Just as strikingly, in the 2020–21 academic year, there were 4,664 undergraduates[41] and 5,066 administrators.[42]

While there are multiple reasons for having so many administrators, it cannot be denied that exceeding the number of undergraduates creates pressure on costs and exerts significant financial pressure on the institution. According to the US Department of Labor, in 2022, the average salary of a postsecondary education administrator was nearly $100,000 per year. That does not include benefits. The cost to the institution, therefore, is significantly higher than $100,000. At UNC, the average salary for the 247 administrative staffers was $165,466 in 2023.[43]

Adding health care insurance, retirement, and other benefits, those staffers likely cost the university $200,000 per year or more on average. The pace of administrative hiring is increasing as well. At UNC, the cost per student of administrative support leaped 50 percent from 2006 to 2011.[44]

Whether the cost of the increased administrators is the primary driver of financial pressure or not, financial pressures are a serious problem with the universities. A survey by the American Association of Colleges and Universities reports that its respondents believe financial constraints are the most significant challenges for colleges and universities.[45]

COST

The cost of a university education continues to increase significantly. In 1980, the cost of a four-year college education, including fees, room,

39. Mousavizadeh, "'Proliferation of Administrators.'"
40. Mousavizadeh, "'Proliferation of Administrators.'"
41. US Bureau of Labor Statistics, "Postsecondary Education Administrators."
42. Mousavizadeh, "'Proliferation of Administrators.'"
43. Mousavizadeh, "'Proliferation of Administrators.'"
44. Warta, "Administrative Bloat."
45. American Association of Colleges and Universities, "Campus Challenges."

and board, was $10,231, adjusted for inflation. In 2019–20, the price was $28,775, a 180 percent increase.[46] According to the Education Data Initiative, tuition inflation was 12 percent annually from 2010 to 2022.[47]

It is also important to note that tuition is published to reflect the cost the student must pay in order to attend a college or university. The published tuition is not the full tuition. In North Carolina during the 2018 academic year, the state subsidized tuition at $12,635 per year per student, one of the highest rates in the nation.[48] This subsidy does allow the UNC university system to keep tuition low, but it also masks the true cost of the educational enterprise. In fact, the cost of a four-year college degree is much higher than what viewing tuition alone might lead one to conclude. While the rate of increase has moderated in the last two years, the long-term rate of inflation in the college and university system has yielded an unsustainable result.

THE EMERGENCE OF PRIVATE SCHOOLS AND HOMESCHOOLING

If the problem facing educational institutions were limited to colleges and universities, it would be easier to solve. The fates have provided no such fortune. The public school system shares in regression as well. While financial collapse is probably not going to force closures of public schools, they face some of the same pressures. The system is regressing.

The homeschooling movement began in the late 1970s and very few children participated, perhaps 13,000 children.[49] Homeschooling was a movement for a small group of fundamentalists. The movement grew in popularity through the 1990s but still had a very small footprint. According to the National Home Education Research Institute, there were 275,000 homeschooled students in the United States in 1990.[50] Although admitting data is difficult to find, *The Washington Post* reports there were between 1.9 and 2.7 million homeschooled students by 2023.[51] The number of homeschooled students grew 51 percent from 2017–18 until

46. McGurran, "College Tuition Inflation."
47. Hanson, "College Tuition Inflation."
48. Robinson, "Did You Know?"
49. National Home Education Research Institute, "Research Facts."
50. Ray, "Research Facts on Homeschooling."
51. Jamison et al., "Home Schooling's Rise."

2022–23. Public schools, by contrast, had a 4 percent decrease.[52] The size of the homeschool movement is substantial as more students attended homeschool than Catholic school in 2023.[53]

What could explain the fact that millions of students have left a free educational system to study at home? Some of the issue is clearly ideological, as many homeschooling parents believe their children are being indoctrinated into a worldview different than their own. Some of the issue, however, is quality or the perception of quality.

Michael Cogan, director of institutional research and analysis at the University of St. Thomas, notes that homeschooled students performed better on standardized admissions tests, earned more college credit before attending college, had higher first-semester college GPAs, and higher fourth-year GPAs.[54]

If parents, many without a degree in education, can generate results for their children exceeding the results of the public school system, must there not be a defect in the system? Are not those parents, then, vindicated by their student's academic performance?

One could argue that the results are skewed because the students whose parents are most involved are taking their students out of the system, leaving students with lesser parental involvement in the system. Taking students with precursors for success out of the system would make the public-school data worse and the homeschooling data look better. This still does not answer the question. What motivates parents to take their children out of a system they pay taxes to support?

It is not just homeschooling that is reducing the number of children in public schools. There is a strong history of private, Catholic, and other religious school systems in the United States. These systems, along with homeschooling, educated approximately 8.1 million students in 2022–23.[55]

INEFFECTIVENESS

Part of the issue is the uneven effectiveness of public schools. In Illinois, for example, recent studies reveal that a full fifty-three schools had zero

52. Jamison et al., "Home Schooling's Rise."
53. Payne, "As Home Schooling Soars."
54. Cogan, "Exploring Academic Outcomes."
55. Jamison et al., "Home Schooling's Rise."

students able to do math at grade level.[56] Those schools are not only fail-ing society; they are failing the students. In a society increasingly reliant on the technical skills of STEM graduates, these students are locked out of high-paying jobs and good futures. These students will be hampered by their inability to do math for their entire adult lives. Notice these scores are not about excelling at math. These scores are for students who can do mathematics at *their grade level*. This failure of education is an institutional failure with dire consequences for students and society.

It is not just math that is a problem for the Illinois school system—it is not teaching reading well either. A mind-boggling sixty public schools had no students reading at grade level.[57] The failure of the Illinois school system is nothing short of catastrophic.

As of yet, there has been no definitive response from educational authorities. Many blame the COVID response for the institutional fail-ure. Neither the state government nor the federal government, however, has intervened. Due to constitutional restrictions, there is little the fed-eral government could do in response to a failure like this. It does seem a failure of this magnitude, however, would merit congressional investiga-tion at a minimum. Based on the data and the failure to react alone, these schools and these students are not a priority for the institutional leaders who ought to be concerned.

Another large-scale failing of public instruction is in Philadelphia, Pennsylvania. Advocacy groups looking at public data estimate that 52 percent of Philadelphia adults are "functionally illiterate."[58] The data demonstrate that not only did the school system fail, it has been failing for a generation or more. To overcome this failure, governments and pri-vate groups are working feverishly. The problem remains, however, that the single best predictor of success in schools is parental involvement. If the parents are not literate, then how could one expect their children to succeed in school? There are exceptions to this rule; however, they are uncommon. The long-term effects are stark. Adults with limited reading skills face difficulties in healthcare and gaining job opportunities.

Worse than failing to educate students is giving them a credential saying they have an education when they do not. In 2021, Oregon aban-doned its essential skill requirement, which required passing standardized

56. Dabrowski and Klinger, "Illinois Education."
57. Griffith, "Damning Report."
58. Sitrin, "How 'Reading Captains.'"

tests for high school students. Since then, graduation rates have soared. 81.3 percent of Oregon's students graduated in 2022. Only 43 percent of those students were proficient in English, and only 31 percent were proficient in math, however.[59] Oregon education officials believe that removing the testing requirement was helpful because not every student who learned would test well.[60] It is difficult to imagine, however, that more than 50 percent of its students are poor test takers. Removing the testing requirement only allows poor educational outcomes to be hidden.

In Charles Dickens's classic *A Christmas Carol,* Ebenezer Scrooge notices something protruding from beneath the Ghost of Christmas Present's robe:

> "Forgive me if I am not justified in what I ask," said Scrooge, looking intently at the Spirit's robe, "but I see something strange, and not belonging to yourself, protruding from your skirts. Is it a foot or a claw?"
>
> "It might be a claw, for the flesh there is upon it," was the Spirit's sorrowful reply. "Look here."
>
> From the foldings of its robe, it brought two children; wretched, abject, frightful, hideous, miserable. They knelt down at its feet, and clung upon the outside of its garment.
>
> "Oh, Man, look here! Look, look, down here!" exclaimed the Ghost.
>
> They were a boy and a girl. Yellow, meagre, ragged, scowling, wolfish; but prostrate, too, in their humility. Where graceful youth should have filled their features out, and touched them with its freshest tints, a stale and shriveled hand, like that of age, had pinched, and twisted them, and pulled them into shreds. Where angels might have sat enthroned, devils lurked, and glared out menacing. No change, no degradation, no perversion of humanity, in any grade, through all the mysteries of wonderful creation, has monsters half so horrible and dread.
>
> Scrooge started back, appalled. Having them shown to him in this way, he tried to say they were fine children, but the words choked themselves, rather than be parties to a lie of such enormous magnitude. "Spirit, are they yours?" Scrooge could say no more.
>
> "They are Man's," said the Spirit, looking down upon them. "And they cling to me, appealing from their fathers. This boy is Ignorance. This girl is Want. Beware them both, and all of their

59. Withe, "Oregon Just Dropped."
60. Associated Press, "New Oregon Law."

degree, but most of all beware this boy, for on his brow I see that
written which is Doom, unless the writing be erased. Deny it!"
cried the Spirit, stretching out its hand towards the city.[61]

The consequence of ignorance is doom, says Dickens. It is hard to
argue he is incorrect. Ignorance produces want, terror, dread. It is the
bane of all enlightened societies, the specter educational institutions exist to wage war against. If billions of dollars and millions of employees
produce cities whose populations are functionally illiterate or unable to
do high school math, then society teeters on the abyss.

COVID

The decision to close schools during COVID has met with educational
failure. Whatever the public health benefits may or may not have been,
students suffered academically during the shutdown. The average thir-
teen-year-old's math scores retreated to levels not seen since the 1990s.[62]

Students at every level had a statistically significant decrease in
performance, but those at the bottom suffered a more pronounced reduction.[63] While some educators correctly note the COVID response
accelerated ongoing trends, the results of the decision were harmful to
the students' education.

COVID did produce a reduction in student performance. Students
who were not prepared to make the shift suddenly had to learn at home.
Educators who were not prepared for the shift suddenly had to teach
students remotely while juggling their own responsibilities in their own
homes. The results were poor.

ACT scores in 2022 fell to their lowest level in over thirty years, and
SAT scores fell as well.[64] Janet Godwin, CEO of ACT, notes that 40 percent of test takers meet none of the college-readiness benchmarks of the
ACT, and scores have fallen for five consecutive years.[65] Certainly part of
the issue is the COVID disruption. High school graduates were also less
prepared for academic and social success than those who completed their

61. Dickens, *Christmas Carol*, 47.
62. Mahnken, "NAEP Scores 'Flashing Red.'"
63. Mahnken, "NAEP Scores 'Flashing Red.'"
64. Bushard, "ACT College Admission Test Scores."
65. Godwin, "Average ACT Score."

courses before the pandemic. That observation, while true, can miss the point.

Just as with other institutional regressions, COVID was not the only cause. COVID only accelerated the problems that already existed. Godwin states:

> These declines are not simply a by-product of the pandemic. They are further evidence of longtime systemic failures that were exacerbated by the pandemic. A return to the pre-pandemic status quo would be insufficient and a disservice to students and educators.[66]

While COVID caused significant harm to learners, the institution of education was already regressing. The failures in education were "longtime systemic failures" long before COVID.

COLLAPSE

Education as an institution is teetering on collapse. Universities are scrambling for students and funding; many large-scale educational public school systems are failing to educate; and generations of people are not learning basic skills. In Washington, DC, 25 percent of adults are illiterate,[67] and in Buffalo, New York, 30 percent of residents are functionally illiterate. A staggering 130 million American adults read below a sixth-grade level.[68]

Many educators and policymakers are in denial about the situation. Blaming COVID is not sufficient, as the problems predated the pandemic. Blaming testing instruments is insufficient as test disparities are on the margins. Wholesale failure to pass tests, as in Oregon, is not the fault of the test.

Immigration is a significant problem as well, as many of those who struggle with reading speak a language other than English at home. Knowing that should cause a change in strategy. It has not. Instead of changing strategy, leaders of many states seek to blame tests, income levels, racism, or other outside forces. Blame is a telling indicator of regression.

66. Godwin, "Average ACT Score."
67. Washington Literacy Center, "Left Behind."
68. Chernikoff, "1 in 5 Americans."

The system is not educating, and many parents are fleeing it to private schools or starting to homeschool their children. The regression of education is toxic for society.

4

Work in Regression

Deprived of work, men and women lose their reason for existence; they go stark, raving mad.

— FYODOR DOSTOEVSKY

If one wanted to crush and destroy a man entirely . . . one need only give him work of a completely useless and irrational character.

— FYODOR DOSTOEVSKY

THE ROLE OF WORK IN A WELL-ORDERED LIFE

ON THE FIRST FRIDAY of every month, the Bureau of Labor Statistics (BLS) releases its monthly report on employment. Economists and investors read the reports with the seriousness of an oracle from Delphi. Except these oracles are not the wisdom of Apollo concerning the future—these oracles are the estimations of the BLS about the past. Notoriously inaccurate, these oracles are updated monthly to reflect changes in previous months. One hundred thousand new jobs in March might get updated to 120,000 or 75,000 depending on the data the BLS gets. In

August 2024 the BLS revised its 2023–24 numbers down 818,000, meaning the economy created 818,000 fewer jobs than originally reported.

What investors call the "headline number" is the unemployment rate. As of August 2024, that rate was 4.3 percent. Even though the number looks quite good and is one of the lowest unemployment rates in the developed world, it is an increase over previous months and is alarming to investors.

Often not noticed in the BLS data is what is called the workforce (or labor force) participation rate. The workforce participation rate is the percentage of working-age persons who are in the workforce or are looking for work. In June of 2024, that number was 62.6 percent. The figure was up from the pandemic era, but a longer-term look at the data shows some disturbing trends. Since 1990 the number has fallen from 66.5 percent to 62.6 percent. The decline in the work force participation rate demonstrates that a substantial number of working-age adults are not working and are not looking for work.

If factoring for just men, the work rate has fallen by 18 percent from the early 1950s until the present.[1] Factoring for just men is important to get the whole picture. In the 1950s, the traditional model of husband at work with wife and children at home was still the norm, and substantially more people lived in that model than now. The increase of women in the workforce has grown steadily, so a comparison of the total number of people in the workforce in the 1950s with the 2020s is not helpful. Isolating for men, however, shows a long-term trend of fewer people in the workforce by percentage.

WORK IS VITAL

Philosophers from King Solomon to Karl Marx have agreed on one thing if nothing else: work is a central part of the human experience. To be disconnected from work is to lead a life of boredom and shame.

Without work, one's life becomes listless. Finding entertainment on social media, playing video games, and endless chasing of pleasure become the norms. Most of those not in the workforce spend seven hours per day watching TV, playing video games, or other forms of leisure activities.[2] Women who are in this group spend even more time in these

1. Eberstadt, *Men Without Work*, 41.
2. Dokoupil and Finn, "Millions of Men."

activities than their male counterparts. On average they spend 11.5 hours on personal time, most of that sleeping.[3] Spending one's life in these kinds of activities is not the norm in human history, and is by no means a harbinger of mental health.

There is value at getting up in the morning, dressing for work, and presenting oneself for work. If nothing else, it provides a structure for existence. The human mind needs order to thrive. Without the quotidian acts of work, the mind fixates on the unimportant and finds destructive ends.

Ennui and nihilism are ever-present for those who choose to not work. Those attributes are seldom associated with mental health or long-term wellbeing either. A sign of this negative association is the lack of caring for other members of the household. Shockingly, working women spend more time caring for members of their households than men who are not employed even though the unemployed men have much more disposable time.[4]

Those who do not work are also more likely to abuse substances.[5] While the data here reflect those who have lost work and may be using illegal drugs as a coping mechanism, the larger point remains. Working people tend to use illegal drugs less often. Lack of work, then, is connected to illicit drug and the bad behaviors associated with it.

One underrated consequence of missing work is missing personal growth. When one works, one develops knowledge, expertise. Over years of work in a field, an employee develops specialized knowledge that a newcomer to a field could not know. Millions of people not working means a loss of human potential on a massive scale. This loss of potential does affect each of the individuals, but it also affects society as a whole.

The absence of work necessarily leads to a life of consuming what others have produced. A British man describes his nonworking life this way:

> I currently finance my life through benefits, which I don't particularly enjoy. When I meet new people, I sometimes feel embarrassed about my situation. They tell me about all the cool things they've done and achieved. Then come the questions and I have to justify myself. I think they don't see the emotional reasons behind my decisions, but I certainly won't do nothing forever.[6]

3. Eberstadt, *Men Without Work*, 29.
4. Dokoupil and Finn, "Millions of Men."
5. Generes, "Recession, Unemployment, and Drug Addiction."
6. Theis, "We Asked NEETs."

Perhaps his "do nothing" phase of life is temporary, but the longer he remains in it, the less employable he becomes, and the more likely he is to never return to work. What a person does affects their character. The longer a person persists in inactivity, therefore, the more inactivity defines his or her character.

Like most of those who are not working and are not in the educational system, the man in question finances his life through taxpayer benefits. He takes from the public system even though he is fully capable of working or developing a marketable job skill.

Others finance their lives by familial support, living with their parents or other family members. Still others finance their lives by living off the support of a partner.

In her haunting "Fast Car," Tracy Chapman describes a life with a partner who remained unemployed. In Chapman's wrenching song, the unemployment of her partner created the conditions for poverty, neglected children, and misery. Perhaps her character found the courage at the end to force her partner out.

If the data are to be believed, this is the lot of millions of those who choose to have nonworking partners. If in the context of a relationship where one spouse is involved with work and the other takes care of the home, this arrangement can be quite helpful. If, however, in the context of a relationship where one spouse refuses to work overall, it is destructive.

Those who work are more invested in society and its future. The act of working and paying taxes means that one is contributing to society. Taxes fund roads and schools, hospitals, and social programs. Taxes fund the military and scientific exploration. Those who do not work contribute very little to the corporate ventures of society. While they may care immensely about them, their contribution is minimal, if any. In fact, they become a net drain on society. Working and producing something of societal good is a cornerstone responsibility of adulthood. Unwillingness to work is the functional definition of selfishness.

THE DATA ON MEN AND WORK

Occasionally, a new acronym is born. The acronym describes a new reality or gives a handy term for a common experience. Born in the United Kingdom in the 1980s, "NEETS" describes the reality of a growing subset of the populace. NEETS means "not in employment, education, or training."[7] NEETS have dropped out of the basic structure of living, employment. In 2023, approximately 11.2 percent of Americans aged 15–24 were NEETS.[8]

Men Without Work is a significant study on the problem of men outside the workforce. The author, Nicholas Eberstadt, critically examines the data and alerts his readers to the problem.

The data for men not in the workforce is shocking. Between 1948 and 2015, the work rate for men twenty and older fell from 85.8 percent to 68.2 percent.[9] More disturbing is the number of men over twenty without paid work doubled from 14 percent to 32 percent. Factoring in retirement, by 2015, 22 percent of men between twenty and sixty had no paid work, constituting a 230 percent increase from 1948.[10] The number of men not in the workforce is at levels not seen since the Great Depression.[11]

The raw number of prime, working-age men not in the workforce was 7.2 million in 2014. Factoring for those in educational programs, the number is 6.4 million.[12] 6.4 million men outside the workforce is simply breathtaking. This is a mass of people living outside the normative structure of life. For comparison, there are just over 2 million people in the US military.[13] Men outside the structure of work number about three times the size of the US armed forces. Once the productivity of US male workers was the envy of the world. In 2015, however, the US ranked twenty-second among twenty-three countries in work participation.[14] The problem is not a lack of opportunity. According to one report, 770,000 manufacturing jobs were available in 2023.[15]

Supposing that these are men undereducated who cannot find an opportunity would be a mistake. True, most of them have a high school diploma or less, but two-fifths of them had some college and one-sixth of them had at least a bachelor's.[16] These millions of men are not seeking

7. Theis, "We Asked NEETs."
8. Dickler and Solá, "'NEETS' and 'New Unemployables.'"
9. Eberstadt, *Men Without Work*, 44.
10. Eberstadt, *Men Without Work*, 44.
11. Eberstadt, *Men Without Work*, 47.
12. Eberstadt, *Men Without Work*, 61.
13. USAFacts, "How Many People."
14. Eberstadt, *Men Without Work*, 68.
15. Dokoupil and Finn, "Millions of Men."
16. Eberstadt, *Men Without Work*, 78.

opportunities. Content to stay out of the workforce, these men survive by other means.

The data also present a perverse incentive for men who do not work. Due largely to social assistance programs, they have higher income than other groups. Particularly striking is that they have higher incomes than many single mothers who work or are seeking work.[17]

WORK AND MORALITY

Eberstadt insists that he is only describing the financing of the NEETS when he notes most of them receive public assistance. He notes others misread him by suggesting he states the public assistance is the cause of the problem.[18] He actively avoids making a causal connection between assistance and not working.

Unfortunately, this is to misread human nature. When people are given money to not work, they will choose not to work. In other words, financial incentives work. If someone has a financial incentive to stay out of the workforce, that incentive is at least part of the cause.

In California, land of the golden sun and misbegotten policy ideals, the city of Stanton ran a pilot program for universal basic income.[19] Although initial reports of the program were positive, the program ignores a basic fact of human life: humans respond to financial incentives. Giving people financial incentives to refrain from working contributes to people not working. Giving such assistance to a broad swath of the population will result in more people out of the workforce.

Much like rent control makes it more difficult to find places to live and price controls are inflationary, a well-meaning investment to give universal income only serves to increase the number of people not working and reduce the efforts of those who do. Why work harder to get a raise when one already gets a stipend?

Getting the NEETS an income is not the problem, nor is it a technical problem about employment. The primary problem is not even the technical problem of how NEETS manage to do so well. The primary problem is an ethical and moral problem with the NEETS themselves.

17. Eberstadt, *Men Without Work*, 130.
18. Eberstadt, *Men Without Work*, 176.
19. Brady, "California Unveils."

Because the NEETS are primarily men, an alternative way to look at the data is to be concerned about the moral and ethical collapse of millions of men. What is it that has happened to them?

Eberstadt writes:

> [The data point to] an almost revolutionary change in male attitudes toward work and dependence in post-war America. It is impossible to imagine any earlier generation in which such a huge swath of prime-age men would voluntarily absent themselves from the workforce, living on the largesse of women they knew and taxpayers they did not.[20]

The 2005 movie *Cinderella Man* pictures the change in mindset well. In the award-winning film, Russell Crowe portrays professional boxer James Braddock. Braddock was a champion boxer in the pre-Depression era. Braddock was not only a champion boxer: he was financially secure from his winnings. All of that changed with an injury. With an injury to his right hand, Braddock spiraled, eventually struggling to survive. In deep shame, Braddock ended up on welfare.

Braddock finally found work on the docks. Able to shield his injured hand from prying eyes and further injury, he was able to provide for his family again and heal from his injury. Eventually, someone remembered Braddock and asked him to stand in for a fight. He would have been notorious. The washed-up fighter now was fodder for young, talented boxers on the journey to fame. Unexpectedly, Braddock won the fight. He continued to win fights, finally becoming world champion again.

The movie is some of director Ron Howard's best work. One aspect of Braddock's mindset that Howard and Crowe portray well is Braddock's revulsion at being on public assistance. Once Braddock could support his family again, he paid back the entire sum he had received from public assistance. For a man of Braddock's generation, it was unthinkable, unmanly, even shameful to depend on public assistance. Due to overuse, the term "revolutionary" has lost much of its punch. Everything from diet drinks to mild advances in dishwashing detergent get the label. It hardly seems powerful enough to describe the phenomenon.

It is not just living off of government assistance that would have shamed a man of Braddock's generation. Living off of his wife or girlfriend's wages would have been deeply shameful. It is quite novel that men would be willing to live off of a partner's income.

20. Eberstadt, *Men Without Work*, 131.

Recent data suggests that men whose wives make more than them experience more stress in their relationships. The situation damages their self-worth and can cause harm in the relationship.[21] Even in the era where women have significant earning power and one-fourth of them out-earn their partners, couples where the woman makes more money tend to hide it.[22] Even in a normal relationship, a wife making more than her husband is a significant complication. It has to be much more complicated with the NEETS. The male NEET is not just making less than his partner: he is contributing nothing financially to the relationship. That millions could live in a situation like this is a striking change in society.

Few large changes happen in society quickly, and this change in work has developed over a generation. It is not, however, a technical problem. Social scientists tend to see problems like this one and immediately suggest a response through the educational system. Education, it seems, can cure any societal ill. Except it cannot. Believing the problem of NEETS can be solved in education is a kind of magical thinking.

Of course, here, education means the learning that takes place in the US educational system. Much of that occurs in a moral vacuum. Yes, the system teaches tolerance, diversity, and multiculturalism, and the system is fairly successful at that. Teaching, however, as a moral pursuit is absent. Missing is Plato's goal that education is the process of teaching the student to love the beautiful or Aristotle's desire that students pursue the good. The educational system does not emphasize any kind of connection between morality and work.

Worse, one has to hear the overused business maxim, "Your systems are precisely designed to get the results you are now achieving." If the maxim is true, one has to see the educational system as part of the problem and needs significant reform.

The problem is not a lack of learning or a lack of opportunity. There is plenty of opportunity for people who are willing to work, even if they have limited education. Work in the trades can be lucrative. Working in technology-related fields can produce solid income. Neither of these fields require extensive education. They simply require work.

21. Stieg, "Men Get More Stressed."
22. Leonhardt, "When Women Make More."

THE PROBLEM IS MORAL

In his review of Charles Dickens's corpus, George Orwell notes that Dickens does not seem too familiar with work and that the occupations of his characters is seldom their reason for existence.[23]

> That is the spirit in which most of Dickens' books end—a sort of radiant idleness. Where he appears to disapprove of young men who do not work . . . it is because they are cynical and immoral or because they are a burden on somebody else; if you are "good," and also self-supporting, there is no reason why you should not spend fifty years in simply drawing your dividends.[24]

Life's goal in Dickens's work was to live in a strange eighteenth- and nineteenth-century dream world. It was a dream of *complete idleness.*[25]

While contemporary US society bears sparing similarity to Dickens's England, work has become quite displaced from morality and meaning as well. That is the primary reason why the NEETS are not working. They find no moral meaning in work, and perhaps not in life in general.

The dream of a life of complete idleness is just that—a dream. It cannot be achieved except under very odd circumstances. When achieved, it seldom produces happiness. Winners of the lottery are seldom happy years after the event.

More than the impracticability and unhappiness in it, it does not produce the virtues necessary for the good life. Whatever one believes about God, it is a shared observation that humans do not do well without work. In the Judeo-Christian tradition, work is a gift from God. Frequently misunderstood, the Genesis narrative of the fall does not teach that work is a curse. Adam had an occupation before any curse. The curse frustrates work. It does not mean work is a curse.

On this point, believers in the Judeo-Christian tradition and unbelievers can easily agree: a life without work is far from idyllic. It is tedious and full of boredom. It is a life spent in the pursuit of pleasure. Pleasure, however, is self-defeating. Once a pleasure is attained, it stops producing the same pleasure. A new car becomes old, and a favorite dessert stops whetting the appetite. Gaining pleasure cannot yield happiness because pleasure is only temporary. A life spent in the pursuit of pleasure only ends in meaninglessness.

23. Orwell, *All Art Is Propaganda*, 37.
24. Orwell, *All Art Is Propaganda*, 44.
25. Orwell, *All Art is Propaganda*, 44.

IS WORK FUTILE?

Many younger workers do have a strain on them. The economic downturns of 2008–9 and the economic chaos from COVID have produced a sense among them that working is futile. Looking back in fondness, they see the wages their parents and grandparents earned and wonder how they could afford the lifestyle.

In the fall of 2023, a video by Brielle Asero went viral. Asero, a college graduate with a degree in marketing, took to TikTok to vent about her life. With her perfectly coiffed blonde hair and manicured nails, Asero wept when she thought about work. Working an ordinary nine-to-five job, Asero has to get up in the morning and prepare for work, gets on the train for her commute at 7:30, works a full day, and gets home at 6:15. Then she has chores and self-care to accomplish. There is little chance for a social life or personal pursuits. Asero is miserable.

Many responded to her video with disdain. "Work is hard," they sneered. Many noted how others worked longer and harder and had less to show for it. Unfortunately, comments like that cannot help. Asero was living under the illusion that life would be like college, which it assuredly is not. Worse, she seemed disconnected from her work. She did not find energy from work; it was just another drain.

She, like many, seemed to long for a world where work's rewards are enough to outweigh the sacrifice. She wanted to earn enough money to live and work substantially fewer hours. Many of her peers who grow frustrated with work look back at previous generations with envy. They want the world of the 1950s and 1960s, at least the part where one forty-hour-per-week income was enough to support an entire family.

Of course, the world they envision did not really exist. As with any retrospection, some of the assumptions are flawed. While previous generations did earn less and still have the necessities of life, they lived on less as well. They ate in restaurants less frequently; they owned fewer clothes; cable TV with its $100-per-month price point had not yet been invented; and not all of them owned a TV. Many of them owned only one car, and kept it longer. The houses were much smaller. Their lives were spartan in comparison.

Because they envy a world that never existed, they do not see their grandparents and great-grandparents as inspirational. They are intimidated by their success. Believing they cannot emulate what their grandparents and great-grandparents achieved, they give in to despair.

Others have a belief system that work is too tedious. Work is supposed to connect them to purpose, and if it does not, it is merely an obstacle. Why go to work when it is not enjoyable? In one sense they are mistaken: work is not usually fun. That is why someone has to pay employees to do it. If work were fun, it would be called "play" and everyone would sign up. No, pay is an exchange of labor. One should not expect work to be fun, exactly.

While not necessarily fun, though, finding work tedious is problematic, although this is a modern problem. Generations of people who worked in factories, mines, and farms probably thought work was quite tedious. Finding meaning in making a spool of yarn seems quite unlikely. What they did, however, was either find meaning in the work or endure it.

The data about work enjoyment is not promising. In a 2022 Gallup poll, 60 percent of workers report being emotionally detached at work and 19 percent report being miserable. Working fewer hours and even working remotely do not affect the misery.[26] "Workers are unhappy at home, at the office, working thirty-hour weeks, and sixty-hour weeks."[27] The key factor in the Gallup poll is management. Good management makes the difference between good employee experience and misery. Certainly, good management makes a difference; however, it cannot explain all of the data.

Employees are more distracted than ever. They have thirty-one interruptions per day and 1.96 hours of unproductive task work.[28] For the average employee, only 53 percent of work time is devoted to doing productive work.[29] Distractions do not, however, only mean tedious meetings and unnecessary tasks. Distractions can be from an employee's personal life, employees' interactions with each other, and even ever-present social media.

Distractions are powerful. They prevent completion of tasks. They create unnecessary workplace stress as employees' efforts to overcome distractions frustrate work. Energy spent to overcome distractions is not only a drain: the process itself causes frustration. In other words, a distracted employee is not productive, not engaged, and is usually not happy.

26. Collins, "Job Unhappiness."
27. Collins, "Job Unhappiness."
28. Schwantes, "New Report."
29. Schwantes, "New Report."

PROTESTANT WORK ETHIC

While distractions are more common now than they were in the past, finding meaning in work has nearly always been a challenge. For those who are Christian, finding meaning in work was connected to the belief that work was from God and for God. Providing all gifts, God provided work as a means of provision. Any work, therefore, was to be done with one's best efforts for the glory of God. Seeing work in that way helped keep many of them engaged even in repetitive tasks.

Others simply found ways to endure the tedium. Bonding with co-workers or simply keeping their focus on the end result of work helped them to work even though the work was not engaging.

While it may not be a wholly modern problem to see work as not engaging, it should be noticed. If one cannot find enjoyment at work, the solution is to find a different field of work. Changing occupations or careers is perfectly acceptable, and often, it should be encouraged. If one dreads going to work, it is perhaps time to change. With the variety of work and careers available and the many different training opportunities available for those who are willing, there are few reasons for people to not find something they enjoy doing.

Taking years off of work in the vain hope that sometime in the future one might find a fulfilling job, however, is immoral. To change careers is to actively work in a new field or gain training for a new field, not pine away for a perfect job. Spending years out of the workforce hoping that one will happen upon the "right" field is magical thinking.

INFLATION AND WORK

In the aftermath of the COVID pandemic, the US experienced something that had long been tamed: inflation. Inflation is the loss of purchasing power. Items cost 20 percent more in 2024 than they did in 2020.[30] That number was debilitating to families and family budgets. It contributed to the sense that work is worthless.

Inflation is, in effect, a tax hike. When the government spends money it does not have, it must get the money in one of three ways. It must raise taxes, borrow money, or print money. Printing money has the effect

30. Foster, "Inflation Accelerated."

of devaluing the currency. Once devalued, the money does not have the power it once did.

It could be called a stealth tax hike. With an open tax hike, officials vote to raise taxes. With inflation, governments simply print money, devalue it, and the result is the same. People have less purchasing power.

The power of inflation can be seen in home prices. In 2020 the median house price was \$317,000. In \$2024 it was \$412,000.[31] From 2021 to 2022, the average thirty-year mortgage payment went from \$1,400 per month to \$2,045 per month.[32] By 2024, the average thirty-year mortgage payment was \$2,715.[33]

Much of that increase is inflation, but the rest of that increase is the result of interest rates. To tame rising interest rates, the Federal Reserve raised interest rates. Home mortgage rates skyrocketed from 3 percent to over 7 percent. Historically, these rates do not seem high. The sudden increase, however, has made home ownership much more difficult.

Transportation costs are equally debilitating. From 2020 to 2024 the purchase price for the average new car has increased 21 percent and the price for used cars has increased 32 percent.[34] Higher prices and higher interest rates drove the average car payment from \$563[35] to \$735[36] per month in four years. In that same time frame, fuel costs went from \$2.25 per gallon[37] to \$3.43,[38] pillaging the bank accounts of US households. Inflation has increased the cost of groceries, energy, restaurant meals, higher education, healthcare, cars, homes, and virtually every other budget category for the American worker.

Work, then, has lost much of its reward. With good governance and fiscal stewardship, inflation will recede and interest rates will fall. Eventually, rising incomes should catch up to the inflated prices and the pressure on citizens will release. The painful reality for many families is that as of the summer of 2024, while inflation has gotten lower, there is a long way to go before their budgets have recovered.

31. Federal Reserve Bank of St. Louis, "Median Sales Price."

32. Witkowski, "Average U.S. Mortgage Payment."

33. Grace and Yale, "What Is the Average Mortgage Payment?"

34. Krisher, "Auto Prices."

35. Noel, "What Is the Average."

36. Davis, "Average Car Payment."

37. Troderman, "Retail Gasoline Prices Rose."

38. YCharts, "US Retail Gas Price."

Inflation, then, is a moral issue as well. It robs workers of their purchasing power. The harm it does to those on fixed incomes is worse, as their peak earning years are over. Living off savings when inflation is high is debilitating.

Inflation effectively discourages work. Why work when the reward for working loses value? Why work when the wage is suddenly not enough? For work to have importance, it must be valuable. Controlling inflation is a key to making work meaningful as inflation is a significant disincentive to work.

SOCIETY AND WORK

No society can function this way for long, and no healthy society would tolerate these conditions. Work is valuable and healthy. It is good for both the society and the individual.

5

Family in Regression

INSTITUTION OF MARRIAGE

PERHAPS ONE OF THE greatest intellectual follies of American life is the devaluation of words. "Sticks and stones may break my bones but words will never hurt me" is a slogan reflective of the mindset. Most people have uttered the old cliché, but their therapists spend much of their time helping them recover from noxious words spewed in their direction. Speech is not lifeless; it is powerful. Speech is one of the most powerful actions a person can take. Words can break, and words can heal. Words can transform, and words can create new realities.

Among the most powerful of words are words of institution. Millions of Americans witness words of institution in ceremonies every year.

> Dearly beloved: We are gathered here in the sight of God and in the presence of these witnesses to join together this man and this woman in holy matrimony, which is an honorable estate instituted by God, and signifying unto us the mystical union that exists between Christ and his Church; which holy estate Christ adorned and beautified with his presence in Cana of Galilee.
>
> Will you have this man to be your wedded husband, to live together in the holy estate of matrimony? Will you love him, comfort him, honor and keep him, in sickness and in health; and forsaking all others keep only to him so long as you both shall live?

> Will you have this woman to be your wedded wife, to live
> together in the holy estate of matrimony? Will you love her,
> comfort her, honor and keep her, in sickness and in health; and
> forsaking all others keep only to him so long as you both shall
> live?
>
> To have and to hold, from this day forward, for better for
> worse, in sickness and in health, to love and to cherish, till death
> us do part, according to God's holy ordinance; and thereto I
> pledge you my faith.[1]

Penned by Thomas Cranmer in 1549, these words and variations of
them have been used by millions of couples over the last half millennium
to begin something new: a marriage. It is a profound mistake to think
that marriage is a celebration of the love a couple has shared already.
No public words or witnesses are necessary for such a celebration. No
celebrant, priest, pastor, or judge needs to be called. No bridal gown, no
tuxedo, no florist or caterer is required for a celebration of love already
shared. What makes a marriage is a promise for the future.

Marriage begins with a promise to love even in the uncertainty of
tomorrow. The future is always unknown, and the conditions the couple
will face are always uncertain. Will they find success in their work or
failure? Will they have children or will infertility's cruel shadow darken
their nursery? How long they will live, and how well, is a mystery. All they
have is each other and a series of promises easily made and only kept with
difficulty.

Little wonder most couples, even those with little religious bent, seek
out Cranmer's words. The promise itself is imposing, and divine help is
warranted. Beyond their beauty, these promises remind the couple of what
marriage is: a commitment to remain together for life, come what may.

MARRIAGE'S EFFECT ON INDIVIDUALS

Not mentioned in Cranmer's ceremony is what marriage does to individuals. Sociologist Brad Wilcox writes that marriage

> is also an institution that transforms people, bonding men and
> women to a particular person, to a whole way of life. In doing
> so . . . it endows their lives, day in and day out, with more mean-
> ing, prosperity, stability, and solidarity, all of which typically
> boost the sense of satisfaction that men and women take from

---

1. Abingdon, *United Methodist Book of Worship*, 31.

their lives after they enter our civilization's most fundamental institution. In other words, the effect of marriage on the human happiness of people . . . is also causal.[2]

Married people are happier and wealthier. They also have greater meaning and purpose in their lives. Not only that, marriage has positive behavioral implications. Men who get married tend to work harder and perform better at work.[3] They also are less likely to get involved in destructive behaviors such as drug abuse or criminality.[4] Women who marry tend to report greater happiness and wealth.[5] They also report greater meaning and purpose in their lives. These data points are especially true of married mothers.[6] In short, marriage makes for healthier, happier people.

MARRIAGE'S EFFECT ON SOCIETY

Viewed from the lens of society, marriage is not only foundational: it is an unquestionable good. Marriage is the single best anti-poverty program. Families headed by a single mother are five times more likely to live in poverty than a married couple.[7] Further, children in two-parent homes do dramatically better on almost every measure.

"Marriage is the most reliable institution for delivering a high level of resources and long-term stability to children."[8] Being in a two-parent household is the single biggest predictor of upward economic mobility for children.[9] Further, children interact with their parents much more in two-parent households. This interaction includes reading, playing, and talking.[10]

While the data may not prove causality, there is a link between single-parent households, particularly households with absent fathers, and crime. Specifically, violent crime and homicide are much more common

2. Wilcox, *Get Married*, 91.

3. Wilcox, *Get Married*, 16.

4. Wilcox, *Get Married*, 86.

5. Wilcox, *Get Married*, 7.

6. Wilcox, *Get Married*, 8.

7. Kearny, *Two-Parent Privilege*, 44.

8. Kearny, *Two-Parent Privilege*, 14.

9. Wilcox, *Get Married*, 8.

10. Wilcox, *Get Married*, 117.

where there are fewer two-parent homes and many absentee fathers.[11] Marriage is, therefore, not just for the wellbeing of individuals: it is for the wellbeing of the community and society.

Against this backdrop, articles like "Why We Should Abolish the Family"[12] make very little sociological sense. Lily Sánchez, who penned the article, argues families are an impediment to human freedom and can impose harm on their members. Families are places of abuse, molestation, partner rape, and psychological torture.[13]

While it is true that relational difficulties often present themselves in families, that does not mean the institution itself is unhelpful. No sane person would eliminate all doctors because some of them were quacks, nor would any rational person give up on the idea of friendship because friends can betray each other. Eliminating family because some use family for evil ends is equally foolish. Those who commit abuse within a family are not only abusing the members of the family—they are doing damage to the institution itself. Further, the data are very clear about those outside family structures. The children in the greatest danger of abuse are those without intact two-parent homes.[14]

Sánchez is not alone. Famed commentator David Brooks argues that the nuclear family was a mistake.[15] Claire Chambers argues in *Against Marriage* that marriage is a violation of gender equity, is a sexist institution, and that the state should not recognize it.[16] One George Mason University professor argues marriage is a structural support of white supremacy.[17] Lest one think arguments against marriage are new, back in 1966, Mervyn Cadwallader referred to marriage as a "wretched institution."[18]

Those who want to argue against marriage have to do so based on ideology. Arguments like "marriage is sexist" or "marriage is heteronormative" abound in such literature. What they cannot do is argue based

11. Wilcox, *Get Married*, 108.

12. Sánchez, "Why We Should Abolish the Family."

13. Sánchez, "Why We Should Abolish the Family."

14. Sedlak et al., "Fourth National Incidence Study."

15. Brooks, David. "The Nuclear Family Was a Mistake" The Atlantic. March 2020. https://www.theatlantic.com/magazine/archive/2020/03/the-nuclear-family-was-a-mistake/605536/

16. Chambers, *Against Marriage*, 2.

17. Walker, "Professor Argues."

18. Cadwallader, "Marriage as a Wretched Institution."

on outcomes. The single best predictor of happiness and prosperity for individuals is a happy marriage.

FAMILY AS THE NORM IN HUMAN HISTORY

While it is tempting to say that marriage has not always existed in the way it does in the modern West, marriage as a relationship between one man and one woman is the norm in human history.[19] In ancient civilizations, families tended to gather in extended household groups that included multiple generations. This mode of living had advantages in antiquity but gradually gave way to the nuclear family.

The nuclear family has been the norm of civilization. Even the critics of marriage would concur. The nuclear family is not just an imposition of 1950s capitalists. It is not the consequence of a bourgeois class brimming with malicious anti-women forces. The nuclear family is the way humans have ordered existence from the beginning.

FAMILY DELAYED AND DENIED

An ill wind is blowing against marriage in the US, however: marital delay. In the 1950s the median age of men at their first marriage was 22.5 years. The average for women was 20.1 years. In 2023 the average for men was 30.2 and the average for women was 28.4.

Young people delay marriage for many reasons; chief among them is education. More young people attend college and graduate from college now than in 1950. More are also getting graduate degrees. Completing one's education at twenty-five versus eighteen would be a significant reason to delay marriage. Those who complete their education at twenty-five also often choose to find meaningful employment and to be significantly settled in their careers before getting married.

Other causes for delaying marriage include societal norms about sexuality. In the 1950s, premarital sex was verboten, at least publicly. In contemporary society, premarital sexuality is most often part of the ordinary dating process. Losing this stricture means that those who are dating can enjoy some of the benefits of marriage without the commitment.

This is not to say that widespread premarital sex has been a net benefit; far from it. It enables people to behave without responsibility. The

---

19. Chambers, "Against Marriage."

most extreme version of widespread premarital sex, hookup culture on college campuses, has hardly been a benefit. Crushed souls abound in the rubble of hookup culture. Rampant premarital sex and the culture around it divorces the act of sex from love and commitment and therefore enables young people to treat each other as commodities. As Kant might assert, it has enabled people to treat each other as objects, not ends in themselves.

Another cause of marital delay is cohabitation. Why go through the trouble to get married when moving in gets roughly the same end, or why not see if a couple can live together first before marriage? The problem is, however, that cohabitation is not a precursor of successful marriages. It is a precursor to divorce.[20]

Another cause for delay is the endless search for the right person. Perhaps the most difficult concept for individuals to process is that marriage is not so much about finding the right person but about being the right person. While it is important to find a good match who shares one's values, faith, and aspirations, all couples have places where they disagree. All couples have irreconcilable differences, differences they cannot repair. Successful marriages are not those without them—they function well despite them.

Contributing also to the delay of marriage is a curious phenomenon among marriage-aged men. 63 percent of 18–29-year-old men are not in a romantic relationship.[21] Not only are they not in a relationship, but increasing numbers of them are not interested in one. Spending significant time on social media and being able to fulfill their sexual desires through pornography, developing relationships with women is not a high priority for many men.[22]

For many women, advancement in their careers is a reason to delay marriage. While the option may seem good, it does have consequences. Women who delay marriage can find themselves in their late thirties and early forties wanting to be married but having difficulty finding a suitable partner. The dating pool is not as deep for them as it was in their twenties. If they want to have children, waiting is perilous as well. The single biggest predictor of being able to conceive is age.[23] Even with assisted reproductive technology, the possibility of being able to carry children

20. Atkinson, "New DU Study."
21. Gelles-Watnick, "For Valentine's Day."
22. Matos, "Why So Many Young Males."
23. Cha, "Cruel Twist of Fate."

declines rapidly as women age. For many women, delaying marriage and children for the sake of their careers has led to a single and often childless future.

CONSEQUENCES OF DELAYED MARRIAGE

The delay in marriage is having side effects in other parts of society. Delayed marriage often means delayed parenthood. For those who wisely wait to be married before having children, waiting means fewer opportunities to have children. A woman who marries at twenty-two, for example, has more time to have children than a woman who marries at thirty-two. If for no other reason than less time, families are having fewer children.

Delay in marriage, however, cannot be the only explanation. The birth rate in the US has fallen 20 percent since 2007,[24] and people were already delaying marriage by then. One explanation is the high cost of children. In an agrarian society, children were partners in the family enterprise. In a technological society, children are a cost. Treating children as a cost, however, is only credible in the most materialist calculation. What children provide has always been more than a financial calculation. Treating them as such is to think of them as a means.

Whatever the reason, fewer births means a bleak future. The US' birth rate, along with other developed nations, is now below replacement levels. Were it not for massive immigration, the US population would be shrinking.

ANTI-FAMILY CULTURE

US culture has become more anti-family. This observation is not so much about policy but about outlook. Only about 25 percent of Americans believe getting married or having children is extremely important in having a fulfilling life, while over 40 percent say these are not too important.[25]

When one looks at the data of happiness, meaning, and fulfillment in life, the single most determinative factor is marriage, however. 40 percent of adults see the most important factor as not too important. This disparity between perception and reality is almost Orwellian.

24. Kerney et al., "Mystery."
25. Kim and Minkin, "5. What Makes."

Some of this disparity is hyper-individualism in American culture. Americans tend to see happiness as the pursuit of pleasure. Happiness cannot be found by chasing pleasure, however. Happiness is a by-product of a life lived in pursuit of noble ends. Chasing pleasure leads to frustration when pleasure cannot be achieved or to disappointment when pleasure loses is intensity.

The best indicator of long-term happiness is in the quality of relationships. One revealing sign of the failure to live in relationships is the lack of sexual activity. Despite sexual partners being easier to find and the wholesale acceptance of the sexual revolution, young people are having less sex than previous generations at the same time in their lives.[26] While having multiple sexual partners is a recipe for divorce,[27] it does not seem that millennials or Gen Z have suddenly become puritans. What appears to be happening is that they are disconnected from each other relationally, too busy to form relationships, sometimes not having the skill to develop relationships, and preoccupied with trivial pursuits.[28] Relationships are secondary to career goals and educational goals. Further, young people seem to be too distracted by social media and technology to be connected. If relationships are what makes for human happiness, many in these generations do not perceive it.

MARRIAGE AND LOVE

Some of the disparity between what people perceive will make them happy and what is statistically more likely to make them happy is the notion that romantic love is the foundation of marriage. Some scholars have argued that romantic love is the creation of the medieval poet Chaucer and his reflections on courtly love. Whatever its origin, romantic love is a wonderful feeling. However, it cannot serve as a serious foundation for marriage.

Romantic love can ebb. A disagreement that turns into a serious argument can reduce romantic feelings. Busy work schedules and the challenges of parenting young children can chill libido. Because relationships are complicated, couples can get frustrated or angry with one another as

---

26. Fry, "'Failure to Launch.'"
27. Smith and Wolfinger, "Testing Common Theories."
28. Fry, "'Failure to Launch.'"

part of life. If one were to base marriage solely on the fleeting feelings of romantic love, few marriages would survive after the oxytocin wears off.

Love, specifically romantic love, does not sustain marriage. Marriage sustains love. What marriage does is allow for feelings to ebb and flow. The commitment and promise of marriage give love the chance to mature. It overcomes moments of failure and anger. The foundation of marriage means that couples have the security to pursue reconciliation when hurt.

In dating, if a couple finds themselves in a profound disagreement and harsh words have been said, it is quite easy to end the relationship. Without marriage, romantic relationships are disposable. From there, it is no great stretch to conclude that people are disposable. What marriage does is bring committed couples back together to work through their issues and create a better, healthier relationship. In the commitment of marriage, love can change and grow.

This kind of love transcends romantic love and can create it. Knowing that one's spouse will always seek the best allows that kind of love in return. Seeking the highest for the other is often quite costly to the self. Love seeks it anyway. Knowing that the other always seeks union empowers unity in response. If one were to base marriage on love, Aquinas's vision of love as seeking the highest and best good for the other is superior to Chaucer's vision.

FAMILY FIRST

One of the great fears in relationships is the loss of self. Many feminist authors recoil against marriage and traditional family precisely because they see marriage and the sublimation of the self to another or to the institution itself. In one sense their fears are warranted. In marriage, in love, one readily sacrifices the self for the other. In good marriages and families, it is all the members who make the sacrifice.

This family-before-individual mindset is counter to much marriage advice which focuses on making sure the self gets taken care of first. Teresa Newsome, writing relationship advice for *Bustle*, claims, "Self-care leads to a happier relationship," and "being in a relationship isn't about becoming a pleasing machine that works for everyone but yourself. You deserve self-care, damn it!"[29]

29. Newsome, "Little Self-Care Tips."

She continues:

> Continuing with the idea that the speakers in the car are yours
> half of the time, remember that so is the TV, the credit card, the
> vacations, the weekends, and the home. And so is the free time.
> Make sure to get your wants and needs met, too. Use your half!
> Your partner won't die if they have to watch a show they don't
> like. You didn't. They'll survive a date you planned. . . . You have.
> Even if it is just buying the kind of cookies you like sometimes.
> Make sure you're getting your half.
>
> If you do all of these things or even just a handful of them,
> you'll be so full of joy and relief that it will spill over into your
> relationship. And your partner will have a new respect for your
> "yes" because they'll know you really mean it.[30]

On the surface, she does have a point. After all, healthier people do
create healthy relationships, and the loss of one's person will destroy relationships. All humans need self-care. What is not expressed but assumed
is that relationships are places where people, particularly women, never
get their way and never get their needs met. Her logic is that one has to
fight for their needs or they will never be met.

It is odd, however, to think of a relationship this way. Yes, one
should be free to say what he or she needs. Her logic, however, assumes
a domineering relationship fitting for a Neanderthal and his prize rather
than a couple. She is much more concerned with power than love.

The article is not "11 Tips to Make Your Spouse's Day." At least in
this article, that is not in view. The article assumes the nature of relationships is a constant drain. Her point is, "Fight for what you need or
you and your relationship will suffer." If one has to constantly fight for
her needs to be met, what kind of relationship is it? In relationships that
practice Aquinas's version of love, one needs only say what his or her
needs are and the other will do their best to meet them because he or she
is seeking their highest and best good.

Also missing is that people get the greatest satisfaction in life in giving. It is better to give than receive. Giving of the self is not the path of
misery—it is the path of happiness. Healthy marriages are not the one
where each spouse makes demands for the sake of individual needs.
Healthy marriages have a "we before me" mentality.[31]

---

30. Newsome, "Little Self-Care Tips."

31. Wilcox, *Get Married*, 144.

Marriage is not founded on a balance of needs but on mutual self-sacrificial love. Both partners, although fallible, make their best efforts to do what is right for each other. Yes, there are times when there are competing needs and great disagreements about what is best, but the happiest persons and marriages are those where each is genuinely seeking the wellbeing of the whole. The family comes first.

SACRIFICIAL GIVING IS JOYFUL

It is more typical than usually acknowledged. A man will give up something he loves for the people he loves. Ray[32] was an excellent bowler. His team recognized and celebrated his contribution to their success. In their small town in the late 1970s, Ray's team was well known for their winning ways. Ray had several trophies for his bowling success that he kept on display in his home. One night after a team win, Ray came home to his family. His six-year-old daughter was fast asleep, but his four-year-old son waited for Dad to come home. He could barely keep his little brown eyes open as Ray came and sat in his favorite chair in the family living room. Climbing up in his dad's lap, he peered into his dad's eyes and said, "I don't want you to go bowling anymore. I want you to stay home with me." Rubbing his little eyes, he fell asleep in Ray's lap.

With that, Ray reconsidered his choices. Going out bowling several nights per week was what he had always done, even before marriage. There was nothing wrong with going bowling. In fact, using Newsome's advice, he could say he had the right to go. It was good. Going out could even be helpful for the family as it was self-care. Ray intuitively knew better. For the sake of his son, he chose to stop going bowling multiple nights per week. He sacrificed something he truly enjoyed for his son. Ray's choice was what everyone focused on the "we" of the family would gladly make.

Families are not without joy because of the self-giving, however. The exact opposite is true. Self-giving gives and sustains joy. In 2023, my youngest daughters, then six and four, were playing in the guest room. Unbeknownst to me, they were jumping on the bed. The older of the two came running to me reporting that the youngest had fallen off the bed. I ran to the room and picked up my terrified child. Holding her for an

---

32. "Ray's" name has been changed to protect his identity.

extended period, I noticed that she could not be comforted and that she would shriek in pain if I touched her elbow. She had broken her arm.

One week later at school, she was playing on the sliding board. Due to another child roughhousing with her, she fell, breaking her other arm: two casts. The next several weeks were difficult as we managed a child with one cast on each arm. Fortunately, she healed quickly.

When the casts were removed, however, she had a fear of getting hurt again. She was particularly afraid of being on the bed as she thought she might fall off and break her arm again. She wailed every night at bedtime.

Eventually, I found a solution. I would make a pallet on the floor between my girls' beds to comfort her. I would grab one of the mermaid pillows, lay on the floor, do our nighttime prayers, and hold her hand until she fell asleep. Realizing what I was doing, my six-year-old wanted to hold my hand too. So, I scooted the beds a little closer together so that I could reach both of them. For a few months, I lay on the floor holding my girls' hands as they went to sleep every night.

The hardwood floor did not make for a comfortable place to lay. I would frequently curse the stiffness in my joints as I struggled to get up once the girls fell asleep. I also had other responsibilities that had to wait while I lay on the floor. I would, however, trade nothing for those few months. It was a joy to be with my girls, and I was a little sad when they no longer needed my attention. The memory of those weeks remains joyful. Giving up my time was good for them, yes. It was also very good for me.

The truth of love is that doing the loving action creates the loving feeling. People sacrifice for whom they love, but they love those for whom they sacrifice. Doing the loving thing creates loving feelings.

MISCONCEPTIONS

One of the misconceptions about family that permeates society is that children are a net drain. Actor Seth Rogan and his wife Lauren Miller have chosen to be childless. In an appearance on *The Howard Stern Show*, Rogan noted that children would have limited his availability for work and that the responsibility of parenting children would dampen some of his preferred activities. Most importantly, according to Rogan, parents have to make children their priority. He adamantly does not want to do that.[33]

With Rogan's mindset, perhaps he made the right choice. After all, for him, kids are a burden. No child needs a parent who sees them that way. Rogan's mindset, however, is a mistake. Children do require attention, but they are a gift.

Rogan is just one of many who share his view. Not only do many see children as a drain, but they see children as bad for marriage. That view is not reflective of the whole. Marital satisfaction does decrease with small children and when they are teenagers, but on the whole, adults with children are more likely than their childless peers to report that they are happy or very happy.[34] The adults who report the greatest happiness and meaning in their lives are those with children.[35]

Other misconceptions include boredom. Somehow committing to one person and to one's children makes life tedious in the view of some. What is odd about that is that psychologists and spiritual thinkers have long taught that meaning and purpose are found in relationships. Having a variety of pleasures and new experiences without a family to share them with might be attractive for a while, but is not consistent with long-term happiness.

DIVORCE LAWS

Led by social influencers like Andrew Tate and Hannah Pearl Davis, there is a movement against marriage among those who see it as a bad bargain for men. Tate focuses more on men needing to be more masculine and gain more money and pleasure, while Davis focuses more on the devolution of women. For Tate, women are a complication to be avoided. They can come along when a man has gained sufficient wealth, but tying oneself to a marital partner is a mistake.

Davis argues that modern women have become too sexually active, insufficiently feminine, and lack homemaking skills. In her thought, men should not marry because modern women are not worth marrying.

Davis and Tate have a surprising reach, especially with young men. Young men who are alienated from society and have a jaded view of

---

33. Guerrasio, "Seth Rogen Explains."

34. Wilcox, *Get Married*, 168.

35. Wilcox, *Get Married*, 168.

women resonate with their views. Their views are influential, but they hardly help alienated listeners. Tate and Davis's success is the terminal point of the sexual revolution. Women who are sexually liberated are a commodity to some and an object of revulsion to others. In either case, women are not persons of value.

Marriage is terrible for men, they argue. A man can commit to a woman, have children, and then the woman can leave the marriage for any reason and leave him without access to his children and financially ruined.

If Tate and Davis have a point, it is that divorce laws are very anti-father. Judges in many states are notoriously bent toward giving custody and financial support to women. In US divorce cases, fathers gain custody only 18.3 percent of the time.[36] This is true even though children who get abused are more frequently abused by a mother than a father.[37] The data could be skewed because more mothers have custody, but one would think that a recognition of the data would lead to a better balance in deciding which parent gets custody. A balanced society would value both parents' contribution to the development of children and would have a more even custody breakdown.

Many politicians have made their careers deriding "deadbeat dads." There certainly are many of those, but few politicians would attack "manipulative mothers" in their advertisements; it would be a sure loser. While many people know mothers who deliberately make relationships with their children's fathers more difficult, society's mindset is skewed toward mothers.

There is a movement in more conservative political circles to do away with no-fault divorce laws. They want divorce to be harder to achieve and to restore the shame of divorce. Also among their proposals is lengthening the time it takes to get a divorce.

What the movement is missing is that making divorce take longer makes it even more bitter. Few who get married do so cavalierly. So they are already broken when they get to the place of seeking a divorce. Making a divorce take longer only makes fights more destructive. The longer it takes to get a divorce, the less likely it is to be amicable.

Dragging a divorce out is also bad for the children involved. As their parents have longer and worse fights and court sessions, they often make

36. Divorce Lawyers for Men, "Facts About Child Custody."
37. Zuckerman and Pederson. "Child Abuse and Father Figures."

children pawns. Even if they can avoid doing that, the protracted court cases often put the intense pressure and sadness of the divorce on children for longer.

While lengthening the process could be destructive, there are steps beyond balancing the divorce laws that could help. Policies that make martial counseling more affordable could be helpful. The availability of professional counseling at early levels of conflict could prevent conflict from spiraling.

Making counseling more affordable for children would be helpful too. Since the data show that children suffer greatly in a divorce, the prudent thing to do would be to make sure they have access to the help they need. Professional counselors and therapists for children could help children going through their parents' divorce better navigate their challenges.

SOCIETAL AND SPIRITUAL IMPLICATIONS

Marriage and family are the single best predictors of happiness in individuals. The two-parent family is the most reliable way to nurture and educate children. Children from these families are more likely to succeed in life. Because family is the best way to nurture healthy children, family is the best arrangement for society.

Where marriage is delayed or avoided completely, society finds less well-adjusted adults and more criminal activity. It makes little sense, then, to treat marriage and family as secondary issues. Regression in the family is a persistent danger to society and imperils the lives of individuals.

6

Regression in Science

Trust the science.[1]

Our science has outrun our spiritual power. We
have guided missiles and misguided men.

—MARTIN LUTHER KING JR.

WHAT IS SCIENCE

STANDING IN A LAB wearing a white coat and a face shield, a blue-eyed
scientist pours a chemical from a beaker into a cylinder. Stepping away
from the table, he picks up the brown clipboard to document his work. He
sets aside his presuppositions like an ill-fitting coat to pursue the truth.
Observation, hypothesis, experimentation, result: these are the tools of
his trade. At least that is how many in the pubic think science works.
Many philosophers of science conceive of the discipline differently and
doubt that anyone can set aside their worldview and make experiments
based on facts alone. Science, for all the wonder it creates, is a discipline
whose foundations are difficult to state.

1. Simons, "'Trust the Science.'"

74

Philosophers of science debate exactly what constitutes science, what the meaning of a scientific theory is, whether Baconian induction is possible, if Kuhn is right about paradigms, and whether Popper is right about falsifiability. Like most other disciplines, those who think about science itself find the discipline difficult to define.

Whatever the correct definition, one fact remains: science has enlightened humanity about the nature of the universe and made human life substantially better. Scientists have discovered the germ theory of disease and the laws of planetary motion. They have enabled human flight and decoded DNA. The Hubble and Webb Telescopes peer into the depths of space, alerting humans to the impossible size of the universe and rewriting scientific beliefs about its origin. Webb and Hubble gaze into the unknown and focus on the billions of galaxies and trillions of stars. Only the foolish can see the images they produce and not gape in wonder. Creating antibiotics, treatments for cancer, and medicines for diabetes, scientists have extended human life. Creating air conditioning and delivering indoor running water, scientists have made life more comfortable. If these achievements were the totality of their work, humans would need to express eternal gratitude. These achievements are but grains of sand on the beaches of scientific discovery. Not only have scientists created billions of terabytes of information, they have also enabled uninterrupted access to it through the Internet. More than that, they have created a device that can access that information but is small enough that it can be carried in a pocket: the smartphone.

One way to understand the high regard society and other disciplines hold science in is by how they attempt to use the term for their respective discipline. The great German philosopher Immanuel Kant famously wanted to make metaphysics a science.[2] In the twentieth century, Karl Barth thought of theology as a kind of science.[3] Even the infamous economist Karl Marx wanted the label "science" for his theories even though they have led to claims that have not come to pass.

Despite all of the admiration from other disciplines and all of the accomplishments of science, the discipline has suffered regression. Some scientists see large sections of the public as being "anti-science." Others note that the public treats them with great suspicion rather than gratitude. Some polling gives credence to their concern:[4] the public perception of

2. Kant, Critique *of Pure Reason*, 23.

3. Barth, *Church Dogmatics*, 1.1.3–11.

4. Habeshian, "Distrust in Scientists Rises."

science has deteriorated.[5] This deterioration is not merely the result of overzealous theists protecting precious doctrines. Political ideologues who reject precious tenants of science are not powerful enough to remove science from its perch. There are important causes for the regression of science, and scientists themselves share significant blame.

THE INTERNET AND SOCIAL MEDIA

The Internet and social media are mixed gifts. They connect people and inform people from distant countries, and they help develop relationships in ways that were impossible before their invention. Unfortunately, social media and the Internet can also spread information without context. Social media enables a throng of would-be experts to state scientifically inaccurate information online.

On any given day, cranks and crackpots will flood social media with preposterous nonsense. One can readily find charlatans arguing nonsense, such as Jesus never existed, the moon landing was faked, or 9/11 was an inside job. Disturbing conspiracies float in online spaces too. One can find horrendous anti-Semitism in those arguing that the Jews are the cause of the world's ills. Even silly falsehoods abound. Some argue, with apparent seriousness, that the earth is flat. It would be tempting to silence those peddling falsehoods, but attempting that comes with costs.

During the height of the COVID pandemic, social media executives often tried to silence "disinformation." The trouble is that defining "disinformation" is as difficult as viewing Pluto with a magnifying glass. Who gets to decide what is true? Who gets to decide what is disinformation?

Social media executives, alarmed at conspiracies about COVID, suppressed the "lab leak" theory of COVID's origin. Frequent reports stated the theory was "debunked." Now, in retrospect, the "lab leak" theory seems to be the most plausible explanation for COVID's origin. While scientists continue to study COVID (and in the future, the "lab leak" theory may be disproven), there was no good reason to suppress the theory or to call it debunked. The effect was to give credence to conspiracy theories. "If they will suppress the 'lab leak' theory, what else might they suppress?"

The net effect was that federal agencies and social media executives lost credibility, and the scientists who supported their actions lost face.

5. Viswanathan, "Americans' Trust in Science Declining."

Suppressing disinformation is very difficult to do without suppressing the minority report of credible persons who disagree with the public narrative.

COVID AND DECISION MAKING

It was March 10, 2020. A high school student at Oakland High School was wearing a burgundy hoodie as if she were going to a football game at the University of Southern California. Her slightly disheveled brown hair framed her cheeks as it peeked out from beside the hood. Her long gold necklace dangled over her zipped hoodie. Somehow her brown-rimmed glasses were not fogged even though she was dutifully wearing a yellow paper mask. She stared off into the distance and leaned on her arms when the harsh crackle of the intercom pierced the quiet.

"Good morning, Oakland High. This is Mr. Abdul," said the flat-toned voice over the school intercom. "Please excuse this interruption for the following announcement. We just got off the phone with the super-intendent, and she has closed schools effective at six o'clock for the next three weeks until April 5." In a sudden, awkward attempt at humor, the voice said that if the students had any questions not to ask them because the teachers and staff at Oakland High had no answers.[6]

Two male students danced with glee at the prospect of three weeks with no school, oblivious to the stress and frustration that awaited the students of Oakland High. Others seemed confused. Only a precious few understood the gravity of the decision. None of them could have expected the school to close for eighteen months.

The teachers and administrators began to give instructions to students on what to do if they had no Internet or smartphone. They counted on the students to be resourceful. Oakland High is in a high-poverty area. Students in these areas performed the worst both before and after the COVID shutdown. Many students simply disappeared.[7] Even upon returning, the students' response to the educational process has remained damaged. Chronic absenteeism at Oakland High is now 58.4 percent.[8]

6. Powell, "March 10, 2020."
7. Tones and Lurye, "Thousands of Kids."
8. Powell, "Chronic Absentee."

School closures had a significant negative effect on student learning.[9] Students lost between a half and a third of a year in math and a
quarter of a year in reading.[10] While the amount of learning lost does
not seem insurmountable, students are having a difficult time catching
up. Learning concepts takes the same amount of time as before the pandemic, so catching up by increasing the pace of learning is very difficult.[11]
The decline in learning is most pronounced in minority and poor communities as they remained virtual longer.[12]

Students also experienced loss of connection to other students
and loss of student activities. The isolation bred by school closures led
to higher rates of depression and reduced social skills.[13] Students were
clearly harmed by the decision to close schools.

In retrospect, school closures had minuscule effects on the transmission of COVID.[14] "Infectious disease leaders have generally agreed
that school closures were not an important strategy in stemming the
spread of COVID."[15]

It could be argued authorities did not know the ineffectiveness of
closing schools during COVID until afterward. There were signs, however, early in the pandemic. COVID was primarily a destroyer of the
elderly, a curse on the corpulent. Those with multiple comorbidities were
its most common victims. The young, however, were less likely to get the
disease. When the young were infected, they were much less likely to get
seriously ill. They were also much less likely to transmit the disease. Shut-
ting down the schools came at great cost to the young with a very limited
upside. It was a mistake, and a very costly one.

At the beginning of the pandemic, the public thought highly of the
authorities who were leading the governmental response. That perception, however, changed over time. With the public's diminishing perception of the COVID response and the scientists who managed it, the
public perception of scientists has faded as well.

Several factors led to the general public taking a negative view of science post-COVID. During COVID, Anthony Fauci said that any attack

9. Mervosh et al., "What the Data Says."
10. Harvard University, "New Data Show."
11. Harvard University, "New Data Show."
12. Harvard University, "New Data Show."
13. Woldehanna and Berhie, "Beyond Academic Learning Loss."
14. Mervosh et al., "What the Data Says."
15. Mervosh et al., "What the Data Says."

on him was an attack on science. He was, at least in his mind, the representative of science. The problem with that statement, other than the obvious hubris, is that if Fauci misbehaved in any way, the public would then associate his mistake with the mistake of science. The mantra "trust the science" worked in exactly the same way. The public was supposed to trust the scientists. What would happen to that trust if the scientists were wrong? Worse, what would happen if the scientists weren't acting in accordance with science?

After the pandemic, Congress discovered that one of the most important regulations during the pandemic had no basis in science. Social distancing was not based on science: based on Fauci's testimony, it was his untested idea.[16] Authorities insisted that individuals keep six feet of distance between themselves and others to reduce transmission. Where did Fauci get this information? "It just sort of appeared."[17]

It is hard to overstate how onerous this rule was for the public. Based on social distancing, churches could not meet in their sanctuaries, costing people connection and support during a terrifying period of history. Little wonder, then, that clinical depression surged during the pandemic. The elderly were isolated. Children could not attend school because there was no practicable way for students to maintain social distance in a crowded classroom. School systems immediately shifted to online education, and the results were dismal.

SPEAKING OUTSIDE COMPETENCE

One of the issues is that scientists often will speak or write in areas beyond their expertise. Consider Richard Dawkins. Dawkins is an excellent scientist. He is, however, a terrible philosopher. Dawkins was one of the leaders of the now-floundering New Atheist movement. The movement, not content to merely be atheists, became evangelists of sorts engaging in ridicule of theism.

Attaching a venerable scientist's name to a book on God, Dawkins's publishers sold three million copies of *The God Delusion*. The problem is, however, as a work on the subject of the philosophy of religion, it is sophomoric. He misunderstands the function of Aquinas's "Five Ways," argues Aquinas's natural theology was equivalent to intelligent design,

16. Diamond, "In the Pandemic."
17. Nicole Russell, "COVID Guidelines Caused Millions to Suffer."

and misunderstands Aquinas's argument from motion.[18] Perhaps most important is that the evidence and arguments Dawkins tends to marshal against the existence of God are from physical reality, the universe. There is no sense in which evidence from the physical universe has any bearing on the God who is utterly transcendent.

Writing about Dawkins's work, David Bentley Hart states:

> Dawkins, for instance, even cites with approval the old village atheist's cavil that omniscience and omnipotence are incompatible because a God who infallibly foresaw the future would be impotent to change it—as though Christians, Jews, Muslims, Hindus, Sikhs, and so forth understood God simply as some temporal being of interminable duration who knows things as we do, as external objects of cognition, mediated to him under the conditions of space and time.[19]

Never one to suffer fools gladly, Hart ridicules Dawkins's work with Voltairean cruelty. The difference is, however, unlike Voltaire's noted misunderstanding of Leibniz, Hart reads Dawkins well:

> *The God Delusion* was, if anything, even more of a nursery entertainment: puerile rants, laboriously obvious jokes, winsomely preposterous conceptual confusions, a few dashes of naïve but honest indignation, attempts at philosophical reasoning so maladroit as to be touching in their guileless silliness. And I think it fair to say that nothing Dawkins has written for public consumption has lacked this element of beguiling absurdity—the delightful atmosphere of playtime on a long golden summer afternoon, alive with small figures shouting happily in shrill little voices and stumbling about in their parents' clothing, acting out scenes from what they imagine to be the daily lives of adults. But the bewitching effect has also always been diluted by his unfortunate failure to embody his ideas in a form suitable to their triviality.
>
> And, in general, he reprises all his most familiar "philosophical" gestures. As he has before, for instance, he invokes Hume's argument against the plausibility of miracles, in a sweetly oversimplified form, clearly unaware both of its irrelevance to most religious rationales for belief and of its own formidable internal contradictions. And so on. All of his reasoning is dreadful, of course. Even where he gets something right, it is clear

18. Hart, *Experience of God*, 22.
19. Hart, "Believe It or Not."

that he has done so only by accident, and has reached his correct formulation for all the wrong reasons. Every argument is circular, or incoherent, or simply wrong—which, under normal circumstances, would quickly grow annoying. Once again, however, the book's lispingly infantile prose makes it impossible for the reader not to feel indulgent. Rather than rebuke Dawkins for his vapidity, one almost wants to give him treats.[20]

Another instance of scientists speaking out of their area of expertise comes from Neil deGrasse Tyson. When speaking in his field proper, no doubt Tyson has expansive knowledge. Outside his field, he does not demonstrate such fluency.

In his series *Cosmos*, Tyson does repeated violence to the historical accounts. For him, plucky scientists had the courage to oppose Christian dogma and get to the truth even at high personal cost. He imposes that view on the historical narrative even if it does not fit.

In *Cosmos*, Tyson discusses the Catholic persecution of Bruno. While Bruno was a scientist, his persecution was not over his scientific work. He was persecuted because he was a theological heretic denying the virgin birth, the Trinity, transubstantiation, and the divinity of Christ. Further, he asserted a view tantamount to pantheism.[21] No persecution is moral, and what happened to Bruno was a horrific abuse. Reasoning from Bruno to the assertion that religion or the Catholic church is anti-science, however, is an adventure in missing the plot so profound it makes the *Rise of Skywalker* look entirely reasonable.

Tyson also asserts a calumny against the Catholic church that it opposed Galileo on theological grounds and attempted to hush him. This assertion is also a misstatement of history. It was the Jesuits who helped Galileo confirm his theory by the use of mathematics. The pope wanted Galileo to refrain from calling his theory a fact before sufficient proof had been amassed. Further, there were personal animosities between the pope and Galileo that led to their conflict.[22] The pope was not persecuting him because of the theory itself. In fact, Nicholas of Cusa had made similar observations and experienced no persecution.[23]

Opposition to Galileo came largely on *scientific* grounds. Galileo's opponents were incorrect, but they had contemporary evidence on their

20. Hart, "Richard Dawkins Discovers."

21. Spitzer, "Neil deGrasse Tyson's *Cosmos*."

22. Consolmango and Graney, "What the Story of Galileo."

23. Hart, *Atheist Delusions*, 60.

side. The old theory better comported with most observations and made better predictions at the time.[24]

Galileo was no atheist. He was a Catholic. So to argue, as Tyson does, that Galileo's case was a case of science against religion is anachronistic at best. It was a confrontation within a religious sphere among religious scientists with implications for how the Bible should be read on the cosmos.

Perhaps Tyson is unaware of the totality of the story and is using boilerplate readings of history. In that case, he is using a distorted reading of the history of the mythology of science. The technical name for that is "shoddy research." If Tyson is aware of the fuller history, he is being deceptive. In either case, his use of history in *Cosmos* is not fitting for a person with a scientific zeal for truth.

Will Rogers once said, "There is nothing dumber than an educated man once you get him off the subject he was educated in."[25] Speaking outside their frame, scientists do significant harm science.

OPPOSITE CONCLUSIONS

In January 2019 the *Daily Mail* reported that one egg per day lowers the risk of type 2 diabetes. The article, summarizing a study from a university in Finland, argues that one egg per day would promote fatty acids, protecting a person from the disease.[26] The same publication just two years later posted a completely contradictory story. It cited Australian researchers who argue eating just one egg per day would increase the risk of diabetes by 60 percent.[27]

Which is it? Does the consumption of one egg per day increase the risk of diabetes or decrease it? Diabetes is a destructive and debilitating disease. Untreated, it can lead to the loss of limbs, blindness, or even death. Even when treated, diabetes can lead to kidney disease, neuropathy, and a whole list of comorbidities. It is a major health issue in the United States and the United Kingdom, with millions of sufferers. If consumption of one egg per day would be helpful in preventing the disease, it would be of vital interest for public health. If it is true that eggs increase

---

24. Consolmango and Graney, "What the Story of Galileo."
25. Rogers, "There Is Nothing."
26. De Graaf, "One Egg a Day."
27. Chadwick, "Eating Just One Egg."

the risk of diabetes by 60 percent, then because of the connection to high cholesterol, public health officials should consider putting warning labels on eggs. Eggs would then be a public health hazard.

Of course, with only these studies, it is impossible to tell if eggs are a boon or a bane. Articles like these only teach the public that contemporary scientists are more eggheaded than brilliant. Reading these two articles in succession would lead one to discount both and the process that created them. Further, how is someone without scientific training supposed to differentiate between two studies that directly contradict each other?

It would be helpful for scientists if studies like the egg studies above were not presented to the public as if they were news. Sensational headlines about terrible public diseases with thin research greatly harm the perception of science. Juxtaposing these articles makes science look trivial.

THE SCIENCE OF READING

In 1981, Lucy Calkins became the founding director of Columbia's Teachers College Reading and Writing Project. In her research, she developed the Units of Study curriculum as a method of teaching reading to elementary school children.[28]

Calkins's Units of Study, often called "balanced literacy," was born out of her time observing third-grade children in a rural New Hampshire school. During her observational period, Calkins noticed teachers assigning papers to their students and merely correcting and grading their work. Calkins thought the program was uninteresting. In response, she recommended the teachers allow the children to choose their own topics and write about them with little teacher feedback. The feedback would come from the other students during workshop time.[29]

To teach reading, Calkins's approach was quite different from phonics. In phonics, students learn the sounds of letters and then sound out the word. In Units of Study, students learn by a process called "three-cueing," where students will use clues like pictures to figure out words.[30]

---

28. Winter, "Rise and Fall."
29. Wexler, "Problems with Lucy Calkins's Curriculum."
30. Markovich, "Berkeley Schools."

Among academics and administrators, Calkins's program was very popular as up to 25 percent of US elementary schools used her methods.[31] In a poll of educators, 67 percent cited "balanced literacy" as their educational philosophy.[32] In New York, Mayor Bloomberg brought Units of Study into the New York City school system,[33] and the results were not good. By 2019, only 40 percent of New York's third to eighth graders were proficient in reading.[34]

The long-standing consensus among researchers is that phonics and vocabulary-building instruction are essential for the development of reading skills. Phonics, they argue, changes children's neural pathways in ways that make them better readers.[35] Phonics education tends not only to produce better readers: it works because it better reflects how children's brains function.

Calkins defended her work by stating the obvious: reading skills were poor among the target groups long before implementation of her system. That observation is true. What is also true is that her system made no noticeable improvement in reading scores, and was quite detrimental to those with dyslexia.[36]

Finally, after years of evidence that the program does not work, the Teachers College is disbanding the Teachers College and Writing Project.[37] In one sense, the problem with this case is not science. The science became clear some time ago. The problem is that with limited and equivocal scientific research, an educational theorist convinced entire school systems that her preferred reading method was scientific and the best way to educate children. In another sense, this case illustrates a problem science has. Once claiming the name science, pseudoscience can entrench itself into a discipline, and eliminating it is very hard.

31. Hurley, "Lucy Calkins's Program Closure."
32. Peske, "Teaching Reading."
33. Hurley, "The Decades-Long Travesty."
34. Winter, "Rise and Fall."
35. Peske, "Teaching Reading."
36. Markovich, "Berkeley Schools."
37. Schwartz, "Teachers College."

REPLICATION SCANDAL

Science is a discipline of publication. Scientists conduct research according to the best of scientific processes and forward their findings to reputable scientific journals, where their work will be subjected to the blind review process. If the work survives the withering eyes of the anonymous reviewers, it will be published. Once published, the scientific community reads the results critically before incorporating the findings into future research, textbooks, or accepted theories about the particular discipline. The process is supposed to create replication. Any scientist testing the same theories, using the same materials and the same processes, should get the same result as the original researcher. At least that is how science works on paper.

In practice, the process has become very messy and sometimes fraudulent. Since 2010 the scientific community has been embroiled in what is known as "the replication crisis." Emerging first in the social sciences and then spilling into the "hard sciences," vast swaths of scientific research have failed replication. As one writer put it, "An entire field of genetics has even turned out to be nothing but a mirage."[38]

It is one thing for a scientific theory to be proven incorrect. That is good for science as it eliminates a false possibility and moves a discipline ever closer to genuine discovery. What is not healthy, though, is for fraudulent research or shoddy methods to be found at the basis of important scientific research. At its worst, the replication crisis threatens the entire scientific enterprise.[39] The depth of the problem is significant. 70 percent of scientists have attempted to reproduce another scientist's research without success.[40]

In physics, a series of papers about superconducting materials had to be withdrawn because all attempts to replicate them failed and some of the research was falsified.[41] In cancer research, dozens of cancer studies had to be withdrawn because they could not be replicated.[42] According to *Nature*, ten thousand studies were withdrawn in 2023.[43]

---

38. Wilson, "Replication Crisis."

39. Hedges, "'Existential Crisis' for Science."

40. Baker, "1,500 Scientists."

41. Padavic-Callaghan, "Physicists Are Grappling."

42. Haelle, "Massive 8-Year Effort."

43. Van Noorden, "More than 10,000 Research Papers."

In an often-cited psychological theory, women prefer men with masculine faces for short-term relationships and men with more feminine faces for long-term bonds.[44] By "masculine faces," the researchers mean wider. Wider faces communicate a higher level of testosterone, indicating dominance. Dominance, however, is not as attractive for long-term bonds because dominant men may not share resources as willingly. The research is common, even showing up on pop-psychology websites.[45]

The problem is, the research cannot be verified. In a recent study published in *Evolutionary Psychology*, researchers studied the phenomenon and found "no evidence"[46] for such claims. In one sense, this is exactly how science should work. Researchers publish a set of findings that support their theory. Future researchers investigate the theory and find no evidence for it, thus disproving it. That is the creative destruction of the scientific process.

What is problematic is the theory was so successful that it was accepted as truth for many researchers and found its way into popular culture. When disproven, a theory with such widespread acceptance is not disposed of readily. It lingers in the societal ethos like Polo in an eighth-grade dance hall. Avoiding it or getting rid of it is extremely difficult. Discredited theories like this one only serve to convince the skeptical that scientists are charlatans. This phenomenon is even more pronounced in social sciences, where the replication scandal hit most powerfully.

Adding to the problem is that studies that cannot be replicated are cited more frequently.[47] Researchers note that frequent citations of these studies are because they are interesting.[48] According to *UC San Diego Today*, researchers speculate that reviewers lower their standards for papers they find interesting.[49] Of course, the right question to ask in response to this is, "Can these findings and this speculation be replicated?"

44. Valentine et al., "Judging a Man."

45. For example: Harrington and Rosa-Aquino, "11 Qualities."

46. Dong et al., "Re-Evaluating the Role."

47. Clark, "New Replication Crisis."

48. Clark, "New Replication Crisis."

49. Clark, "New Replication Crisis."

TRUST

Trust in the enterprise of science has devolved, and for the sake of society, it must be rebuilt. What happens the next time there is a pandemic? Will a trusting public don masks at the behest of the government? Would businesses and churches close because of federal mandates? Would people willingly line up for a new vaccine? Would the public willingly submit to "two weeks to flatten the curve?" At this point, any of that seems very dubious. A public that cannot trust the work of its scientists is vulnerable.

It is perhaps likely there will be another pandemic. There will be a point in the future where the work of scientists will be the difference between life and death. The loss of trust science has generated will be an enormous obstacle to overcome if the public's trust in science is not rebuilt.

Sudip Parikh, chief executive officer of the American Association for the Advancement of Science, writes, "Unfortunately, science and scientists have not consistently earned and nurtured this trust."[50] Parikh understands the gravity of the situation. A public that does not trust science will not trust its doctors, professors, or leaders who base decisions on science.

Unfortunately, it seems that Parikh focuses on academia's usual suspects. Science has fallen into the traps of discrimination, subjugation, and marginalization.[51] That list hardly gets at the problem. The problem is not the sociology of science or its intersectional biases. Scientists made recommendations affecting public life that harmed individuals and groups. It has failed to live up to its own standards of truth and has gone to press with mutually exclusive theories. He sees scientists as presenting evidence-based findings,[52] while society has lost trust that scientists are doing that at all.[53] Being unable to see the problem, it is unlikely that scientists will quickly recover their place in society anytime soon.

50. Parikh, "Why We Must Rebuild."
51. Parikh, "Why We Must Rebuild."
52. Parikh, "Why We Must Rebuild."
53. Kennedy and Tyson, "Americans' Trust in Scientists."

7

National Defense in Regression

THE MILITARY IN THE US

IN WHAT MUST BE considered an outlier in US history, in the aftermath of the Vietnam War, the military was not held in high esteem by the public. Soldiers coming home were told to wear civilian clothes in public, and those who did not heed that advice often faced scorn. Some were spat upon; others were taunted as "baby killers."

In contemporary society, however, the public holds service members in high regard. On occasion, those who have first-class seats will give them to service members in uniform. Many service members in uniform will be greeted by strangers saying, "Thank you for your service to our country." The public is grateful.

Gratitude to individual soldiers is not necessarily a sign of confidence in national defense, however. The public, while being grateful for individuals who serve, has great questions about those who lead the military.

Confidence in the military's ability to complete its mission is falling too. According to a 2023 Gallup poll, public confidence in the military has fallen from 82 percent in 2009 to 60 percent in 2023.[1] The military is not alone in losing the confidence of the public. The public has lost confidence in all institutions, and its confidence in many of them is at

1. Younis, "Confidence in U.S. Military."

or near historic lows.[2] The loss of confidence in the military stands out as the military remains very strong and the public is willing to spend billions on it.

Confidence in the military to succeed in its mission is only 10 percent off of its all-time lows. Looking at the long-term data reveals some interesting trends. Confidence in the military seems to fluctuate considerably with events. In 1980, at the end of the Carter administration, confidence in the military tumbled to its lowest level in the poll's history at 50 percent.[3] This low level of confidence came at the time of the Iranian hostage crisis and the botched military rescue attempt.

On November 4, 1979, Iranian students stormed the US embassy in Tehran, kidnapping fifty-two Americans. The public largely perceived President Carter's response as weak and waffling. Unable to secure the release of the hostages, the administration sanctioned Iran and began to apply diplomatic pressure. Further complicating the problem was that President Carter stopped campaigning and remained in the White House, giving the terrorists the impression they could throw the whole presidency into chaos.[4]

With the election on the horizon and no peaceful means having worked to secure the release of the hostages, Carter committed to a military rescue plan. On April 24, 1980, Operation Eagle Claw began. With the failure of diplomatic means to release the US hostages in Iran, the Carter administration prepared a military incursion. The plan was for an assault team of 118 to storm the US embassy compound, rescue the hostages, and be flown by helicopter to an airfield thirty-five miles to the south. By the time of their arrival, Army Rangers were to have secured the airfield, preparing it for Air Force transports to receive the hostages.[5]

In hopes of rescuing the hostages and restoring the US' reputation, eight US helicopters took off from the USS *Nimitz* on the six-hundred-mile journey to reach the transport planes in the Iranian desert. Two of the helicopters had to abandon the mission because of instrument and mechanical problems. A third continued despite hydraulic problems. Encountering a violent wind storm, the remaining helicopters were delayed by nearly an hour.[6] Disasters continued at the rendezvous point. Encoun-

2. Saad, "Historically Low Faith."

3. Younis, "Confidence in U.S. Military."

4. Kamarck, "Iranian Hostage Crisis."

5. Air Force Historical Support Division, "1980—Operation Eagle Claw."

6. Air Force Historical Support Division, "1980—Operation Eagle Claw."

ters with a passenger bus, a fuel truck, and another pickup complicated securing the airfield. Once reaching the airfield, the helicopter with hydraulic issues could not be repaired, leaving the team with one less helicopter than needed to complete the mission.[7]

On hearing the news, President Carter aborted the mission. Worse, in preparation for the mission, a collision between a helicopter and another aircraft caused the death of eight service members.[8] The mission was an embarrassing failure for President Carter and the military itself. In 1980, confidence in the military would require a suspension of disbelief. Remarkably, confidence remained at 50 percent after the public humiliation of Operation Eagle Claw.

Confidence in the military was at its highest in 1991 in the aftermath of the first Persian Gulf War, when it reached 85 percent.[9] In what many feared to be another Vietnam-like scenario, the US military quickly decimated Iraq. The Iraqi army was a significant foe, at least in terms of size. Fielding ground forces of 1,000,000, the Iraqi army was the fourth largest in the world.[10] The US and coalition forces demolished the Iraqi army quickly, and much of it was broadcast live on CNN. The US military was a juggernaut.

What accounts for the current low level of confidence in the military in recent polling? The poll does not answer that question, but if events are the driver of the public's confidence, there is one event that could explain the data: the withdrawal from Afghanistan.

THE AFGHANISTAN WITHDRAWAL

Although intelligence failures led to 9/11, in the aftermath of the attacks, US intelligence identified the perpetrators quickly. Al-Qaeda, headed by Osama bin Laden, planned and executed the attacks. Hosted by his coreligionists in Afghanistan, bin Laden was able to coordinate the attacks. Bin Laden stayed in Afghanistan after the attacks, hosted by the Taliban. Shortly after 9/11, the US was at war with the Taliban.

---

7. Air Force Historical Support Division, "1980—Operation Eagle Claw."
8. Air Force Historical Support Division, "1980—Operation Eagle Claw."
9. Younis, "Confidence in U.S. Military."
10. Vergun, "Nation Observes Anniversary."

9/11 was a miscalculation by bin Laden. Al-Qaeda's leader thought US civilians would rise in anger not at terrorism but at US policy.[11] His goal was to get the US populace to recreate the Vietnam protests and force the US to withdraw from majority Muslim nations.[12] He could not have been more mistaken. He awakened a rage in the US population unseen since Pearl Harbor.

The US moved quickly to respond. The Taliban was not a strong military force; only significant strategic bungling would have prevented a quick victory. By the time of the 2002 State of the Union address, Afghanistan already had a new leader, Hamid Karzai. The Taliban were routed; most of its leaders were either killed or captured.[13] The Taliban, however, did not disappear. Its remnants went to the tribal areas of the nation where they would conduct attacks on US forces and cause as much carnage as possible.

In December 2001, US intelligence had tracked bin Laden to a cave complex in Tora Bora in the Spin Ghar mountain range. Sometime during the weeks-long battle, bin Laden escaped.[14] By December 2001, Afghan intelligence reported that bin Laden was in Pakistan among al-Qaeda sympathizers.[15]

The initial impetus to invade Afghanistan was to find bin Laden and destroy al-Qaeda. That goal shifted quickly to eliminating the Taliban, to stabilizing the security situation, and to creating a new government.[16] By 2002, President Bush cited the "best traditions of George Marshall" to rally Americans for the reconstruction of Afghanistan.[17]

The plan did not work. In 2021, President Biden said, "We did not go into Afghanistan to nation-build."[18] Perhaps President Biden was correct about the reasons the US entered Afghanistan, but within months of entering Afghanistan, the goal went from finding bin Laden to building a nation. Had the goal been only to find bin Laden, US and coalition troops would have likely left by 2002.

11. Sukheja, "Osama bin Laden."
12. Germino, "Documents Reveal Bin Laden's Bid."
13. Lahoud, "Bin Laden's Catastrophic Success."
14. 9/11 Memorial, "Hunt for Bin Laden."
15. CNN Editorial Board, "Osama bin Laden Fast Facts."
16. Robinson, "Our Biggest Errors."
17. Richburg, "America Tried Nation-Building."
18. Richburg, "America Tried Nation-Building."

The US spent $2.3 trillion and lost thousands of lives in its nation-building quest.[19] US authorities trained Afghan armed services and cultivated assets among the Afghans. By 2020, however, a war-weary public and administration tired of the sacrifice required to sustain Afghanistan. It was America's longest war, and it was time to bring it to a close.

The trained government of Afghanistan was supposed to be able to secure the populace when the US troops withdrew. That, however, was a terrible miscalculation. On April 14, 2021, President Biden announced that US forces would be withdrawn from Afghanistan by September 11, 2021, the twentieth anniversary of the 9/11 attacks. Evacuations proceeded. By August, entire cities began to fall to the Taliban, and on August 15 the president of Afghanistan fled the country. The government collapsed, and chaos ensued.[20]

With US allies and assets trying to flee the country, terrorists attacked the Kabul airport on August 26, 2021. A suicide bomber killed thirteen US service members and approximately one hundred seventy Afghanis.[21] The evacuation plan fell into chaos. Images of people plummeting to their deaths from airplanes as they tried to hold on to the wings for escape haunt the memory and serve as reminders of how badly the withdrawal went. The withdrawal abandoned eight hundred US citizens and numerous Afghanistan partners.

When President Biden announced the withdrawal of US forces, he promised, "There's going to be no circumstance where you see people being lifted off the roof of an embassy . . . of the United States from Afghanistan. It is not at all comparable."[22] The images, if anything, were worse. Nation-building has long been the bane of the US military, and Afghanistan was a horrific nation-building failure.

On August 14, 2024, the Taliban paraded the US military hardware left behind in Afghanistan.[23] The withdrawal from Afghanistan was a dishonorable and shameful event, leaving observers to wonder how a failure of planning and intelligence could be so complete.

19. Robinson, "Our Biggest Errors."
20. Brown, "Timeline of the US Withdrawal."
21. Olay, "Kabul Airport Attack."
22. Biden, "Remarks by President Biden."
23. Walker, "Taliban Parade."

MISSING RECRUITING GOALS

What would it be like if boot camp remained empty for lack of interest? What would happen if the Army's battalions were short-staffed? Imagine a world where US Marines could not storm the beaches in a time of crisis or where carriers and destroyers of the US Navy had to remain in port because they were understaffed. A shortage of volunteers leads to military weakness, which invites aggression. A shortfall in recruiting, then, is a danger for the US. Unfortunately, the shortage of volunteers for military service is not imaginary.

The armed services have developed a recruiting problem. Despite the public's high regard for the military and those who serve, recruiting has become very difficult. In 2023, only the Marines and the Space Force met their recruiting goals. The Army, Navy, and Air Force were a combined 41,000 enlistees below their goals. In 2023, only 51 percent of Americans would recommend a family member join the armed services, a precipitous fall off from 2018 when 70 percent would recommend military service.[24]

Men are much less likely to join the armed services than in previous generations. In 2013, the Army enlisted 58,000 men. In 2023, that number fell to 37,000. That shortfall is not being filled in by women recruits. Women enlisted at a steady 10,000 per year.[25] As a result of the lack of recruits, the Army is considering cutting the number of its brigade command teams, and Navy ships are understaffed.[26]

Florida Senator Marco Rubio argues the causes of the recruitment issues are mission creep, declining quality of life for service members, and what he calls "a dramatic fall in patriotism."[27] Rubio writes:

> Meanwhile, we've seen a dramatic fall in patriotism. Only 39 percent of citizens are extremely proud to be Americans, 12 points down from 2017. Worse, just 18 percent of citizens between 18 and 34, the prime demographic for military service, are extremely proud to be Americans.
>
> This makes sense when you consider that the political Left, the corporate media, many public schools, and the vast majority of colleges have spent the last six years peddling the narrative

24. Sisk, "Military Recruiting Outlook."
25. Sisk, "Military Recruiting Outlook."
26. Rubio, "Military Recruiting Crisis."
27. Rubio, "Military Recruiting Crisis."

that the United States is an irredeemably oppressive and racist nation.[28]

Whether or not Rubio is right about the loss of patriotism causing recruitment issues and right about blaming the decline in patriotism on the progressive left, there is a broader point he misses. Two large sociological events are happening in the US. First is the dropping-out phenomenon. A substantial portion of the working class is dropping out of nearly everything. From college to the church to the military, their absence is striking.

If the data about the gender of recruits is correct, then leaders should also pair it with the data about men in the workforce. These same young men who are not at work and not in the educational system are not in the military either.

Just as ominous is that 77 percent of young Americans, even if they were inclined to serve, could not without a waiver. The biggest issues are drug use, obesity, and mental problems.[29] The single largest issue is obesity with a full third of young people being unable to serve because of their weight.[30] Military recruiters are having to recruit in a less patriotic society, with families less likely to recommend military service, and with a shrinking population of people who can meet the military's requirements.

As a senator, Rubio looks for technical solutions, solutions that can be implemented by the government. Conversely, Rubio looks for errors the government has made and argues for their correction. He may be right on those points; however, missing is the larger issue. The problem is not a technical one. The problem is a moral one.

Men missing in the workforce, educational system, and the military is a moral concern with practical dangers. The solution will not necessarily be a policy solution. It will come when society understands the causes of this moral regression and finds ways to develop courage and industry among its youth, particularly its young men.

Not listed among his main points but noted in his article is politicization. Politicization ruins everything it touches. A politicized military is not a military that encourages young people to enter into a life of service. Examples of the politicization of the military, in Rubio's estimation,

28. Rubio, "Military Recruiting Crisis."
29. Novelly, "Even More Young Americans."
30. Pawlyk, "One-Third of Youths."

included firing service members who refused the vaccine; imposition of diversity, equity, and inclusion ideology in the services; and tying the armed services to controversial social issues, such as transgenderism and LGBTQ+ inclusion.

One may disagree with Rubio's view here, but his closing statement is on point: "If we fail to restore people's trust in the institutions we represent, America's global decline . . . is all but certain."[31]

LOSS OF FOCUS IN THE ARMED SERVICES AND DHS

The lethality of the US military is unmatched. Its ability to marshal conventional and nuclear weapons is unmatched. Its sole superpower status is unique in human history as it does not attempt to enlarge its territory or expand its riches by military conquest. Even in the ill-fated Second Persian Gulf War, the US did not annex Iraq or strip it of its oil reserves. It forced no tribute. Iraq is a freestanding nation making democratic decisions, even as some of them are very disturbing. Iraq's parliament is considering lowering the age of marriage to nine for girls, with little public condemnation from US authorities.[32] Iraq is not a US fiefdom. The US could conquer most of the world, and refrains.

With the lethality of US forces, why would the US military be concerned with anything other than winning wars? It appears the military has competing foci. In June 2023 the US Army Secret Services Battalion sought to monitor social media to look for online threats and "positive or negative sentiment relating specifically to our senior high-risk personnel"[33] as part of its mission to prevent kidnapping, assassination, "injury or *embarrassment*" for those it protects.[34] Why would the military be concerned about embarrassment?

It is not just the Pentagon that worries about social media. In 2020 the Department of Homeland Security (DHS) partnered with Stanford University's Internet Observatory, the University of Washington's Center for an Informed Public, Graphika, and the Atlantic Council's Digital Forensic Research Lab to create the Election Integrity Partnership (EIP).[35]

31. Rubio, "Military Recruiting Crisis."

32. The Times of India World Desk, "Iraq to Reduce."

33. King, "Veterans Slam."

34. King, "Veterans Slam." Emphasis added.

35. Bowman, "DHS Officials."

As NPR reports, the EIP's goal was to track false and misleading information about the 2020 and 2022 elections. The EIP became "the focus of conspiracy theories that it was a front for the government to suppress speech it didn't like."[36]

While NPR suggests that attacks against the EIP were political, emails obtained by the Judiciary Committee show that the EIP was created at the behest of DHS and had regular communications about disinformation.[37]

The Judiciary Committee also claimed, "The federal government and universities pressured social media companies to censor true information, jokes, and political cartoons."[38] Targets of the EIP included Donald Trump, Senator Tom Tillis, *The Babylon Bee*, Sean Hannity, Mollie Hemingway, and Charlie Kirk.[39] In August 2024, Facebook released information that government officials pressured it to censor COVID posts during the pandemic as well.

The EIP's targets tended to be conservative, which accounts for the differing perspectives in press accounts. In NPR's telling of the story, the EIP was a victim of right-wing propaganda. Lawsuits against EIP's coordination with social media are

> just one element in a right-wing legal and political campaign that frames efforts to combat false and misleading information about consequential topics, including voting and health, as censorship.
>
> The assault has already had widespread reverberations, from disrupting the work of government agencies meant to safeguard voting to subjecting researchers studying online harms to harassment and even death threats.[40]

Even if one were to grant NPR's claims about the right-wing nature of the lawsuits against EIP, on what basis would one want to argue that the US federal government has any business being an arbiter of true information? Its track record on truth is sketchy, to say the least.

Even more crucial, why in a free society would the federal government be monitoring speech? Why would it use its considerable ability

36. Bond, "Major Disinformation Research."
37. Bowman, "DHS Officials."
38. Bowman, "DHS Officials."
39. House Judiciary, "Weaponization."
40. Bond, "What It Means."

to pressure organizations to stifle speech it deemed untrue? It sounds almost Orwellian.

The Judiciary Committee viewed the EIP's work this way:

> The EIP's operation was straightforward: "external stakehold-ers," including federal agencies and organizations funded by the federal government, submitted misinformation reports directly to the EIP. The EIP's misinformation "analysts" next scoured the Internet for additional examples for censorship. If the submitted report flagged a Facebook post, for example, the EIP analysts searched for similar content on Twitter, YouTube, TikTok, Red-dit, and other major social media platforms. Once all the offend-ing links were compiled, the EIP sent the most significant ones directly to Big Tech with *specific* recommendations on how the social media platforms should censor the posts, such as reduc-ing the posts' "discoverability," "suspending an account's ability to continue Tweeting for twelve hours," "monitoring if any of the tagged influencer accounts retweet" a particular user, and, of course, removing thousands of American's posts.[41]

A government very concerned about what citizens say on Facebook, Twitter, Instagram, TikTok, or X is a very observant government. It is almost like the government is watching, like a big brother, maybe.

Whether it is censorship or a fight against disinformation, how is this in the purview of DHS? If DHS is monitoring social media to pro-tect against the next terrorist attack, monitor terrorist activity, or even infiltrate terrorist groups, that is fitting. Getting a tweet from October 23, 2020 by Newt Gingrich removed for stating Pennsylvania officials were trying to steal the 2020 election[42] is not remotely connected to DHS work.

These extraneous efforts have kept the DHS off mission and em-broiled in lawsuits. DHS's behavior is much like what Freidman notes about anxious systems. They will take actions that reduce anxiety but produce no actual results. The main result of DHS's missed focus is the loss of trust in the institution by the public.

BUDGETING AND AUDITS

In fiscal year 2023, the US spent .82 trillion on national defense. As a number, one billion is hard to conceptualize. One writer describes it this

41. House Judiciary, "Weaponization," 3.
42. House Judiciary, "Weaponization," 74.

way: a billion seconds is thirty years. A trillion seconds is thirty thousand years.[43] To say that the US government spent .82 trillion dollars on national defense in 2023 is to posit an unfathomable number.

With such a commitment, one would expect that military leadership would prove trustworthy with those resources. Spending in the military, however, has proven to be profligate. In 2023, the Pentagon failed an independent audit of its finances. It has failed this same audit for six consecutive years.

In their annual review, 1,600 auditors conducted twenty-nine sub-audits and made seven hundred site visits assessing $3.8 trillion in assets and $4 trillion in liabilities.[44] The Pentagon only passed seven of its sub-audits, the same number as the previous year.[45] Most disturbingly, the Pentagon cannot account for $1.9 trillion in assets. In fact, the Pentagon has never passed an audit.[46]

"Right now, the Pentagon can't even tell you where all of its buildings are," said an aid to Senator Bernie Sanders.[47] The Pentagon cannot say how many contractors or subcontractors it employs and cannot keep track of all its properties. In a previous audit, auditors discovered a warehouse of aircraft parts that had not been used in a decade.[48]

Pentagon officials maintain the Defense Department is too large and complex to pass an audit. Defense Department officials take the failure as a learning experience. In fact, they were not even trying to pass the audits yet. Their goal is to pass them in 2028.[49] The Pentagon cannot manage its finances and has not been able to for some time. Without accountability, the Defense Department leaves the impression no one is in charge.

MISSILE DEFENSE

The Strategic Defense Initiative (SDI) was quite controversial after its rollout to the US public. President Ronald Reagan called SDI "Star Wars" after the wildly popular 1980s movie trilogy. Often mocked by Reagan's

---

43. Better Explained, "How to Develop."
44. Stone, "Pentagon Fails Audit."
45. Stone, "Pentagon Fails Audit".
46. Chappell, "Pentagon Has Never."
47. Chappell, "Pentagon Has Never."
48. Chappell, "Pentagon Has Never."
49. Chappell, "Pentagon Has Never."

critics, the system's purpose was to shield the US from incoming nuclear missiles. The arms race with the USSR would then be moot, as Soviet missiles would not be able to reach the US.

The vision was for a spaced-based system of sensors, satellites, and weapons partnered with ground-based interceptors to be able to destroy intercontinental ballistic missiles in space before they could unleash a nuclear holocaust on the ground.[50] The plan was ambitious. Its critics called it reckless and implausible.

While the entire program was never implemented, core pieces of the idea became part of the US military defense. The Patriot Missile Defense System was an outgrowth of Reagan's SDI, for example. Since the days of SDI, technology has improved and US missile defenses have become more robust.

According to a report from the Government Accountability Office (GAO), however, the US missile defense system notes that US missile defense systems are not operating well. The system is not making its targets, and its goals are unmet.[51]

Since 2002, the Defense Department has spent $194 billion on the Missile Defense Agency (MDA). Despite all of that funding, the agency has not kept up with foreign threats.[52] Worse, the MDA only completed six of its nine flight tests in 2022, and only one of those tests achieved its objectives.[53]

Currently, there are only forty-four ground-based interceptors.[54] While sufficient to protect the US against a small attack, a larger attack would overwhelm the interceptors.[55] If US citizens think they are protected from a large-scale nuclear assault from China or Russia, they are sadly mistaken.

LOSING WARS

The US military performs many roles very well. It deters most nations from assault and can overwhelm most enemies very quickly. It has

50. Geller and Kraemer, "40 Years After Reagan."
51. Press TV, "US 'Vulnerable.'"
52. Kredo, "America's Missile Defense System."
53. Kredo, "America's Missile Defense System."
54. Missile Defense Project, "Ground-Based Midcourse Defense (GMD) System."
55. Geller, "40 Years After Reagan."

superior technology, firepower, and training than most other nations. It has the near-unparalleled ability to project force quickly into a dangerous and far-flung location. The US is, indeed, the sole superpower.

What the military does not do well is long-term engagements. Against the Taliban in 2002, the military routed the Taliban quickly. It was the long-term rebuild that was difficult. In the rebuild of Afghanistan, the State Department was entrusted with reconstruction efforts. It, unfortunately, had neither the resources nor the expertise for its mission. The Department of Defense had the resources and expertise for rebuilding, but not for greater-scale missions with large economic and governmental components.[56] In short, "The US government was simply not equipped to undertake something this ambitious in such an uncompromising environment no matter what the budget."[57]

The Defense Department implemented a strategy of attrition against the Taliban insurgents. This strategy often used air strikes to eliminate Taliban fighters and leaders. While effective, they created many civilian casualties. These civilian casualties caused friction with the Afghan government and civilians, which erased any military gain.[58]

Modeling the Afghan military after the US military was a mistake. The US created a central structure, and used expensive US equipment and aircraft.[59] Afghanistan's harsh, mountainous topography did not work well with a centralized logistical structure. Afghan soldiers were used to Russian equipment, and it had the advantage of being cheaper and easier to maintain. More tellingly, creating a large standing force was a drain on resources. Creating smaller local forces was easier and more successful. Even with that success, the US insisted on a large centralized army. It failed.[60]

More than a failure of strategy, this was a failure to learn. The US came in with a strategy that did not and could not work in Afghanistan. Instead of quickly adapting, the Department of Defense held on to its failing strategy, even when seeing the success of alternative models in the field.

With the lessons of Vietnam still unlearned, military planners tried to impose solutions that made sense in Washington but made no sense in the field of operations. More than the distant memories of Vietnam,

56. Sopko, "What We Need to Learn."
57. Sopko, "What We Need to Learn."
58. Robinson, "Our Biggest Errors."
59. Robinson, "Our Biggest Errors."
60. Robinson, "Our Biggest Errors."

leadership did not learn from Iraq. After defeating the Iraqi army, the US military disbanded the Iraqi army and did not stop the looting. The lack of security and the lack of feeling like someone was in charge led to a deteriorating security situation. In Afghanistan, planners did not keep the populace secure as they tried to build new institutions. This failure made developing a new nation much more difficult than it should have been.[61]

Another problem with the strategy should have been apparent. The US wanted to completely reinvent Afghanistan but only had the support of an elite group of Afghans.[62] No reinvention campaign can work with only elite support. The US needed to gain the support of the vast populace, but it did not get it.

Looking at US history since World War II, the wars the US faces are different from those in the past. Wars are not large groups of armies massing against one another. Most of the wars the US faces now are civil wars and counter-insurgency operations.[63] Today, much of the military's focus is on the kinds of wars that do not happen anymore.[64] According to the former vice chief of staff of the Army, Jack Dean, "After the Vietnam War, we purged ourselves of everything that had to do with irregular warfare or insurgency, because it had to do with how we lost that war. In hindsight, that was a bad decision."[65] It was more than bad—it was classic anxiety. Anxiety cannot learn from its past, so it cannot bear its mention.

While using military power to deter such wars is helpful, the Department of Defense has not learned to excel in the kinds of wars the US is most likely to fight. World War II ended in 1945. Vietnam ended in 1975. In fifty years, the US military has not figured out a way to excel in the kinds of wars most likely to occur. It has not figured out how to avoid quagmires.

The regression of the US military is unnecessary. The regression in the military is not that it has lost the power to decimate an enemy in the field. It is that, like many other institutions, the military has been unable to adapt to a changing situation. It has not been able to adapt to a changing US populace. Its recruitment woes demonstrate it is not reaching the young people it desperately needs. It also is not able to convince the

61. Sopko, "What We Need to Learn."
62. Robinson, "Our Biggest Errors."
63. Elliott, "'Major American Failure.'"
64. Elliott, "'Major American Failure.'"
65. Sopko, "What We Need to Learn."

public to stay invested in long-term commitments. The American public grows weary of long warfare, even if a long investment is what is required.

The military has not been able to adapt well to changes in warfare itself. No longer facing massive numbers of enemy troops in battalions, the military finds fighting small numbers of insurgents committed for the long term. In short, it is guerilla warfare.

The inability to adapt, inability to recruit, and focus on anxiety-relieving solutions that do not actually help are hallmarks of an institution in regression. When viewed from that lens, the military, like the other major US societal institutions, is in regression.

8

Press in Regression

If I were a father and had a daughter who became a prostitute,
I should not despair over her, I would continue to hope for
her salvation. But if I had a son who became a journalist and
continued to be one for five years, I would give him up.

—Søren Kierkegaard

THE ROLE OF THE PRESS

IN HEALTHY SOCIETIES, THE press has an important role: they provide information to the public. In democratic societies, this role is invaluable. If the press does not provide truthful information to the public, the public is not able to make proper judgments. The public, by their votes, determine the policy of governments in democratic societies. They, therefore, need access to a stream of truthful information about their society.

In the US, the press is specifically mentioned in the Constitution. The press is a free press, guaranteed the right to publish as they see fit. If the press has a commitment to truthfulness, and its reporting has a reputation for fairness, then it is invaluable to the public.

In the US, among other Western societies, the press is undergoing substantial regression. The public is tuning it out, turning to alternative sources of information, and trying to read through reports as if they were reading *Pravda*. Perhaps the truth is in there somewhere.

PRESS IN REGRESSION

The local newspaper was once a staple of American life, serving an important purpose. The reader gained insight into news happening far away. Even with the advent of network news, that purpose remained. Network news shows could not cover every story in thirty minutes and could only give the broadest outline of the news it did cover. The local paper, however, could cover in some detail foreign affairs, business affairs, and local news. To not receive the local paper meant having little knowledge of the world.

Local newspapers are in terminal regression. Now more than half of US counties have no local newspaper. Further, local newspapers are closing at a rate of 2.5 per week.[1] In 2013, US newspaper advertisement revenue stood at $23.6 billion. As of 2023, it was less than $10 billion.[2]

It is not just print where the regression of the press is occurring: it is happening with TV news as well. Just 25 percent of Americans say that TV is their primary source for news. For those under thirty-four, social media has replaced TV as their primary source.[3] In a breathless headline, CNN reports, "News Outlets Are Collapsing."[4] One of the main drivers of the collapse is loss of revenue. Newspapers have lost approximately $40 billion in revenue since 2005.[5]

MORE THAN THE MEDIUM

Part of the problem for the traditional press is that it is bound to its medium. Print and TV are their media of choice, and they have not figured out how to survive in the new era. While online news organizations like *The Drudge Report* and *HuffPost* have navigated the new era and have maintained profitability, traditional news organizations have not done so well. *The Washington Post*, *The New York Times*, and other major news

1. Northwestern, "More than Half."
2. Marketing Charts, "US Newspaper Ad Revenues."
3. Houston, "Social Rapidly Replacing TV."
4. Darcy, "News Outlets Are Collapsing."
5. Pew Research Center, "Newspapers Fact Sheet."

sources have not been able to make the transition. They struggle with profitability despite their status within the industry.

The problem, however, is not just the medium. The problem is that the press has lost the trust of the public. According to Gallup, in 1972, just under 70 percent of Americans had a great deal or a fair amount of trust in the press. That number fell to 32 percent in 2023. That represents greater than a 50 percent decline. Worse than that, the number of Americans who have no trust in the press has risen to 39 percent.[6]

Much more ominously, 50 percent of the American public believes national news organizations intend to mislead or misinform the public.[7] Half the American public believe that the press corps *intentionally* misleads them.

While transitioning to a digital medium has been problematic, the bigger problem is the forfeiture of trust. Media elites have often blamed the late Rush Limbaugh for their issue. Others have blamed President Trump and his "fake news" epithet for the loss of trust. As Freidman notes, however, anxious systems blame, and healthy systems take responsibility. Press failures account for the loss of trust more than any outside force.

MEDIA MINDSET

The press corps, particularly in Washington, DC, and New York City, have a different mindset than the rest of the nation. This difference can be seen in how the two different groups think of the role of the press. While the public wants the press to seek truth, the press corps sees itself as a means of societal improvement.

Katherine Mahr became the CEO of NPR in 2024, having previously been the CEO of Wikipedia. Once starting at NPR, comments she made in a 2022 TED Talk became controversial. In the TED Talk, Mahr talked about the lessons she learned about truth in her time at Wikipedia. She said:

> That perhaps for our most tricky disagreements, seeking the truth and seeking to convince others of the truth might not be the right place to start. In fact, our reverence for the truth might be a distraction that's getting in the way of finding common ground and getting things done.

6. Brenan, "Media Confidence."
7. Knight Foundation, "American Views."

Now, that is not to say that the truth doesn't exist, nor is it to say that the truth isn't important. Clearly, the search for the truth has led us to do great things, to learn great things. But, I think if I were to really ask you to think about this, one of the things that we could all acknowledge is that part of the reason we have such glorious chronicles to the human experience and all forms of culture is because we acknowledge there are many different truths. And so in the spirit of that, I'm certain that the truth exists for you and probably for the person sitting next to you. But this might not be the same truth . . . so we all have different truths. They're based on things like where we come from, how we were raised, and how other people perceive us.

We shift from focusing on one key truth to instead finding minimum viable truth. Minimum viable truth means getting it right enough of the time to be useful for enough people. It means setting aside our bigger belief systems and not being so fussy about perfection.[8]

As the speech continued, Maher noticed that her process of creating minimum viable truth required taking bias seriously. She noted that most of the early work at Wikipedia was written by Western white males. That necessarily led to biases in the work.[9] Repairing the biases led to the need to undo systems that excluded people and allowed for diverse voices to participate in the conversation, Maher argued.

For Maher and others in the press, bias is not about intellectual biases. Bias is the result of socio-demographic status. If a publisher primarily publishes articles by wealthy white males, it will necessarily produce biased research.

The problem with Maher's rhetoric is that it does not touch intellectual biases. What does it matter if a news organization has a very diverse group of writers but they share the same worldview? Sharing the same ideological worldview or political worldview would make them produce similar results. Those results would necessarily be biased against other worldviews. Worse, bias is notoriously difficult for an institution to notice about itself. The definition of "bias" is an unobserved, unnoticed way of seeing data that precludes one from certain conclusions. If it is overt, easily discerned by the institution, it is not bias so much as prejudice.

Bias hides in plain sight. It lurks under the glow of fluorescent tube lights. It multiplies while unnoticed. When most of the group thinks

8. Maher, "What Wikipedia Teaches Us."
9. Maher, "What Wikipedia Teaches Us."

similarly about similar issues, bias is almost invisible. Having a diverse group that shares a worldview ensures that ideological bias continues.

Maher's thinking about truth is problematic as well. While giving lip service to the truth, she claims that each person has their truth. If each person has "their truth," then they do not have *the* truth.

The role of the press, traditionally understood, is to report the facts correctly so that the news consumer can use the facts to interpret the world and make decisions about it. What Maher argues is not an amalgamation of facts or a setting of the facts in a narrative that intends to present the truth. She wants to subjugate the search for truth to the articulation of the minimum viable truth. Minimum viable truth is close enough to the truth to be actionable.

For Maher, the search for truth has led to the inability to "get things done." While her thinking may or may not be useful for an organization like Wikipedia, it is very different from the role of the press in history. The role of the press was not to be enablers of social theorists or politicians. The role of the press is not to create conditions where governments can take credible action on climate change, for example.

Once the press steps into the role of assisting in "getting things done," the press becomes an advocacy group. Advocacy groups are important in a free society. They rally supporters, contact legislators, convince skeptics, and press for legislation. These activities, however important, are not the activities of a free press. A free press gives the public the information it needs to make critical decisions.

Importantly, Maher's work fails at its own criterion. Wikipedia's minimum viable truth has not led to actionable information, nor has it rallied groups to "get things done." If minimum viable truth should lead to action on the issues she mentions, like climate change, then it has failed in its mission.

Worse still is Wikipedia's reputation. Getting to minimum viable truth has not helped Wikipedia's reputation for veracity. Wikipedia is notorious for its incorrect information. Bias remains at Wikipedia as it skews heavily left in its reading of the world. Wikipedia is not diverse in viewpoint. These problems mean that Wikipedia cannot be trusted to provide accurate information. In fact, most educational institutions do not consider Wikipedia to be a reliable source and discourage students from citing it.

NO VIEWPOINT DIVERSITY

The rest of the press shares the same lack of viewpoint diversity. Uri Berliner, business reporter at NPR, writes:

> Today, those who listen to NPR or read its online coverage find something different: the distilled worldview of a very small segment of the US population.
>
> An open-minded spirit no longer exists within NPR, and now predictably, we don't have an audience that reflects America.
>
> The message from the top was very different. America's infestation with systemic racism was declared loud and clear: it was a given. Our mission was to change it.
>
> What's notable is the extent to which people at every level of NPR have comfortably coalesced around the progressive worldview.
>
> And this, I believe, is the most damaging development at NPR: the absence of viewpoint diversity.[10]

Bias is worse at *The New York Times*. The *Times* has always been progressive, but something has happened. Economist columnist James Bennet writes:

> The *Times*' problem has metastasized from liberal bias to illiberal bias, from an inclination to favor one side of the national debate to an impulse to shut debate down altogether. All the empathy and humility in the world will not mean much against the pressures of intolerance and tribalism without an invaluable quality . . . courage.[11]

At its origin, the *Times's* goal was to present its work "without fear or favor." That impulse is now missing. The paper is not only reliably progressive in viewpoint and intolerant of other perspectives—it no longer has faith in Americans.[12]

In a damning line, Bennett writes, "The reality is that the *Times* is becoming a publication through which America's progressive elite talks to itself about an America that does not really exist."[13]

10. Berliner, "I've Been at NPR."
11. Bennet, "When the *New York Times*."
12. Bennet, "When the *New York Times*."
13. Bennet, "When the *New York Times*."

Even in these self-critical reports, vituperative attacks on Donald Trump's character fill line after line. The press was responding to Trump and his manifold lies, lack of character, and belligerency, these reports state. Missing, however, is an appraisal of why Trump won. Trump is not a cause of the lack of trust in the press: he is a consequence.

The loss of trust in the press predates Trump, and the loss of trust in the press accelerated when ordinary citizens learned that the press was actively working against Trump. The press highlighted the Russian collusion story that was later proven to be false. When the story was demonstrably false, the press simply moved on without apology or introspection.

The press actively suppressed information about Hunter Biden's laptop. The reason the press did not cover it was, at least at NPR, that "it could help Trump."[14] Once proven to be true, the press pretended like the story and their complicity in suppressing it did not matter. If Trump was dishonest and belligerent, they were as well.

President Trump is an anomaly in American politics. Republicans have nearly always chosen their Presidential nominees from sitting or former vice presidents, governors, generals, or congressional representatives. Never before had Republicans chosen someone like Trump. Republican primary voters had their choice of typical candidates: Senators Ted Cruz and Marco Rubio and Governors Jeb Bush, John Kasich, Chris Christi, and Mike Huckabee were available to the party.

The primary voters chose Trump because they no longer believed conventional politicians represented their views or dared to fight off a media that they perceived to be poised against any Republican. Trump's willingness to fight with the press, to state the obvious failure of both parties to secure the border, and to engage in cultural fights that had incensed common citizens won him the nomination. Trump succeeded because traditional Republicans failed and partially because the press clearly loathed him.

The press's loathing of Trump made it easier for Trump to side with the ordinary citizen. The ordinary citizen believed the press despised him too. Voting for Trump then meant that he was voting for someone who was on his side.

14. Berliner, "I've Been at NPR."

SUPPRESSION OF VITAL NEWS STORIES

When the press suppresses stories, it not only makes a determination of who it will and will not believe: it breaks trust. During the height of the COVID pandemic, government officials in multiple nations publicized the "wet market theory."

The "wet market theory" was the idea that COVID emerged in a wet market in Wuhan, China. Someone, apparently, ate a bat from the market and the disease went from the bat to the human population. The press treated other theories as nonsense, conspiracy theories, or worse, racist. As recently as 2024, Wikipedia stated that "the lab leak theory and its weaponization by politicians have both leveraged and increased anti-Chinese racism."[15] This entry is not minimum viable truth exactly.

Of course, Wikipedia is not a news source or credible source of information. *The New York Times* is supposed to be, however. In 2021 the *Times's* lead reporter on COVID wrote about the lab leak theory, "Someday we will stop talking about the lab leak theory and maybe even admit its racist roots."[16] Another credible source, *The Lancet*, stated, "We strongly condemn conspiracy theories suggesting that COVID-19 does not have a natural origin."[17]

Now it is common knowledge that the US government through several of its agencies has concluded that COVID originated as a lab leak in Wuhan. That is not the story. The story is how far news agencies, social media companies, and government officials went to control public perception.

Those who articulated the lab leak were racists and conspiracy theorists. They were quacks who ignored data. Only anti-science oafs would conclude such a thing.[18] Repudiation was normal. Worse though was manipulation.

The Wall Street Journal put it this way: "Question: When does misinformation stop being misinformation on social media? Answer: When Democratic government officials give authorities permission." Facebook censored the lab leak theory under pressure from the Biden

15. Wikipedia, "COVID-19 Lab Leak Theory."
16. *New York Post* Editorial Board, "NYT Writer Blames."
17. Calisher et al., "Statement in Support."
18. Turley, "COVID Lab Leak."

administration.[19] Pressure from governmental authorities led social media companies to censor information.

If the press were focused on the truth, several things would have been true. They would have been the ones actively investigating the wet market theory. Why were government officials so concerned about controlling the narrative about COVID's origin? Surely the racism angle is insufficient. One can say a virus originated in a place without treating the residents of a place with contempt. With the "racism" slur, the press worked with authorities to shut down discussion when the press's role is to instigate discussion. Was the press's loathing of Trump so severe that it could not even do a serious investigation? Perhaps a kinder interpretation is best. The press trusts scientists in general and government scientists specifically. With a bias to believe government scientists, believing their word was perhaps not a matter of malevolence but credulity.

An effective press would not have bowed to the cult of consensus and joined in on disparaging those who articulated the theory, however. An effective press would have noticed the connections between government officials and social media executives and questioned why they were working so closely on this issue. Why was the government so intent on controlling the narrative? How is it possible that the government was so terrified of a theory that it wanted to ban even satire of it?[20]

The response from the Biden administration was that it believed social media companies had a responsibility to monitor speech that could cost lives. In all seriousness, how could a differing theory of COVID's origin cost lives? Suppose Americans came to believe false information about COVID's origin. Would that make them less likely to participate in preventative activities? The reasons provided do not make sense, and the press did not investigate. What reason accounts for this?

Uri Berliner claims the reason was politics. Executives at NPR believed they had been fooled by the Bush administration on weapons of mass destruction (WMDs) in Iraq and did not want to be fooled again.[21] How being overly credulous to one administration leads to being overly credulous to another administration, Berliner does not answer. What he says, though, is illustrative: "Again, politics were blotting out the curiosity and independence that ought to have been driving our work."[22]

19. Tracy, "Facebook Bowed."
20. Gaskins, "White House Pressed."
21. Berliner, "I've Been at NPR."
22. Berliner, "I've Been at NPR."

Whatever the reason, the press did not want to investigate the origin of the virus, why the government wanted to control the narrative, and why it pressured social media companies to censor alternative theories.

More recently, President Joe Biden's health has demonstrated a press in compliance. For any onlooker, President Biden's health decline is obvious. Watching a video of him in 2016 followed by a video of him in 2024 demonstrates a significant and obvious cognitive decline. The president seemed to be lost at the G7. He was unsure of when he was supposed to stand and sit during the ceremonies celebrating the anniversary of the D-Day invasion. When he had no teleprompter, the president seemed lost, searching in vain for a semblance of a complete thought. He could get angry and challenge reporters to a fight when confronted.

When reports began to emerge, the majority of the press corps defended the President. When videos of Biden wandering aimlessly began to emerge, the White House press secretary said they were fakes created to do damage to the President. All the while, as the pubic noticed, the press said little and investigated little.

Then came the most monumental presidential debate since Kennedy-Nixon. President Trump quipped, "I have no idea what he just said, and he doesn't either." After the debate, the press was shocked at what happened. Commentator Van Jones of CNN neared tears. Missing, however, was curiosity. Why was the president's health kept secret? Worse, the press nearest the president had to know of his condition. Those who met with him daily had to know. Why was the reporting limited? One of two things must be true. The press corps knew and kept the president's condition secret, thereby earning eternal opprobrium. The other option is the press did not know, forfeiting their reputation of making any obvious observation. Any realistic observation of President Biden would have concluded that his health was deteriorating quickly.

At this point, the press was in a quandary. If they exposed President Biden's health, they risked electing President Trump. The reaction was muffled. For several days, the press shifted the narrative until Democratic Party insiders forced Biden to end his campaign for reelection. The donors were not going to give to his campaign any longer, and he had lost the support of the Democratic apparatus.

Here again the press made a critical mistake. Instead of finding out why Biden stayed in the race too long, they focused on lionizing him for stepping away from power. The press suppressed the story of Biden's deteriorating health for as long as possible and would have continued to do so had the debate not revealed his condition.

TRIBALISM AMONG MEDIA OUTLETS

While ideology and suppression are features of the regression of the press, a significant issue in the regression is tribalism. The press picks sides in an "us-them" way that hinders their way of reporting facts. There are interesting connections among disparate groups the press supports. It is their purported oppression. In modified Marxist ideology, the world is divided between the oppressor and the oppressed rather than the traditional haves and have-nots. This variation of Marxism makes it possible for the press to side with groups antithetical to their purported values.

Consider the story of the purported bombing of a hospital in the Gaza Strip. In the aftermath of Hamas's gruesome attacks on Israel on October 7, 2023, Israel engaged in an offensive to destroy Hamas. Israel's actions would be considered normal for any other Western democracy had the event happened to them. The press, however, despite its duty to report facts objectively, chose to side with Hamas. Interestingly, Hamas would not tolerate a free press in Gaza.

In a horrifying distortion, *The New York Times* reported, "Israeli Strike Kills Hundreds in Hospital, Palestinians Say."[23] *Newsweek* called the Times's reporting "journalistic malpractice."[24]

Announcing the horrifying news of an explosion at a hospital in Gaza, the Times's journalistic choices were outside the boundaries of good journalism. *Newsweek* writes:

> Think of the editorial decisions involved here: repeating an inflammatory claim (an "Israeli strike"), one that is highly likely to provoke a violent response, one that is unsubstantiated and heavily disputed, and subtly bending the rules of writing by burying the extraordinarily suspect source of this allegation as an afterthought at the end of the headline.[25]

It was not Palestinians in general who were the source for the *Times*: it was Hamas. The picture of the building included in the *Times* was not a picture of the hospital. Finally, after the full picture emerged, it was not

23. Sagalov, "Slow evolution."
24. Robinson, "*New York Times*."
25. Robinson, "*New York Times*."

the Israelis who struck the hospital. It was a misfired rocket from Islamic Jihad.[26]

Newsweek could not contain its ire:

> So to sum up, the most prominent media institution on Earth decided to take an unproven allegation from a vicious terrorist group that 11 days earlier had murdered 1,300 innocent people, taken 200 hostages, and burned alive and decapitated their victims including children, and present it in a way that most served the propaganda aims of the terrorists.[27]

What the writer misses is the reason why the *Times* was susceptible to printing something of this nature. He thinks the *Times* printed the article because its audience is left wing and there are business reasons to bend its coverage the way it did.

Missing is the self-awareness of Berliner who notes that the audience's composition is the result and not the cause. The audience is left wing because the reporting is left wing. The reporting is left wing because the reporters are left wing. The absence of ideological diversity and oversight leads to telling stories that are inaccurate representations of the truth.

GROUPTHINK AMONG MEDIA OUTLETS

One of the core attributes of an institution in regression is the herd mentality. Once arranged in a herd, the members of the group cannot function independently. If one member of the herd has a cold, the rest sneeze. Eventually, the herd crowds all independent thought and punishes dissenters.

Notable evidence of a herd mentality in the press includes the JournoList scandal, where members of the press shared their thoughts on stories they would cover and their desire to punish journalists who deviated from their norms.

Other evidence of the herd mentality is the consistent wording and framing of issues across most press outlets. The framing of *The New York Times* will likely be the framing of CNN, ABC, CBS, and other outlets. Getting talking points on how to report a story is not really necessary.

26. Robinson, "*New York Times.*"
27. Robinson, "*New York Times.*"

Sharing the same worldview, personal connections, and sense of the world yields a press whose reporting is strikingly similar.

ELITISM AMONG THE PRESS

In the early days of the American press, the press corps was a working-class group. The contemporary press is a group of elites doing their work for each other. During the events of January 6, 2021, the American press tried to make sense of the unfolding scene. Anderson Cooper of CNN said, "They're going to go back to the Olive Garden and to the Holiday Inn that they're staying at, or the Garden Marriott, and they're going to have some drinks and they're going to talk about the great day they had in Washington."[28]

Cooper was betraying something about himself. His view is elitist. The Olive Garden and Holiday Inn are somehow beneath Cooper. Middle-class restaurants and hotels are *funny* to Cooper, or at least they were funny to him on that day. Cooper's joke points to a serious problem among the press: "One of the greatest problems of modern news: the mass media is not representative of the masses because a class gap impedes the industry."[29]

It is not just that Cooper is of another class than those who he was covering. One could expect that an anchor at CNN would be wealthy and upper class. It is that Cooper viewed those from a lower class with disdain.

Former President Franklin D. Roosevelt was among the elites. He was wealthy, a Harvard graduate who practiced law in New York. Roosevelt could have had disdain for the common worker, and yet he made them the center of his coalition. He ended up not having the support of his class but the support of the public. In other words, being an upper-class person does not necessitate elitism.

The press is no longer the representative of the working classes. It is by and for the elites. Non-elites need not read nor watch, and they don't. In reviewing Batya Ungar-Sargon's book *Bad News*, Mark Hemingway writes:

> The book's key insight is that the media's problems stem largely from the issue of class. . . . Journalism used to be written primarily by the working class for the working class, but as the industry

28. Booth, "'Public' Elite."
29. Booth, "'Public' Elite."

shrinks it has become ensconced in an elitist bubble that serves the interests of its corporate owners. . . . This renders it incapable of accurately describing, much less diagnosing, the problems faced by working-class readers.

By swapping class concerns for narrower and politically correct concerns, this allows major media to preserve their existing business models . . . while still keeping up the self-serving illusion that elite media are holding power to account rather than catering to the ruling class.[30]

The press, then, cannot be a representative of the working class because they are not from the working class, do not understand the working class, have divergent concerns from the working class, and view the working class with contempt. That noxious stew, then, is evidence of the regression.

WHERE DOES ONE GET TRUE INFORMATION?

This state of affairs is deeply problematic. If one cannot trust press accounts, how does one make decisions? It is little wonder that conspiracy theories, once the domain of Internet crackpots, are making a comeback. A society whose press cannot be trusted is a society that cannot self-govern.

30. Hemingway, "News for the Elite."

9

Humanities in Regression

Violence is not necessary to destroy a civilization. Each civilization
dies from indifference toward the unique values which created it.

—Nicolás Gómez Dávila

HUMANITIES IN REGRESSION

One of the side effects of decreasing attendance at colleges and universities is financial pressure. Budget shortfalls are the norm. Administrators have little choice but to engage in cost-saving measures, and some of
those are necessarily painful.

At West Virginia University, addressing a $45 million budget short-
fall meant drastic cuts. The university cut twenty-eight majors and laid
off 143 faculty. Included in the cuts are half the education faculty and the
entire Department of World Languages. Clarkson University is phasing
out liberal arts majors.[1] State University of New York, Fredonia, is cutting
thirteen majors, all of which are in the liberal arts.[2] The University of
North Carolina, Asheville, is particularly interesting as it is well known

1. Grindon, "Clarkson Announces Plan."
2. Freile, "SUNY Fredonia."

in North Carolina for its arts programming. A decrease in attendance of 25 percent, however, forced cuts to smaller majors, among them theater.[3]

When universities make budgetary cuts, their first instinct is to cut humanities programs. That instinct seems reasonable. Because the humanities continue to attract fewer students, they are often the obvious targets. At Ohio State University's main campus, the number of humanities graduates has plummeted 46 percent from 2012–20; Tufts lost nearly 50 percent of its humanities majors; and Boston College lost 42 percent.[4]

Because STEM majors are popular and tend to lead directly to employment, university administrators are loathe to cut them. Looking at the universities that have cut programs, very few of those cuts have been to STEM programs.

EDUCATION FOR EMPLOYMENT

Humanities can become a target because they are not practical, at least not obviously. There are few jobs for a cello performance major. Mastering an A minor arpeggio, while impressive, is not a job skill in high demand. Even if deciding to teach music, the demand for music instructors is quite limited.

Even fewer jobs are available for majors like medieval Russian literature or classics. One could imagine a graduate in either discipline finding work as a teacher, but that would probably require a degree in education as well. The same would be true of English, anthropology, art history, and other humanities.

The disconnect from apparent employment gives the humanities an image problem. An immigrant family of a Harvard student once said, "You don't go to Harvard for basket weaving."[5] They share a perception that humanities, while possibly interesting, have no practical value. The perception is not, however, grounded in fact.

Among the disciplines within humanities, philosophy is often considered the most abstract and disconnected from work. Philosophy majors, however, do quite well in their careers. Out of fifty majors studied by *The Wall Street Journal*, philosophy majors had the sixteenth-highest

3. Atkinson, "UNC Board of Governors."
4. Heller, "End of the English Major."
5. Heller, "End of the English Major."

mid-career earnings.[6] It is important to note that the reference focuses on only those with an undergraduate degree.[7]

Those who study philosophy often do so in preparation for graduate work in other disciplines like theology, political science, business, or law. Philosophical study sharpens the mind and creates habits of thinking that are foundational to many other disciplines.

No, a philosophy major is not headed directly into unemployment. While there is no transcendental idealism factory, a mind that can comprehend Kant is a mind sharpened well enough to comprehend many other difficult concepts. As such, the image of a philosopher as a bespectacled bloviator spouting nonsense about esoteric topics while living in a van by the river is completely false.

Why would a university cut a program whose nature is to create critical thinkers, engaged citizens, and well-employed workers? In part, it is because there are few majors. In part, it is because of budgetary necessities.

The question is one of value, however. What does society value and want for its college graduates? Currently, that answer is "a marketable job skill." In the beloved Robin Williams classic *Dead Poets Society*, Williams's character, John Keating, defended the discipline of poetry:

> We don't read and write poetry because it's cute. We read and write poetry because we are members of the human race. And the human race is filled with passion. And medicine, law, business, engineering, these are noble pursuits and necessary to sustain life. But poetry, beauty, romance, love, these are the things we stay alive for.[8]

In making education primarily about a marketable job skill, lost is the knowledge that life is more than work and that there are questions worth pondering.

Philosophy, unmentioned in Williams's stirring speech, is the discipline of reflecting on the great questions of life. As the love of wisdom, philosophy is the love of life. The ancient Greeks, Plato, Socrates, Aristotle, and others thought and wrote about life's most important questions, including God, freedom, and immortality. They pondered about the

6. *The Wall Street Journal*, "Salary Increase by Major."

7. *Wall Street Journal*, "Salary Increase by Major."

8. IMDb, *"Dead Poets Society* (1989)."

nature of society and what would make the best society. Also looking at the earth itself, they pondered mathematics and geometry.

Philosophers have mused on other great questions of life: the true, the good, and the beautiful. Williams's point is quite right: beauty, love, and wonder are among the reasons humans live; they make life worth living. An education, then, that does not give sustained reflection on what makes life worth living is deficient.

The Greeks and generations of philosophers over the millennia since have not answered every question correctly. That is impossible. Their model, though, is helpful for those willing to ponder the same questions. Failure to ponder those questions betrays a lack of curiosity that should be part of the educated mind. A mind that has not pondered these questions and interacted with those who have pondered them before cannot be said to have been educated, even if it has gained a lucrative job skill.

Reducing education to mere practicality reduces a person's mind to participation in the great machinery of society. If the only value is production, then the lack of productivity means life has no value. Little wonder people find themselves anxious. Gaining a job skill and only a job skill has not helped people conceive of why they work.

The humanities serve another function: they transmit ownership of the society's story from one generation to another.[9] When studying the great works of Western civilization, one gains not only knowledge of history but ownership of the narrative. Their role then becomes protector and transmitter to future generations.

Without teaching the great works of Western civilization, future generations lose investment in its creations. If Western civilization is to survive, the values on which it is built have to become the common wisdom of the populace. If a society creates millions who can work in a field but have little connection to the society itself, it cannot help but regress.

DESPISING WESTERN CIVILIZATION

Beyond the lack of practicality, the humanities have the reputation of being hives of proto-Marxism. This creeping proto-Marxism often hides in the guise of hating Western civilization. This wound is self-inflicted. When one looks at humanities departments or listens to their lectures, one can

9. I am indebted to Dr. Terry York of Baylor University for this observation.

invariably hear litanies about the racism, sexism, homophobia, transphobia, inequality, oppression, and other phobias and isms of the day.

If one wants to count the alleged sins of Western civilization, however, one ought to count its contributions. Further, if one's loathing of Western civilization is so complete as to want it replaced, one ought to note what the alternative is. When academics in the humanities glare at the sins of Western civilization, often missing from their piercing gaze is the failure of their preferred options for replacement: socialism and Marxism.

Venezuela should not be a poverty-stricken nation. Rich in natural resources, the South American nation was the fourth-richest nation in the world after World War II[10] and among the twenty richest nations in the world as late as 1970.[11]

Hugo Chavez and his successor Nicolás Maduro led Venezuela from being one of the wealthiest countries in Latin America to one of the poorest. Chavez and Maduro's policies, including nationalization of industry and increased government spending, were financed by oil proceeds. The policies, however, created collapse in oil production.[12] Worse, these policies led to bread lines, gang violence, hyperinflation, and an untold murder rate.[13] Additionally, Venezuela is caught in an increasing spiral of authoritarianism. The people of Venezuela are not just poor because of Chavez and Maduro: they are now oppressed. Marxism in practice creates poverty and ruin. This is the lesson of the USSR, China, North Korea, and Venezuela. To ignore this reality is to exist in fantasy.

The fantasies of the neo-Marxists ought to be revealed for what they are by noting Marxist results, yet the ideology will not disappear. The fantasies show up in odd places like in university protests about the war in Gaza. A group named Columbia University Apartheid Divest (CUAD), who protest Columbia's investments with Israel, writes:

> We stand in full solidarity with every movement for liberation in the Global South. . . . Our Intifada is an internationalist one—we are fighting for nothing less than the liberation of all people. . . . We reject every genocidal, eugenicist regime that seeks to undermine the personhood of the colonized.

10. Wharton, "How Venezuela Fell Apart."
11. Hausmann and Rodríguez, "Venezuela Before Chávez."
12. Johnson, "How Venezuela Struck It Poor."
13. Grillo, "It Was Once."

As the fascism ingrained in the American consciousness becomes ever more explicit and irrefutable, we seek community and instruction from the militants in the Global South, who have been on the frontlines in the fight against tyranny and domination which undergird the imperialist world order.[14]

If the Latin American militants have their way, much like in Mao's China, there will be a pile of corpses. Decolonization, with its hatred of the West, rests on Marxist premises and Marxist processes. It can do nothing other than produce Marxist results. CUAD is unwilling to see that and is completely willing to join cause with militants in Latin America and with Hamas.

Just as fundamental as their unwillingness to see the failure of Marxism is their misunderstanding of the West. Western civilization is not the story of oppression creeping like kudzu in a field. It is not the story of riches being hoarded by the few on the backs of the oppressed masses. It is quite the opposite.

Western civilization first recognized human rights. The idea that every human being has rights simply because he or she is a human being is relatively new in human history. It was not the position of the Romans or the great empires of antiquity. For the Romans, a slave was not even a person, at least not in the legal sense,[15] and it was only those who had Roman citizenship by purchase or birth that had anything like legal rights.

The evolution in Western civilization is from only a few having rights to the recognition that all have human rights. The notion of rights is a natural outgrowth of Christianity with its emphasis on the image of God. Since every human being is in the image of God, each of them must be treated as such. It is worth noting that these rights progressively unfolded. At first, only white men had those rights in the US. Then women, and then all gained those rights. Western civilization not only expanded rights, but it defeated two of the most evil and oppressive ideologies in human history: Marxism and Nazism.

Not only has Western civilization expanded rights: it has expanded prosperity. At the beginning of the 1800s, the number of people in the world estimated to live in extreme poverty was estimated to be 80 percent. By 2014 the percentage was 20 percent.[16] By 2018 that number had

---

14. Lewis, "Anti-Israel Columbia Students."
15. Hart, *Atheist Delusions*, 168.
16. Beauchamp, "World's Victory."

fallen to 8.6 percent.[17] The number of people in extreme poverty is falling, and the rate of the fall is accelerating.

This is exactly the opposite of what Karl Marx predicted. In his mind, wealth was produced on the backs of masses of poverty, and the wealth of some required the poverty of others. Eventually, the increasing number of the poor would require a revolution. The failure of this prediction is so complete that neo-Marxist writers have shifted from the language of "haves and have-nots" to "oppressor and oppressed."

This victory over poverty was already noticed in the time of George Orwell. He writes, "The tendency of advanced capitalism has therefore been to enlarge the middle class and not to wipe it out as it once seemed likely to do."[18] Where poverty exists most pervasively is in nations that have adopted Marx's ideas.

Also among Western civilization's contributions to the world is modern science. Born in the Enlightenment, modern science has created innovations leading to longer, better, healthier, and more comfortable living. Diseases that once destroyed civilizations, science has nearly eradicated. Simple creature comforts like air conditioning have made hot climates tolerable. Through inventions, modern science has even made work easier and more productive.

Western civilization has spawned hospitals, orphanages, universities, and other educational institutions, and the realization that life is sacred. Western civilization should not merit hate—it merits preservation.

Hating Western civilization is not only based on historical flights of fancy: it is based on a misunderstanding of every alternative. Hatred of Western civilization is a product of envy and racism, not the answer to them. The hatred of Western civilization then leads to forgetting the voices that contributed to the notion of the humanities itself. It is not a serious intellectual position, and its persistent presence in the academic study of humanities is a form of cannibalism. It is using the tools of study to consume the object of study. It is a regression of the humanities.

POSTMODERNISM AND DECONSTRUCTION

Postmodernism and deconstruction are other self-inflicted wounds in the humanities. *Intellectual Impostures* makes the argument that "vast

17. Tupy and Bailey, "End of Poverty."
18. Orwell, *Why I Write*, 42.

sectors of the humanities and the social sciences seem to have adopted a philosophy that we shall call, for want of a better term, 'postmodernism.'[19]

If one had to pinpoint the beginning of the regression of the humanities, a leading candidate would be 1988. In that year, Stanford University substantially changed its Western culture program.[20] Before the change, Stanford required its undergraduates to take Western civilization. Deemed by students and some professors as Eurocentric, or white-male indoctrination, the university expanded its offerings to be more global and more diverse.[21]

Stanford's change "set off a 'multiculturalist' movement that swept away Western civilization courses at most major American colleges."[22] While the underlying claim that Western civilization was a nativist movement was false, the changes came with scant opposition.[23]

Students, however, stopped taking the classes. The humanities are now "a minor activity."[24] Now only 12 percent of undergraduate degrees are in the humanities, and part of that reason is that professors with a diversity bent cannot give a central thread to the story of Western civilization.[25]

The lack of a central theme is an important component of postmodernism. The term "postmodernism" was coined to describe a movement in art and only later was used to describe movements in English and philosophy. Postmodernism is a rejection of many cherished notions of the Enlightenment.

Illustrating how researchers work in the new environment, Barry Wimpfheimer, associate professor of religious studies and law at Northwestern University, writes:

> In popular perception, elite institutions of higher education exist to discover or name "truths" that can then be disseminated to society at large. In this perception, knowledge is presumed to be a concrete, discrete entity like a dataset or a fact pattern. This perception is more accurate with respect to the "hard" laboratory sciences like physics or biology and significantly less

19. Sokal and Bricmont, *Intellectual Impostures*, 3.
20. Inside Higher Ed, "What Took the Place."
21. Inside Higher Ed, "What Took the Place."
22. Inside Higher Ed, "What Took the Place."
23. Inside Higher Ed, "What Took the Place."
24. Inside Higher Ed, "What Took the Place."
25. Inside Higher Ed, "What Took the Place."

accurate with respect to the humanities, with the social sciences falling in the middle of the continuum. Within higher education humanities in the United States—in fields such as literature, history, philosophy, and religion—we think of knowledge not as a concrete discrete entity so much as a mode of analysis or a way of thinking. Scholars in the humanities no longer see themselves, as their predecessors in the nineteenth century did, employing scientific methods to uncover truths about the history of texts, ideas, or society/culture. Rather, we use theoretical techniques to critique texts, ideas, or society/culture and to draw meaning out of them. Reasons for this transformation include general agreement that it is impossible to fully recover the original intent of an historical actor or author, as well as the feeling that while there is some value in aiming for objectivity, there is also a lot to be gained from acknowledging the existence of multiple subjectivities, including one's own. Different readers always encounter and understand texts considering their own settings, values, and interests; in today's humanities, we embrace this reality rather than pretending it is possible to read from a neutral standpoint.[26]

Neutrality, objectivity, and discerning the authors' original intent are not his focus. It is critiquing texts and ideas to draw meaning out of them.

In postmodern thought, the Enlightenment, or modernism, was fixated on *metanarratives*, the idea that one overriding truth or narrative could explain every human phenomenon. In the Enlightenment, the metanarrative was reason. Human reason could overcome every superstition and give to all rational human beings truth and define right and wrong. For the postmodern thinker, this metanarrative was impossible from the outset. To find truth, one had to have an objective point of view, a view from nowhere. That view is not available to an individual thinker. Individuals are too grounded in their cultures for that. There is no view from nowhere. One of the most pervasive ideas of postmodernism is the incredulity toward metanarratives.

Postmodernity's core tool is deconstruction. The tool, however, is quite difficult to define. Of course, that is natural within postmodernism. Postmodernism is a strategy of not making identity stances and not being fixed.[27] Even though defining deconstruction is difficult, Syracuse University Professor of Religion John Caputo tries:

26. Wimpfheimer, "What Is Happening."
27. Thompson, *Karl Barth*, 4.

> It [deconstruction] simply tells the truth, meticulously, un-
> compromisingly, without disguise, amelioration, or artificial
> sweeteners. In a deconstruction, things are made to tremble by
> their own inner impulse, by a force that will give them no rest,
> that keeps forcing itself to the surface, forcing itself out, mak-
> ing the thing restless. Deconstruction is organized around the
> idea that things contain a kind of uncontainable truth, that they
> contain what they cannot contain. Nobody has to come along
> and "deconstruct things." Things are auto-deconstructed by the
> tendencies of their own inner truth. In a deconstruction, the
> "other" is the one who tells the truth on the "same"; the other is
> the truth of the same, the truth that has been suppressed, omit-
> ted, and marginalized, or sometimes just plain murdered, like
> Jesus himself.[28]

Of course, that definition actually says very little. It is verbiage in search of a thought. It is a cascade of words signifying nothing. "Something contains something it cannot contain" it is a figment. He does not describe the process, as is typical.

The more concrete definition of deconstruction one can find, the more likely it seems postmodern thinkers will reject it. As for Caputo's question in the title of his book, *Who Would Jesus Deconstruct?*, the answer for him is those on his theological and political right. If Jesus would deconstruct everyone an author wants to reconstruct, chances are he has made Jesus in his image, to borrow a phrase.

The question remains, however, "What is deconstruction?" Deconstruction looks at texts and sees the tensions in them as a way to find the claims to power in them. Deconstruction will also look at the way texts function, not just their content. The question is not just "What does this text mean?" but "How does society use this text?"

Postmodernity exchanges truth for relativism. This relativism applies to the way postmodern thinkers read texts. For the thoroughgoing postmodern thinker, meaning in a text is not found within the text itself. The reader of a text provides the meaning. Further, meaning in the text is not the most important part of a text. The important item to notice in a text is how society uses the text. If a society uses a text, for example, to support structures that oppress minorities, then the text is racist.

Reading texts this way is how supporters of critical race theory find racism in just about any document. Of course, many of them could find

---

28. Caputo, *What Would Jesus Deconstruct?*, 29.

racism in two dandelions swaying in the sweltering summer breeze or even something as banal as a requirement to be at work on time.[29] Lest one think only fringe madmen would promote such an idea, none other than Duke Medical School adheres to that madness.

Despite its prevalence on university campuses and in humanities programs, many thinkers have concluded that postmodernism is dead, or at least the conditions that produced postmodernism have died. Whether dead or living, the concepts of postmodernism still fill the humanities and influence readers across disciplines.

THE POWER OF A HOAX

In *Intellectual Impostures*, authors Jean Bricmont and Alan Sokal reveal the bankruptcy of much postmodern thought. The origin of the book was a hoax. The authors, wanting to demonstrate the pervasive nature of postmodern influence, wrote an article entitled "Transgressing the Boundaries: Toward a Transformative Hermeneutics of Quantum Gravity."[30] The paper was an absurdity but somehow was published in *Social Text*, a reputed journal of social theory.

The hoax was constructed around quotations from postmodern intellectuals about the philosophical and social implications of math and the natural sciences.[31] What made the article so much worse is that the author, Alan Sokal, merely connected quotes from postmodern thinkers. It was a fiasco. It concludes, "The π of Euclid and the G of Newton, formerly thought to be constant and universal, are now perceived in their ineluctable historicity."[32]

To those not involved in postmodernism, the quote is gibberish. Those in the movement, however, could be fooled. The pompous rhetoric and often nonsensical writing of postmodern thought is quite easily parodied. Richard Dawkins, famed scientist and mediocre philosopher, wrote a review of *Intellectual Imposters* and utterly savaged postmodernism. He writes:

> Suppose you are an intellectual imposter with nothing to say,
> but with strong ambitions to succeed in academic life, collect

29. Curl, "Expecting People."
30. Sokal and Bricmont, *Intellectual Impostures*, 1.
31. Sokal and Bricmont, *Intellectual Impostures*, 3.
32. Sokal and Bricmont, *Intellectual Impostures*, 2.

a coterie of reverent disciples, and have students around the
world anoint your pages with a respectful yellow highlighter.
What kind of literary style would you cultivate? Not a lucid one,
surely, for clarity would expose your lack of content.

Given their own standards of relative truth, isn't it rather
unfair to take them to task for fooling around with word games,
and playing little jokes on readers? Perhaps, but one is left won-
dering why their writings are so stupefyingly boring. Shouldn't
games at least be entertaining, not po-faced, solemn, and
pretentious?[33]

Dawkins is merciless in his rebuke of postmodernism. Postmodernism is vague because it is empty, boring because it has nothing to say. Its
expansive verbiage masks a poverty of ideas. It is ChatGPT for men in
corduroy blazers.

There is a postmodern thought generator. As Dawkins notes, a
visit to the website https://elsewhere.org/pomo will yield an impressive
parody of postmodern thought, almost enough to create a convincing
short essay.

Dawkins is not simply ridiculing postmodernism for the sake of
ridicule, however. He, Sokal, and Bricmont are making the point that
postmodernism in the humanities is vapid and destructive. This vapidity
is particularly obvious when postmodern thinkers employ scientific or
mathematical concepts in their work.

Embedding postmodern thought into the humanities is a regression. It takes away from the study of the canon of a discipline and incul-
cates those who would read it into abstruse jargon.

POMPOSITY AND OBSCURITY

Although often tied to postmodern thought, pompous language and
obscure wording are also often present in the humanities even without
postmodern connections. There is a thought among some humanities
scholars that difficult concepts require difficult language.[34]

Writing at its best, clearly communicates. The worst kind of writing obscures. In his famed essay *Politics in the English Language*, George
Orwell describes poor writing style as an unfortunate by-product of
bad thinking. The bad writing, however, contributes to poor thinking.

33. Dawkins, "Postmodernism Disrobed."
34. Butler, "A 'Bad Writer' Bites Back."

Thinking badly and writing badly feed off of each other in the worst of symbiotic relationships.

For Orwell, one constant in bad writing was the use of euphemisms. Using euphemisms was a way to cover up horrors to make them less likely to be noticed. Euphemisms could also replace actual thought. For him, writers should eliminate euphemisms and write clearly. The absence of clear writing was evidence of bad thinking.

Sokal and Bricmont would concur with Orwell. They "deconstruct" the idea that some texts are difficult because they contain difficult ideas: "In some cases . . . if the texts seem incomprehensible, it is for the excellent reason that they mean precisely nothing."[35]

Pointing to the work of Jaques Lacan, Sokal and Bricmont make their case that postmodern writing is not filled with impressive thought. Lacan was an influential French psychologist of the 1900s. His work, always controversial, used frequent references to mathematics. His references, however, show no understanding of mathematics. His use of math is simply pompous. He writes:

> No doubt Lévi-Strauss, in his commentary on Mauss, wished to recognize in it the effect of a zero symbol. But it seems to me that what we are dealing with here is rather the signifier of the lack of this zero symbol. That is why, at the risk of incurring a certain amount of opprobrium, I have indicated to what point I have pushed the distortion of the mathematical algorithm in my use of it: the symbol $\sqrt{-1}$, which is still written as "i" in the theory of complex numbers, is obviously justified only because it makes no claim to any automatism in its later use.
>
> Thus the erectile organ comes to symbolize the place of *jouissance*, not in itself, or even in the form of an image, but as part of lacking the desired image. That is why it is the equivalent of the $\sqrt{-1}$ of the signification produced above, of the *jouissance* that it restores by the coefficient of its statement of the function of lack of signifier.[36]

If a non-scholar wanted to create a parody of the humanities and its desperate search for relevance, he or she would have a difficult time competing with Lacan's verbiage. Trying to derive support for a theory in the humanities from mathematics is fraught with peril, a pursuit best left

---

35. Sokal and Bricmont, *Intellectual Impostures*, 5.

36. Sokal and Bricmont, *Intellectual Impostures*, 25.

avoided. Even if one were to attempt it, why think of an "erectile organ" as an *i*?

What has an imaginary number to do with Freudianism? The correct answer is, "Nothing." Worse, it gives the reader with some knowledge of math the impression that the entire enterprise is balderdash, and rightly so. It might also give the reader the impression that the humanities themselves are balderdash.

That impression is toxic and self-induced. The humanities are very much what Robin Williams's Keats describes: they are *life*. Why do we love? What is love? Is there a meaning in life? Where is there meaning in life? What is the human personality? What is God like, and how could one know? Is there a truth? If so, how could one find it? What economic structures best create human flourishing? Is there any benefit to government intervention in the economy? What is the good life? These are among the questions of greatest importance in life. The humanities are the study of these questions and myriads of questions like them.

Allowing the humanities to descend into well-earned derision among other disciplines is shameful. Sakol and Bricmont write, "We are not attacking philosophy, the humanities, or the social sciences in general; on the contrary, we feel that these fields are of the utmost importance and we want to warn those who work in them (especially students) against some of the manifest cases of charlatanism."[37]

Theirs is a rescue attempt of sorts. Why is this rescue needed? It is needed because the humanities in US institutions have fallen under the spell of an extraneous ideology hostile to them.

Because of the nature of the humanities, studying them and writing about them should bring clarity and understanding to the most important parts of life. Sadly, in much of the work of the humanities, that is not so.

IDENTIFICATION WITH POLITICS

The humanities have developed a reputation of connection with the politics of the American left. Some argue that political posturing in the humanities is a result of trying to be useful.[38] Perhaps there is truth in that assertion. Whatever the reason, the connection to partisan politics is a crisis equally as pressing as the problem of relevance.

37. Sokal and Bricmont, *Intellecutal Impostures*, 5.
38. Harper, "Humanities Have Sown."

One scholar cited in *The New York Times* notices the problem and questions, "How did anyone think we could get away with being nakedly ideological for years without any chickens coming home to roost? Universities have always been tacitly left-leaning and faculty have always been openly so, but institutions have never been this transparently, officially political."[39]

The connection to politics is not accidental. Steven Mintz, professor of history at the University of Texas at Austin, writes:

> The vision put forward by a number of my junior colleagues—a conception of the humanities that is more self-consciously political, more activist, more presentist [sic], more attentive to the issues of power and inequality, more focused on the voices and agency of the marginalized—may not be everyone's cup of tea. But the efforts to broaden the humanities, to encompass new subjects, to reach out more assertively and determinedly, and think more comparatively and internationally, strike me as exactly right. That way lies the future.[40]

Only if the future is death. In that same article, Mintz argues that resistance to change is the way of stagnation. That is of course true as far as it goes. The problem is that the humanities are entering a death spiral. The humanities have already suffered a collapse in attendance. Significantly fewer students are interested in them precisely because of the direction Mintz and his junior colleagues advocate. Failing to recognize the state of the humanities is academic malpractice. The solution he provides will sound good to many of his fellow academics, but that is only because of groupthink and the academic acceptance of polysyllabic attacks on the English language.

Politicizing any branch of academia is fatal. It cannot be otherwise. Why would a society continue to fund overtly activist institutions especially when the activism is contrary to the values of approximately half of the society? Why should the humanities tie itself to ideologies that are tangential to its subject matter? Mintz bemoans that "ideologues" caricature much of the work in the humanities as "faddish, impractical, and politically motivated claptrap."[41] The problem for Mintz is that what critics say about much of the work in the humanities is not caricature.

---

39. Douthat, "Why Liberal Academia Needs Republican Friends."
40. Mintz, "Humanities Are in the Midst."
41. Mintz, "Humanities Are in the Midst."

It is fact. For the sake of the humanities, institutions would be wise to abandon the political project of the humanities, or else, there will be little left standing of the discipline.

UNREAD ARTICLES

Publishing in academia can be a lonely venture. It will not make one famous or wealthy. It is, however, a requirement for becoming a scholar in the humanities. The often-cited figure that 50 percent of all articles are never read by another human post-publication is most probably false.[42] What is true, however, is that academic journals have a very small distribution and few people will read any academic piece. A blog on Patheos could easily have a larger audience than a prominent journal in religious studies.

So, when academics learn to write for publication, they are learning to write for a miniscule audience. As a result, when a scholar of the humanities has an impressive list of publications in academic literature, he or she may not have compelled many people by blinding logic or original thought. As *Intellectual Impostures* demonstrates, being able to take on the correct verbiage and cite the correct sources can get someone published.

Of course, this is unfortunate for the humanities. The study of Shakespeare, the Gospel of John, the *Enneads*, or the history of the United States should not be a matter of creating proper-sounding words and critiquing the right groups. Inasmuch as it is, the humanities are devouring themselves.

The humanities might be in the worst state of regression of all the institutions studied here. They are in decline in the number of students; they have alienated politicians and taxpayers; they have lost sight of their aim; and they have tied themselves to the progressive political movements. Few leaders in the humanities have the foresight to address the issues, much less change course.

42. Jago, "Can It Really Be True."

10

Cause 1

Herd Mentality

> A society cannot evolve no matter how much freedom
> is guaranteed when the citizenry is more focused on
> one another than their own beliefs and values.
>
> —EDWIN FREIDMAN

> The instinct to protect the human race is the es-
> sence of the species, the herd.
>
> —FRIEDRICH NIETZSCHE

BOWEN THEORY: A PRIMER

A HELPFUL WAY TO look at institutional regression is through the lens of Bowen theory, often called family systems theory or systems theory. Formulated as a theory to describe and treat family dysfunction, Bowen theory offers insight into how societal institutions devolve.

Created by the late psychiatrist Murray Bowen, the theory focuses not on individual behavior but on individual behavior as part of a system of relationships: "Systems theory strives to look at the emotional process going on among people, while never losing sight of the facts of the situation.

Rather than trying for control or blaming the other, one tries always to better manage oneself and one's own contribution to the situation."[1]

Emotional systems have a profound power over the behavior of the individuals in the system. In writing about metaphysics, Catholic philosopher Robert Koons writes, "In quantum mechanics, particles lose their individual identities as a result of being incorporated into quantum systems."[2] While people are not particles and do not behave like particles in a quantum system, something similar can be said about people in emotional systems. Emotional systems have great power over their participants. It is easy for the emotional system to overwhelm individual persons.

Bowen theory focuses on eight concepts: the family as an emotional system, self-differentiation, emotional triangles, emotional cut-off, the family projection process, sibling position, and societal emotional process.[3]

One of Bowen's observations about society is relevant here. Societies vary in emotional stability during different moments in their history. In times of higher anxiety, individuals in society tend to behave more irresponsibly and create more anxiety as a result.[4] What is needed when societies become more anxious is a more self-differentiated leader.

In his book *A Failure of Nerve*, Rabbi Edwin Freidman argues that American society has become so chronically anxious that it is toxic to well-defined leadership.[5] It is helpful to note this use of anxiety does not have the same meaning as in the medical or psychological field. In those settings, anxiety is intense worry and the physiological and mental consequences of worry. In this sense, anxiety is emotional intensity born of a sense of threat. In practical terms, high anxiety is revealed by emotional intensity. The greater the intensity, the higher the anxiety.

It is important to note that there is an important difference between acute anxiety and chronic anxiety as well. Acute anxiety is situational, tied to worries over specific events. Chronic anxiety resides in the person or institutions. Any event, therefore, can provoke an anxious response in the chronically anxious.[6] Chronic anxiety is debilitating for societies,

1. Gilbert, *Eight Concepts of Bowen Theory*, 2.

2. Koons, *Is St. Thomas's Aristotelian Philosophy*, 90.

3. Gilbert, *Eight Concepts of Bowen Theory*, 3.

4. Gilbert, *Eight Concepts of Bowen Theory*, 92.

5. Friedman, *Failure of Nerve*, 53.

6. Steinke, *Congregational Leadership*, 10.

institutions, and individuals. Worse, it actually prevents the cure: well-differentiated leadership.

There are five characteristics of anxious societies, according to Freidman:

1. *Reactivity, the automatic, unthinking reaction to other people and events.* Some reactivity is normal. It is a shortcut for the brain. When reactivity is the norm, however, anxiety emerges. When societies are regularly reactive to events, they become unstable and use forced togetherness to regulate anxiety.

2. *Herding, the process of compulsory togetherness instead of individual thinking.* Herding is the process of enforcing the norms of a group and crushing dissent. Norms may be enforced by shaming, ostracizing, and insulting.

3. *Blame displacement, where societies focus on those who have harmed them rather than taking responsibility for their own choices.* Highly anxious societies will find scapegoats.

4. *A quick-fix mentality; the low threshold for pain requires these societies to find solutions that relieve symptoms.* These solutions provide temporary relief but cannot address long-term causes or create fundamental change.

5. *A lack of well-differentiated leadership.*[7] A well-differentiated leader knows his or her convictions, is capable of managing internal anxieties, and does not yield to conformity.

ANXIETY

Societies with chronic anxiety tend to identify the wrong poisons. The poisons in society are not drugs, guns, violence, crime, or any of the other issues society faces at a given moment. Many fixations that seem like pressing issues are not really issues at all. For example, every so often a terrible event like a plane crash will occur. Society will obsess about the event, studying it from every angle. Eventually, press accounts will compare that crash to an earlier one and seek to find commonalities between them. If suddenly multiple crashes occur over a short period, reports will emerge questioning the safety of air travel. All the while, air travel is

7. Friedman, *Failure of Nerve*, 88.

statistically much safer than travel in cars. That fact, however, will be lost in the panic. Society and the press will treat the ones who try to see the event objectively as insensitive or worse.

Sometimes, however, society does have a real issue and seems powerless to solve it. Part of the reason that is the case is that the forces of anxiety prevent clarity and objectivity. Whatever problems society has, anxiety fuels them and can render them unsolvable.

Anxiety in an individual or group is a very uncomfortable emotional state, and those affected by it must regulate it. Some regulate anxiety by bringing in another person. Bowen theorists call this triangulation. Tactics for triangulation include gossip, sharing secrets, and creating alliances. What triangulation does is allow the person who has the anxiety to displace it onto a third party.

Another way to regulate anxiety is by control. People with high anxiety seek to control their environment and the people around them. Unable to allow others to have an opinion differing from theirs, they cajole, manipulate, argue, and intimidate their way into dominance:

> They make hostages of their gifts, attendance, and participation. They employ their stewardship as brinkmanship. Their ultimate threat is to run away from home—transferring or terminating their membership if an action is not rescinded, a person is not removed or a demand is not satisfied.[8]

Best-selling author Robert Greene argues that "emotional states are as contagious as diseases."[9] Anxiety is not only contagious as family systems theorists teach[10]—anxiety is among the most contagious of emotional states. The anxiety in one is quickly experienced by the other and can quickly be the default emotional state of the group. Anxiety cannot remain in one single person as it necessarily takes over others. Everyone who lacks self-regulation will perpetually invade the space of others.[11]

HERD MENTALITY

Originally published in 1999, *A Failure of Nerve* accurately describes some of the challenges societal institutions in the US face. Most pointedly,

8. Steinke, *How Your Church Family Works*, 22.

9. Greene, *Daily Laws*, 145.

10. Steinke, *Congregational Leadership*, 10.

11. Friedman, *Failure of Nerve*, 137.

it describes herd mentality. The herd mentality is the process by which groups attempt to force conformity on all of its members. The herd can tolerate no dissent. Dissent makes its anxiety go higher. Those who have the temerity to dissent must be brought into agreement with the group or neutralized. In the words of Friedrich Nietzsche, "Ultimately, however, it is indifferent whether the herd is commanded to have one opinion or permitted to have five. Whoever deviates from the five public opinions and stands apart will always have the whole herd against him."[12]

THE HERD IN PRACTICE: CANCEL CULTURE

There is a phenomenon in the US known as cancel culture. Cancel culture is the process by which someone can say or post something outside the norms of the group and be "canceled" for it. "Canceling" can be termination from a job, ostracism from a community, or even losing the ability to post on social media. Actor Rowan Atkinson, known for his character Mr. Bean, described cancel culture quite well. He said, "It is like a medieval mob looking for someone to burn."[13]

In 2012 the CEO of Chick-fil-A, Dan Cathy, responded to a question about gay marriage in the way one would have expected. He, a person of outspoken Christian belief who runs a company that is closed on Sunday, said he was against it. His position should have shocked no one. What was shocking was the response. While some who opposed his position attempted to create a boycott, those who supported him decided to do the opposite and purchase from Chick-fil-A. Protesters decided to get in line and order a free cup of water to register their opposition.[14]

One such protester was Adam Smith. Smith recorded his protest and posted it online. Speaking to the drive-thru operator, he said, "I don't know how you live with yourself and work here. I don't understand it. This is a horrible corporation with horrible values."[15] The video was seen by many, and after a bomb threat to his workplace, Smith was fired from his job. Smith found getting employment nearly impossible after the

12. Nietzsche, *Gay Science*, 202.
13. Sadler, "Top 10 Recent Examples."
14. Mooney and Sherman, "How 'Cancel Culture' Changed."
15. Mooney and Sherman, "How 'Cancel Culture' Changed."

video. Finally, after two years, Smith told his story on TV and was hired as a CFO at a software company.[16]

In one respect, Smith had a significant lapse in judgment. He recorded himself having an interaction with a food service worker that was anything but gracious. Questioning a food service employee's judgment in her choices is not an effective way to communicate displeasure with the CEO. He was also denying service to paying customers by taking a spot in line, thereby slowing service for those who wanted to pay. All of that frantic activity was to protest the thoughts of a man he did not even know.

Putting the interaction on video was another misstep. Why would he expect his video to be received positively? Chances are he rarely interacted with others who thought differently from him. Living in his comfortable bubble where opinions varied as little as the tonal range of a boy band, Smith was offended that others might think differently. So then, he was in for a shock when many supported Cathy's position. While he might not have expected the number of responses or their ferocity, Smith should have expected some negative feedback. He seems oblivious to that. He was trying to cancel Cathy and could not understand why others would not as well.

In another sense, he was most certainly a victim of cancel culture. Bomb threats at his workplace, termination, and two years of unemployment for a protest are quite cruel, even when his protest was misguided. In every respect, the problem in the Smith case is that people were unwilling to allow others to have differing opinions.

Why was it necessary to protest Chick-fil-A? Cathy simply answered a question. Why was it necessary to terminate an employee for his protest? He is entitled to his opinion. In modern US society, however, opinions must be hushed if they differ from the herd. In Freidman's words:

> As with any chronically anxious family, there is in American society today an intense quickness to interfere in another's self-expression, to overreact to any perceived hurt, to take all disagreement too seriously, and to brand the opposition with ad hominem personal epithets (chauvinist, ethnocentric, homophobic, and so on).[17]

Cancel culture has attacked Elon Musk, J. K. Rowling, Gina Carano, Ralph Northam, Kevin Hart, Bill Maher, and many others. In these cases,

16. Mooney and Sherman, "How 'Cancel Culture' Changed."
17. Friedman, *Failure of Nerve*, 64.

it is insufficient to disagree with the content of their words. Cancel culture attempts to destroy them for disagreement with the herd.

If highly anxious families are a panic in search of a trigger,[18] then highly anxious societies are just the same. When societies are highly anxious, togetherness is comfort and independent thinking is a trigger.

In the greater sense, the herd mentality and the resulting cancel culture result from having poor interpersonal boundaries. Those without boundaries cannot face the anxiety that comes from others thinking differently. As Freidman notes in *Generation to Generation*, one of the best tests to see if someone has appropriate boundaries is to make an "I believe" statement. "I believe" statements define the speaker and the speaker's boundaries. A person with appropriate boundaries will respond to statements of self-definition with curiosity or by defining themselves in response. A person without boundaries will respond with pressure to conform, "How can you think that when . . ."

The herd mentality forces adaptation to weakness when what society needs is adaptation toward strength.[19] What would it be like if instead of trying to break nonconformists, society listened to them? It is the nonconformists who have the possibility of leading society back to health.

LOSS OF AUTHENTIC SELFHOOD

Humans are social beings. Born into families, humans require contact with the family for survival and development during their first years. As people mature, they seek out some differentiation from the home; however, they need some sense of connection or community to thrive.

Despite the need to be connected to a group, to be a whole person, one needs to be able to differentiate oneself from the group. Human maturity is the process of being able to separate one's individual mental and emotional functioning from the group.[20] According to Bowen, there are two counterbalancing relationship forces: a togetherness force that craves attachment and a separateness force that craves autonomy.[21]

Some loss of the individual self can be seen in group events. Sporting events, popular concerts, and political rallies offer individuals the

18. Friedman, *Failure of Nerve*, 63.
19. Friedman, *Failure of Nerve*, 98.
20. Gilbert, *Eight Concepts of Bowen Theory*, 28.
21. Brown and Errington, *Bowen Family Systems Theory*, 12.

opportunity to lose self in the group. While these events are not dangerous in themselves and can be enjoyable, loss of self to the group is powerful. Like all other powerful instruments, they can be used to cause harm. Consider riots after soccer matches in Europe or mob violence from intoxicated revelers at a concert. The loss of individuality these events provide makes a turn toward bad or even criminal behavior much more possible.

Humans have the capacity to self-differentiate. As anxiety and the fusion between persons increases, the ability to remain a self decreases. As anxiety in the group increases, the emotional distance between each member decreases. What happens to one is experienced by all. One's anxiety affects the whole group, and the group's anxiety affects the one.

Applied to anxious societies or organizations, the herd makes demands. It stifles individuality; it shutters the eyes of the mind. Anxious herds cannot tolerate differences.

THE HERD IN ACTION: CULTURAL REVOLUTIONS

Gao Jianhua grew up in communist China and had the good fortune to attend a "key school" where 90 percent of the students went to college. Studious, Jianhua worked to create the kind of academic record that would gain him admittance to Beijing University.[22]

At his school, Jianhua developed friendships with Fangpu, a classmate of his and a passionate communist. Although Fangpu was four years older, they connected over literature. While friends, they did have important differences. Fangpu's work, poetry, centered on political issues. He worshiped Chairman Mao and attempted to emulate his writing. Jianhua, however, had little interest in politics.

In May of 1966, Fangpu made an unexpected visit to Jianhua. Animated, he described a literary debate covered in Beijing newspapers. Some well-known intellectuals had accused respected writers of hiding counterrevolutionary themes in their work. "Certain people are using art and literature to attack the party and socialism," Fangpu said.

Far from remaining an academic debate in far-off Beijing, the story gripped the nation. After the Communist Party secretary made a speech recounting an editorial, Jianhua's school became gripped by the controversy as well. The students made posters attacking those who opposed

22. This story is recorded in Greene, *Laws of Human Nature*, 391–402, and the text that follows is a summary of it.

the communist revolution, parroting the posters other students had plastered in Beijing.

Eventually, the campaign in Beijing spread nationwide. If there were counterrevolutionaries in Beijing, surely they were elsewhere also, so the logic went. Students began to scrutinize their teachers, analyzing their ideas and work to see if they were sufficiently loyal to Mao. Some of them made posters critiquing their teachers. The party secretary banned such posters, suggesting it trivialized the debate.

By June the movement in Beijing had a name: the Great Socialist Cultural Revolution. Secretly, Mao initiated the movement by placing articles in newspapers. Motivated by the fear that China would return to its feudal past without intervention and wanting to revive the spirit of the revolution, Mao encouraged young people to question everything.

Inspired by Mao's thinking, Fangpu created a poster attacking the local Party secretary. Fangpu thought that protecting the teachers from inquiry into their anti-revolutionary beliefs revealed that the party secretary was part of the counterrevolution. Shortly after Fangpu posted his poster, teams from Beijing came to supervise the cultural revolution at the school. They ordered Fangpu to apologize but lifted the ban on posters critiquing teachers. They suspended academic work so that students could devote themselves to the revolution.

Once free of academic obligations and the requirement for obedience, students began to attack teachers who did not exhibit enough revolutionary zeal or treated the students poorly. As the campaign intensified, so did the anger of the students.

Some teachers began to confess minor sins against the revolution. Rather than slaking the student's wrath, it only intensified it. Students began to use humiliation techniques derived from Mao's work to coerce confessions. Even that was not enough. Eventually, students would force teachers into a "jet plane" position. A student would stand on either side of the teachers and push them to their knees. Then a student would pull the teacher's hair back while others held their arms out and back, imitating the appearance of a jet plane. The position was quite painful. After being held in that position for sometimes hours, many of the teachers confessed. Eventually, some teachers fled, and others committed suicide.

Beatings and torture commenced. Students began to gather in armed groups using torture to force confessions and betrayals. Once groups began to develop insider and outsider mentality, there was little room for rational thought. Eventually, revolutionaries tortured both Ji-anhu and Fangpu.

A terror gripped the entire nation. The only ways of thinking were the dichotomy between insider and outsider, supporter of the revolution or counterrevolutionary, worthy of humiliation and torture or a good soldier of the revolution. The revolution eventually had to be stopped lest the country devour itself.

While the Cultural Revolution was a case of forced conformity, it would be foolish to conclude that forced conformity is limited to Marxist revolutionaries. In response to the October 7 terrorist attacks in Israel, students at George Washington University held mock trials for profes-sors, administrators, and trustees whose support of *Hamas* was suspect.[23] The protesters were recorded supporting the *guillotine* as punishment for them.[24] Students chanted, "Guillotine. Guillotine. Guillotine. Guillotine." Calling the provost by name, they chanted, "Bracey, Bracey we see you. You assault students too. Off to the motherf***** gallows with you."[25] These calls for violence and show trials are tools not only to intimidate, but they also enforce conformity.

Forced conformity is a powerful tool and can lead to violence. At the height of the Black Lives Matter movement, a group of teenagers in Ohio grabbed a fellow student to force him to recite the mantra "Black lives matter." One student grabbed one of his smaller peers, dragging him toward the playground. Eventually, five others joined in the assault as they took the boy to an area around the swing set and beat him. Picking him up over his shoulder, the largest student threw the child to the ground. Other students were assaulted as well. One parent said her son was forced on the ground and required to kneel and say "Black lives matter."[26]

BLAME

In highly anxious families, anxiety can result in over-focusing on one particular child's negative behaviors. An anxious society can manifest a group to blame for its ills. At various points in US history, politicians and political groups have made a pariah of the rich. If the rich were not

23. Collins, "GW President."
24. Perdomo, "At Least 33 Pro-Palestine Vandals Arrested."
25. Stu, "At the George Washington University." Censor mine.
26. Brown, "Black Kids Forced White Kids."

greedy, there would be more than enough resources to go around. If the rich would only pay their fair share, then more benefits would be available to the poor and middle class. Occasionally, blaming the rich can manifest itself into policy. In 1991 Congress passed a 10 percent luxury tax that included the boat industry. The result of the tax increase was that many of those who built and sold luxury boats lost their businesses. It was not the rich who suffered the most. Sales of luxury boats plummeted, and boat builders, small businesses, and employees were hurt the most.[27]

Other examples of societal scapegoating include the status of Jews in Europe from the Middle Ages onward,[28] African Americans in the US, and landowners in South Africa. In all of these instances, it is not necessary that the scapegoats are actually to blame for any societal issue. It is only necessary that they are different enough for them to become the focus of society's anxiety.

FIX IT. NOW.

One of the great temptations in leadership is the desire for a quick fix. Anxious institutions and societies cannot take a long-term view of their problems. In 2011, JCPenney had forfeited its place among successful American retailers. It was clearly struggling for relevance and sales. After the tenure of CEO Myron Ulmman, the company hired Ron Johnson, who had successfully led Target and Apple Stores to become extremely profitable.[29]

Johnson was not content to just make the company more profitable, he wanted to completely redesign it. With speed his aim, Johnson skipped important verifications for his vision. There was no test marketing or staged rollouts.[30] JCPenney changed logos, store designs, pricing structure, and advertisements without seeing how their customers would react.[31]

Johnson eliminated much of JCPenney's leadership, bringing in executives from other retailers. The problem is that they and Johnson

---

27. Goldberg, "Boat Luxury Tax."
28. Friedman, *Failure of Nerve*, 92.
29. Bolman and Deal, *Reframing Organizations*, 387.
30. Bolman and Deal, *Reframing Organizations*, 387.
31. Meyersohn, "How It All Went Wrong."

both gave off an air of not liking the company or its customers.[32] Johnson assumed, according to Mark Cohen of the Columbia Business School, that he could walk away from his former clientele and a new one would appear instantly.[33] That new clientele did not appear. In one sense, Johnson's issue was magical thinking. More importantly, though, it was a case of seeking a quick fix.

There is a difference between knowing what will sell in a season and quickly transitioning to that merchandise and a quick fix. A quick fix assumes that a sudden change will correct most of what ills an institution. Speed and flexibility assume that an institution is steadily focused on a goal and can quickly adapt to changes.

JCPenney's was indeed struggling when Johnson was hired. It needed an overhaul. Johnson's overhaul was not carefully considered, though. It was a series of mistakes, alienating his customer base and damaging the brand. Johnson's fix of JCPenney's was a quick fix destined to fail.

Quick fixes are notorious in the sense that they seem helpful. They usually, however, are no more than distractions from the problem at hand. Quick fixes are really not even designed to be solutions—they are designed to resolve anxiety, to make pain stop.

What they fail to do is develop the processes that will lead to long-term success. An institution that cannot face its anxiety will forever fall for the promise of a quick fix.[34]

Some of JCPenney's competitors were able to transition. Ross, Kohl's, and Nordstrom managed to reinvent, but JCPenney's reinvention was a failure.[35] JCPenney's problem was it had a "lack of understanding about what it is, what it stands for, and who it wants to serve."[36]

LEADERSHIP PHOBIA

Regressing societies end up undermining the institutions that could produce leaders with the ability to lead the society out of its devolution.[37] This process reveals a fear of leadership. Leaders, after all, have to be able

---

32. Bolman and Deal, *Reframing Organizations*, 388.

33. Meyersohn, "How It All Went Wrong."

34. Friedman, *Failure of Nerve*, 84.

35. Meyersohn, "How It All Went Wrong."

36. Meyersohn, "How It All Went Wrong."

37. Friedman, *Failure of Nerve*, 90.

to self-differentiate. The last thing an anxious herd wants is for a person to self-differentiate.

A self-differentiated leader is exactly what an anxious society needs. It is a perverse reality that anxious societies undermine what they need the most. For a society to experience a rebirth, it needs leaders who can separate themselves from the emotional climate.[38] For leaders to succeed, they need vision. They need to avoid continual crisis management mode and be able to take well-defined stands. They need enough differentiation to be separate from the emotional processes in their institutions, a willingness to be vulnerable, tenacity, and regulation in the face of emotional sabotage.[39]

Because anxiety is contagious, leaders have the role of limiting the contagion. Some may in the group may develop anxiety, others my bear the anxiety of the herd, but well-defined leaders will do neither. By refraining from anxiety, leaders become a "non-anxious presence." Their presence in the system, then, brings the ability to think with logical clarity.

What the herd desires most is safety, and what frightens it the most is danger. The way out of stuck systems, though, is a spirit of adventure, and there is always some danger in adventure. As modern US society and institutions have become intoxicated with safety, they have become intolerant of adventure. They are, therefore, intolerant of leadership.[40]

Leadership threatens the established order. It threatens the emotional safeguards of the most anxious. What it provides, however, is a new way of thinking about the world, rendering some problems moot and resolving others in surprising ways. Neither of these can the herd tolerate.

38. Friedman, *Failure of Nerve*, 33.
39. Friedman, *Failure of Nerve*, 89.
40. Friedman, *Failure of Nerve*, 34.

11

Cause 2

Ideological Repurposing

WHAT IS THE PURPOSE OF AN INSTITUTION?

MANY INSTITUTIONS ARE AGREEMENTS or ways of behaving. Marriage, family, and religion are all institutions that exist beyond the organizations that sustain them. Organizational institutions function differently. Their role is particular to their organizing principle. When formed, institutions have a particular aim. If an institution is educational, its purpose is to educate students. If an institution is religious, its purpose is to expand the number of adherents of the religion, provide worship experiences, explain the tenets of the religion, or even assist its adherents in their efforts to influence society.

In postmodern thought, every institution supports society as it is. Since society is fundamentally violent toward the oppressed, *every institution is violent.*[1] Because of this violence, every institution must be destroyed or repurposed to change society. These theorists do not want to use institutions for the perseverance of society but for its total transformation. As such, they use their institutions for purposes for which they were never intended and for which they are poorly suited. A significant reason for the regression of institutions is this ideological repurposing. "Repurposing" in this chapter is the ideological transformation of an institution to use it for a purpose different from its founding.

1. Hart, *Beauty of the Infinite*, 2.

CHANGING PURPOSES IN THE MODERN UNIVERSITY

The University of Massachusetts at Boston is located on the Boston waterfront next to the John F. Kennedy Library and Presidential Museum.[2] As the only public research university in Boston,[3] the university has prided itself for its diversity and its urban setting.[4] In 2022, the university began to craft a new mission and vision statement. The initial controversial draft states:

> We aspire to become an anti-racist and health-promoting public research institution where:
>
> - Diversity, equity, shared governance, and expansive notions of excellence are core institutional values.
>
> - Wellness and an ethic of care are embedded throughout our campus culture and all policies and practices.
>
> - We invest in a resource-rich learning environment to support the development and success of students of plural identities and from diverse socio-economic, racial, ethnic, and cultural backgrounds.
>
> - Climate, environmental, and racial justice align with sustainable economic and planning decisions with local and global effects.
>
> - Community-engaged scholarship, service, and reciprocity are embedded in University practices that promote the economic, social, and cultural wellbeing of the communities we serve.[5]

In response to the draft, seventy-five professors signed a document saying that the primary purpose of the university cannot be political or ideological activism and that the main purpose of the university is to foster the search for knowledge.[6] "The search for truth can never be subjugated to social or ideological beliefs," they wrote.[7]

---

2. Forbes, "#278 University of Massachusetts Boston."
3. Forbes, "#278 University of Massachusetts Boston."
4. Lu, "Should Colleges Make Anti-Racism."
5. Hayward, "UMass-Boston Faculty Says 'Enough.'"
6. Lu, "Should Colleges Make Anti-Racism."
7. Lu, "Should Colleges Make Anti-Racism."

Professor of Sociology Vega Martinez responded, "In academia, there is this notion that we are objective researchers, that we aren't activists, we're trying to be objective and produce new knowledge. . . . But that is a reasoning that is very steeped in whiteness."[8] For Martinez, the notion of objectively seeking truth is steeped in racism.

One student was shocked by the opposition and it would make her reconsider how she viewed the professors. "The fact that they think politics and research can be kept separate is disturbing and even hurtful," she said.[9]

This re-visioning of the University of Massachusetts at Boston is an effort to codify its repurposing. The seventy-five professors who signed the document opposing it feared, with good reason, that the university would cease producing scholars as its primary mission. It would become an indoctrination center for politically left activists.

BOSTON UNIVERSITY

Boston University Wheelock College of Education and Human Development states, "At Boston University Wheelock College of Education and Human Development, our faculty, staff, students, and alumni are changing society through action. Our academic programs prepare professionals who dismantle systemic barriers and create positive change for all students and families."[10]

What is interesting here is what Boston University does not say. It does not talk about creating excellent teachers, principals, or administrators. The purpose is to change society. In what way does Boston University want to change society? On the "Guide Star and Values" page, Boston University answers the question: "We empower agency within ourselves, each other, and community partners to address privileges and inequalities in education and human development (such as race, gender, sexual orientation, ability, hearing status, socioeconomic status, among other factors)."[11]

Addressing privileges and inequalities is beyond the scope of an educator's work. The role of an educator is not the same as a sociologist. The culture this kind of mission statement creates is stifling to any words

8. Lu, "Should Colleges Make Anti-Racism."
9. Lu, "Should Colleges Make Anti-Racism."
10. Boston University, "Guide Star and Values."
11. Boston University, "Guide Star and Values."

or values that are not of the political and social left. Both the University of Massachusetts at Boston and Boston University have been repurposed.

Of course, they are not alone. The University of Minnesota,[12] Rutgers University-Newark,[13] California State University Channel Islands,[14] DePaul University,[15] and many others make commitments to social justice, anti-racism, and addressing inequalities in their mission and values statements.

SOCIAL JUSTICE

"Social justice" is among the most difficult words to define in modern political discourse. Early American ideals of justice were equality before the law and a world without favoritism. Social justice, however, can mean something very different than the early American sense of justice. It can mean fairness. "Social justice" can also mean a relatively equalized distribution of goods among the classes or preventing wealth or income inequality. "Social justice" can mean the elimination of racism or prejudice, and it can mean relatively equal outcomes among different ethnic or racial groups. It can mean all of these at the same time. The term is as vague as a freshman essay.

Reading the term, it is very difficult to ascertain how the writer is using it. In his famous essay *Politics and the English Language*, famed novelist and essayist George Orwell argues, "The term *Fascism* has now no meaning except in so far as it signifies 'something not desirable.'"[16] Like the terms "justice," "democracy," "freedom," "socialism," and "realistic,"[17] "social justice" has so many differing, mutually exclusive meanings that it is now a euphemism for "something desirable for society." It has become a meaningless term writers use to create positive feelings for their institutions or ideas when used in a colloquial sense.

12. University of Minnesota, "Mission."
13. Rutgers Newark, "Social Justice Champion."
14. Channel Islands University, "What Is a 'Social Justice Framework?'"
15. DePaul University, "University Mission Statement."
16. Orwell, *Politics and the English Language*, 276.
17. Orwell, *Politics and the English Language*, 276.

Lurking beneath the positive feelings in the colloquial sense, however, is a desire for restructuring, a desire to take items from one group and give them to another.[18] A technical meaning is for social justice is as follows:

> Social justice-oriented approaches in education refer to standpoints and scholarly traditions that actively address the dynamics of oppression, privilege, and isms, recognizing that society is the product of historically rooted, institutionally sanctioned stratification along socially constructed group lines that include race, class, gender, sexual orientation, and ability. Working for social justice in education means guiding students in critical self-reflection of their socialization into this matrix of unequal relationships and its implications, analysis of the mechanisms of oppression, and the ability to challenge these hierarchies.[19]

When social justice appears in an institution's mission or values statement, one can be assured that the mission of the institution has been repurposed for social or identity politics. This is true if the institution uses the term colloquially or technically. The original mission is the mission no longer.

Social justice, anti-racism, and critical theory are all terms and concepts borrowed from neo-leftist thinkers who revile capitalism and societies where it flourishes. Their mission is the transformation of the whole of society by using the institutions on which society rests.

OPPRESSORS

What is common among repurposed institutions is the view that social justice, whatever it is, can only be gained by reversing power structures. These power structures, however, are only reversed through domination.

Domination, exertion of power and control, is the goal because of the values, processes, and underlying vision of those who repurpose institutions. There is no other way for neo-leftists to achieve their vision without dominance. Neo-leftists almost uniformly share the logic that there are oppressors in the world who must be disempowered or eliminated.

The oppressors are rich, usually white, male, and have entrenched power. Their power is not earned: it is stolen, as are their resources. The

18. Scruton, *Fools, Frauds and Firebrands*, 11.
19. Sensoy and Diangelo, "Developing Social Justice Literacy."

racism latent in this power is destructive to people of color and is the reason for the differences in group outcomes between those with privilege and those who do not have it. The oppressor must be outed and shamed.

Outing the oppressor is important because the oppressor hides in pleasant words and familiar documents. The Declaration of Independence, for example, is not a document liberating colonists from an oppressive power an ocean away. Rather, it establishes and protects the oppression of blacks as evidenced by the institution of slavery.

For the neo-leftists, it matters little that many of the founders were opposed to slavery. It matters little that at the time, slavery was a universal institution. Unmoved are they by the fact that 50 million people live in slavery now,[20] and that the United States was one of the first nations to eliminate the ghastly evil.

The carnage and gore of Gettysburg and Vicksburg, the March to the Sea, Operation Anaconda, and the 700,000 fatalities of the Civil War notwithstanding, the press for justice means that documents like the Declaration of Independence and the Constitution must be deconstructed.

Seldom noticed by the neo-leftists are the phrases in the documents that virtually guaranteed the end of slavery and oppression. Frederick Douglass called the statement in the Declaration of Independence "all men are created equal" the "ring bolt."[21] For him and those who followed, that simple statement meant slavery was not propped up by the Declaration of Independence but that slavery was *fully incompatible* with it.

The same is true with Martin Luther King Jr. His "I Have a Dream" speech is a masterpiece of American rhetoric. Under the glare of the August summer sun and the glare of vile segregationists, King came to the Lincoln Memorial to remind Americans of their founding. In religious language and with a cadence born from the pulpit, King began to speak.

Decades after the event, one can still feel follicles raise hearing him say, "So even though we face the difficulties of today and tomorrow, I still have a dream. It is a dream deeply rooted in the American dream. I have a dream that one day this nation will rise up and live out the true meaning of its creed: 'We hold these truths to be self-evident, that all men are created equal.'"

For King, as with Douglass, the founding documents were not locks of oppression and racism. They were the key to liberation.

20. International Labour Organization, "50 Million People."
21. Douglass, "Frederick Douglass's 'Fourth of July' Speech."

Facts, however, matter little to neo-leftists. The 1619 Project by Nikole Hannah-Jones is a testament to the distortion of facts for a political end. For its author, one of the main purposes of the American Revolution was to protect the institution of slavery.[22] The American Revolution, however, disrupted slavery.[23] This is no small problem with the project. If the project exists to reframe the discussion of US history and suggest that slavery is the central lens by which to read American history,[24] then being wrong on this fact undermines the whole case. Even more provocatively, Hannah-Jones argues that slavery was *the* institution on which America was built; *America's very origin is slavery* for her.[25] Her assertions cannot withstand an honest assessment of the facts.

More telling is her comment, "Our job as journalists is to tell the truth."[26] Truth is an undiscovered country in the 1619 Project. Missing in her report is that in the 1800s, public opinion began to shift against slavery, and much of this change can be directly tied to the Declaration of Independence.[27] Further, the pro-slavery contingent was also aware of the destructive force of the Declaration's language on the institution of slavery.[28]

John Calhoun, a defender of slavery, called the "all men are created equal" line in the Declaration "utterly untrue."[29] "There is not a word of truth in the whole proposition," he exclaimed. Further, he argued that Jefferson's inclusion of the line was a consequence of Jefferson's belief that blacks were entitled to liberty and equality.[30] Even more dishonest, is that the 1619 Project does not include John Quincy Adams, William Jay, Joshua Giddings, Charles Sumner, Frederick Douglass, or Salmon Chase's efforts to resist pro-slavery "perversions" of the Declaration of Independence and Constitution.[31]

The purpose of the 1619 Project and other neo-leftist projects is not to describe reality or give a simple retelling of the facts. The purpose is to

22. Harris, "I Helped Fact-Check."
23. Harris, "I Helped Fact-Check."
24. Venugopal, "'1619 Project.'"
25. Sandefur, "1619 Project."
26. Venugopal, "'1619 Project.'"
27. Sandefur, "1619 Project."
28. Calhoun, "Speech on the Oregon Bill."
29. Calhoun, "Speech on the Oregon Bill."
30. Calhoun, "Speech on the Oregon Bill."
31. Sandefur, "1619 Project."

change the present. Hanna-Jones's long-term goals are to end "whiteness," to start reparations, and to bring an end to the power of the oppressor.

OPPRESSED

For neo-leftists, there is a second camp in the world. They are the oppressed. The oppressed are poor. Their poverty, however, is not the result of the structure of the world, or individual choices spread over a large group. Poverty is systematic, and the wealthy benefit from it.

It is hard to underestimate the economic illiteracy of such an opinion. If a merchant, a rich person, wants to sell his wares, to whom shall he sell them? A merchant needs people with the means to purchase. Those in abject poverty have no such means. Still, however, they persist. The rich are the oppressor and their wealth must be shared.

Also oppressed are the non-white. This would include Blacks, Hispanics, Asians, Middle Easterners, Pacific Islanders, and all other ethnic groups. The only constant among them is that they are not white. There are the white oppressors, and then there is everyone else.

Women are oppressed, as are gays, bisexuals, and transgender individuals. Inventing a new term, the ones who are not oppressed are the "cisgendered" white males.

ODD RESULTS

This division of the world into oppressor and oppressed makes for interesting partners. For example, in the war in Gaza, the LGBTQ+ community has sided with Hamas. This is despite the fact that Hamas would *throw every one of them off a building for sport.* Hamas despises with murderous venom all who would fly the rainbow flag. Israel, however, is welcoming of the LGBTQ+ community. How can the LGBTQ+ community, Black Lives Matter, and other "oppressed groups" support Hamas? They have concluded Israel is the oppressor and the Palestinians are the oppressed.

The horrors of Hamas's October 7 barbarism leave them unaffected. Seeing Shani Louk's twisted, lifeless body paraded on the back of a white pickup truck while cheering mobs spit on her and celebrated her death leaves them unmoved. Whatever means the oppressed use to throw off the oppressor is appropriate. The colonizer is not a civilian and can be killed barbarously. Black Lives Matter even published posters with Hamas terrorists on their gliders to show support for the attack.

If all of this sounds familiar in some way, it should. Karl Marx famously divided the world into the haves and the have-nots. What neo-leftists do is divide the world into the oppressor and the oppressed. Once accounting for that language switch, the language and the practices are the same.

"LIBERATION"

In what must be the most Orwellian of switches, neo-leftists use the term "liberation" for what they want to happen to the oppressed. This "liberation" has created manifold laws, regulations, rules, and codes, however.

On college campuses, administrators regulate what people can say and where they can say it. Microaggressions, "everyday slights, insults, put-downs, invalidations, and offensive behaviors, that people experience in daily interactions,"[32] are strictly verboten. These microaggressions include denying one's racism if he or she is white, insisting on color blindness, and believing in the "myth of meritocracy."[33] Simply saying "I believe the most qualified person should get the job" is a microaggression.[34] In effect, this stifles speech. It shames, in many cases, ordinary people. It assumes that white people are racist simply because they are white and that meritocracy is a racist lie.

PRAYING WITH PLANTS

It is not only neo-leftists who repurpose institutions, and the targets are not always universities. In 1836, nine Presbyterian ministers founded a new theological training center in New York, Union Theological Seminary, to train Christian ministers in New York's urban culture.[35] Union today, however, does not now have a specifically Christian mission. Union's website states, "Today, the Seminary lives out this formative call to service by training people of all faiths and none who are called to

---

32. UNC School of Medicine, "Microaggression/Microaffirmations."
33. School of Public Health, "Examples of Racial Microaggressions."
34. School of Public Health, "Examples of Racial Microaggressions."
35. Union Theological Seminary, "About."

the work of social justice in the world."[36] Missing in its statement is the Gospel, Trinitarian language, or Christian works of compassion. What is there is the commitment to social justice.

On September 17, 2019, in the seminary worship service, worshipers brought plants into the chapel and confessed their ecological sins to them.[37] Dr. Cláudio Carvarlhaes, who designed the worship service, writes:

> We processed into the chapel carrying plants and placed them on soil. Immediately people started to come to the plants, to confess their forms of relation or non-relation. One student said something that stuck with me: "I don't know how to relate to you in this subjective way. I am afraid that if I do I might discover a level of pain that I don't know whether I can bear."[38]

Plants, however, bear no evidence of consciousness. They may respond to pleasant and unpleasant noises, but they do not do so as conscious actors. Even if they could, apologizing to a particular plant for the relationship one has to all of creation implies the plant could be conscious of all other plants and could forgive on their behalf.

In his opening remarks, Carvalhaes spoke of the sacredness of life, extending it to plants and rocks. While an interesting thought, how is someone supposed to eat a sacred plant or build with a sacred rock? His logic would seem to rule out the logical and necessary use of creation. If all of creation is a manifestation of the sacredness of life, then what about bacteria? As with his more favored parts of nature, humans could not live without bacteria. If one is serious about all creation as a manifestation of the sacredness of life, should not one refrain from tilling the ground as it would kill billions of microscopic creatures, along with grubs, earthworms, and plants?

Carvalhaes hoped his worship service would create a "new relationship with the earth, and thus with God"[39] for the students. Christian theology maintains the reverse sequence. One has a relationship with God that renews and restores. Based on that relationship, one has a new relationship with the world around her. There is no Christian way to go from apologizing to plants to a new relationship with God.

---

36. Union Theological Seminary, "About."
37. Huleatt, "Progressive Seminary Students."
38. Carvalhaes, "Why I Created."
39. Carvalhaes, "Why I Created."

Whatever god one worships by confessing to plants, is not the God of the Christian faith. What Carvalhaes is doing is using Christian-sounding terminology and practices to create a new religion. The god of that religion has not emerged yet.

WORSHIPING THE "STRANGE ONE"

Duke University Divinity School is one of the premier mainline seminaries in the US. Affiliated with the United Methodist Church, Duke has educated ministers for nearly a century. Duke has long had a reputation for excellent scholarship, high-profile professors, and a bent toward the theological left. In recent decades, however, that bent toward the theological left has become more pronounced.

While it made a giant splash on social media and in blogs, Duke Divinity's chapel service on March 22, 2022, barely made a ripple outside those spheres. Hosted by the Divinity School and Duke Divinity Pride, the chapel service began with remarks from a second-year Master of Divinity student.

Unable to contain her excitement, she gestured enthusiastically with her hands as she bellowed, "Good morning, the holy and queer One be with you." The worshipers seemed to enjoy her comments. Some greeted them with approving laughter. A mumble of "And also with you" can be heard in the background.[40]

With her gold sequined jacket glittering from the light filtered through the windows, she continued her greeting for a few moments, reminding the worshipers her pronouns were she/they. She then encouraged the group to stand and share the morning prayer.

> Strange one, fabulous one, fluid and ever becoming, do not allow us to make our ideas of you into an idol. You are as close to us as our own breath and yet your essence transcends all that we can imagine. You are mother, father, and parent. You are sister, brother, and sibling. You are drag queen, and trans man, and gender fluid, incapable of limiting your vast expressions of beauty, embodied in us, your creation. We recognize flesh, in all its forms, is made holy in you. With thanksgiving, we celebrate your manifestation in all its glorious forms. Blessed are our bodies, blessed is our love, blessed are we when we celebrate that

40. Duke Divinity Live, "Service of Word."

which the world turns away. Fill our hearts with a pride rooted in resistance to all that seeks to destroy.[41]

One does not need to be fluent in the intricacies of Christian theology to note this is not a Christian prayer. God is not "ever-becoming." This notion, articulated by philosophers like Alfred North Whitehead and others, makes God to be less than what Scripture affirms God is. God does not become because God is the ever-existing one. Created beings become. God remains. Compare her ever-becoming god to this traditional definition of God as articulated by Christian philosopher David Bentley Hart. Hart states that God is "the infinite fullness of being, omnipotent, omnipresent, and omniscient, from whom all things come and upon whom all things depend every moment for their existence, without whom nothing at all could exist."[42]

The "god" of this prayer, "fluid," "fabulous," and "ever-becoming," is not the God of the Christian tradition. It is a fabrication, a projection. Even pagans would have difficulty conjuring a deity more profoundly emanating from their psyche. Somewhere Feuerbach is smiling.

Next, after asking God (or better, "god") to keep the gathered Duke students from making their ideas of god into an idol, the worship leader articulates some of the most gobsmacking projections about God's being. "You are a drag queen and a trans man," she says without expressing any observable suspicion that she is making her ideas of God an idol.

God cannot be what the worship leader suggests because God is spirit. The spirit of God has no gender because gender is a part of the created order. God is transcendent; therefore, his nature is not gendered. Projecting gender onto God is bad enough, but projecting the kinds of gender practices Scripture would call sinful, even abominable, is quite shocking. For those gathered at this Duke worship service and their leader, "god" is transgender. This "god" is "*not* man shouted in a loud voice":[43] this "god" is *trans* shouted in a loud voice.

The prayer continues. Addressing God, the leader says, "You are unable to limit your vast expressions of beauty, embodied in us." This is gibberish. God may do what God chooses to do. While theologians normally maintain that God is limited by what is logically possible—unable

41. Duke Divinity Live, "Service of Word."

42. Hart, *Experience of God*, 7.

43. This is a paraphrase of Karl Barth's maxim: "One can *not* speak of God simply by speaking of man in a loud voice." Barth, *Word of God*, 196.

to make a round triangle, for example—self-limiting his creative power is not that. God can choose to create or not create. In the infinite mind and beauty of God, what God may create in the future is unknown to humans. What humans can know, however, is that since the created objects she is speaking of are humans, and humans are made of matter, matter limits what can be created. A God who is unable to limit creative expressions while working with limited matter is nonsense.

The loss of orthodoxy continues: "Blessed are our bodies," which sounds very different from St. Paul's "O wretched man that I am! Who shall deliver me from this body of death?" (Rom 7:24 KJV). The point of Christian worship is not to declare how blessed the worshipers are but to declare the eternal blessedness of God. To the extent that humans are blessed, it is because they are created in God's image, share in the divine life by the power of the Holy Spirit, and live in obedience to the divine command.

One might be tempted to think the worship leader was speaking off the cuff. Most who speak in public frequently have had the experience of their brains not functioning at the wrong time, especially when speaking extemporaneously. It is a deeply frustrating experience.

In futility, they utter a mishmash of syllables hoping some of them stick together well enough to form a cogent sentence or at least save them from humiliation. They keep grasping in a vain search for thought as their brain freezes in panic. Finally, with all the grace of a wounded duck, they find a way to stop speaking and prevent further embarrassment. When such a moment happens, the proper response is assurance, not correction. "It is OK. It happens to everyone. No one will remember."

Although in reading the transcript or listening to the video these words might sound like they were impromptu, they were not. The prayer was printed in the worship guide. That means someone, presumably the worship leader, took time to compose these words.

If student worship functions at Duke the way it does in other seminaries, another person proofread the prayer before printing the worship guide. In other words, this prayer was not an accident. This prayer was deliberately planned and willfully penned. Whoever penned these words did so with all the theological subtlety of an addled Alzheimer's patient and all the ebullience of a sophomore writing a paper on Wicca. Shockingly, the worship leader led the prayer, *and no one walked out.*

This prayer *redefines* God according to the dictates and necessary metaphysical grounds of the LGBTQ+ agenda. This makes God into to the writer's image, into her likeness.[44]

It would be tempting to call these events at Union and Duke heresy. Heresy is not the right word though. The prototypical Christian heretic, Arius, functioned within the bounds of a Christian definition of God. What he refused to do was apply that definition to Jesus. What is happening here is different. The god so defined, particularly in the case of Duke, bears less resemblance to the God of the Bible than a brick bears to a mongoose. The god here is not God. Heresy, then, is not the right word. They are worshiping a different deity; they have a different religion.

These religions have different definitions of God, different attitudes toward worship, different perceptions of morality, and different aspirations of love than orthodox Christianity. They differ in soteriology and eschatology as well. While they are being birthed in erstwhile Christian seminaries and practiced in Christian chapels, they have no essential connection to Christianity.

What is happening at both of these seminaries is a repurposing. Professors, students, and administrators of these institutions are using the Christian faith, its language, its symbols, and its heritage for another purpose foreign to the founding intent and content of the gospel. Even if these institutions survive the acids of time and denominational decline, they will have become something contrary to their founding purpose.

44. It is important to note that the student was a second-year divinity school student at the time. While that does not excuse the prayer, it does mean the student ought to be given time and direction by orthodox mentors. The student does not deserve derision. Her prayer, however, is beyond the pale of the Christian faith. Those who enabled it, reveled in it, and have not corrected it are blameworthy.

12

Cause 3
Scandal

SCANDAL

"SCANDAL" IS A DELICIOUS word. It slides through the lips with the ease of chocolate. It whispers "naughty pleasure" and hints at secret rendezvous. The sight of the word attracts the eye like a red dress. The hint of its presence quickens the pulse like a furtive glance. Scandal captivates. Scandal enchants. Scandal, however, is a cruel seductress. It levels those entrapped in its enchantments. Scandal hollows out reputations and institutions. Scandal destroys the innocent, crushes the weak, and empowers monsters. Like poison in a delicacy, scandal slides across the lips and descends into the soul. No one who tastes scandal escapes unharmed. Of the poisons of the soul, scandal may be the most delicious and the most ruinous.

Institutions in the United States are beset with scandals. The story of the regression of institutions cannot be told without giving careful attention to them. Institutions are human constructions. They are liable, therefore, to do ill, to ingest the poison of scandal. While that should not be the practice of institutions, it is not surprising.

Poorly managed scandals have the potential to cause immediate ruin, and well-managed scandals can be mitigated. Scandals that directly undercut the values of the institution, however, are normally ruinous even when handled well.

MANAGING SCANDALS WELL

In 1992 Bill Clinton emerged as a credible candidate for the Democratic presidential nomination. Scandals, however, seemed to dog him. Clinton already had a reputation for marital infidelity and dissembling. His charm and charisma, however, sustained his candidacy past such whispers.

Before the New Hampshire primary, a scandal emerged. Actress and model Jennifer Flowers publicly claimed to have a long-running affair with Clinton. She had evidence, including taped phone conversations. The revelations rocked the campaign. With his wife Hillary, Clinton went on TV to put an end to the story that could have ended his campaign. His strategy was to be assertive, even aggressive. Clinton developed a "war room" whose purpose was to win the day's news cycle. Every rumor was denied, and every lapse in judgment was spun. With great skill, Clinton staved off the Flowers scandal.[1] With a bit of hyperbole, Julian Zelizer wrote an opinion article for CNN titled "Bill Clinton's Nearly Forgotten 1992 Sex Scandal." Zelizer is incorrect. The scandal is not forgotten. It was managed well enough, however, to prevent it from ending Clinton's campaign.

MANAGING SCANDALS BADLY

Hillary Clinton was not so fortunate. Her behavior in those public interviews began to seal a very unflattering public image of her as unlikable. In defending Mr. Clinton against Flowers's accusations, Mrs. Clinton said, "You know, I'm not sitting here, some little woman standing by my man like Tammy Wynette. . . . I'm sitting here because I love him, and I respect him, and I honor what he's been through and what we've been through together. And you know, if that's not enough for people, then heck—don't vote for him."[2] The interview was high-stakes and complicated. The affair had the potential to destroy Mr. Clinton's campaign, and it was Mrs. Clinton's task to save it. She needed to appear strong in his defense but not overly abrasive.[3] The task was nearly impossible, and the "Tammy Wynette" quip did not go over well.

Tammy Wynette, deeply offended by the remark, wrote, "With all that is within me, I resent your caustic remark. . . . You have offended

1. Zelizer, "Bill Clinton's Nearly Forgotten Sex Scandal."
2. Kruse, "TV Interview."
3. Kruse, "TV Interview."

every woman and man who loves that song—several million in number. . . . I believe you have offended every country music fan and every person who has 'made it on their own' with no one to take them to the White House."[4]

Seven weeks later, on March 16, 1992, Mrs. Clinton made a comment that cemented her status as unlikable. A reporter asked her about the possibility of conflicts of interest during her time as a partner at a prestigious law firm and her husband's time as a governor. Mrs. Clinton responded, "I suppose I could have stayed home and baked cookies, but I decided to do was fulfill my profession, which I entered into before my husband was in public life."[5]

Mrs. Clinton's response was a failure of crisis communication. The public is not often angry about a crisis. The public will get angry over refusal to take responsibility, incomplete or inaccurate information, or private interests being placed above the public interest.[6]

What Mrs. Clinton did not do was acknowledge the obvious: there could have been a conflict of interest. She could have mentioned strategies she and Bill Clinton used to mitigate that. If she had, the story would likely have been a blip. Instead, she took no responsibility. Further, she presented the public with a false dichotomy. She could work and have a conflict of interest or stay home and bake cookies. A college freshman with an introduction to logic class would have noticed her error. This false dichotomy is, at best, inaccurate information. At worst, it is cynical manipulation.

Unstated in the rules of crisis communication is the need for humility. The public at large recoils at elitism. Both the "Tammy Wynette" comment and the "bake cookies" comment unmask an elitist hubris in Mrs. Clinton. It is unfair to judge a person's character based on two comments. Mrs. Clinton may not be an elitist. She may not be afflicted with hubris. The comments, though, stuck. They became part of the way the public viewed her.

In 2016 Mrs. Clinton made a comment about supporters of Donald Trump that similarly harmed her public perception. She said, "You know, just to be grossly generalistic, you could put half of Trump's supporters

4. Husock, "Hillary Clinton Still Owes."
5. Kruse, "TV Interview."
6. Robertson, "Telling It All?," 4.

into what I call a basket of deplorables." The remaining supporters felt
"that the government had let them down."[7]

With the two previous comments cemented in the public's perception of her, Trump's campaign used the comments to depict Mrs. Clinton
as having elitist hubris. One of Trump's advisors said, "Just when Hil-
ary Clinton said she was going to start running a positive campaign,
she ripped off the mask and revealed her true contempt for everyday
Americans."[8]

SOMETIMES SCANDALS ARE RUINOUS NO MATTER HOW WELL MANAGED

Part of the lesson, then, is to manage scandals well. The other part of the
lesson is that some scandals have more power than others. If a scandal
clashes with the purported values of an institution or an individual, the
scandal will wreak ruin. Sexual scandals are more powerful against politicians whose stated values are culturally conservative, for example.

Some scandals, however well handled, undermine the institution
because they undermine the stated reason for the institution's existence.
Judges who accept bribes lose credibility because they are tasked with being impartial. Unfortunately, most major institutions have had scandals
that directly undermine the institutions themselves.

EPSTEIN AND ABC

Jeffrey Epstein will be remembered as the most prolific pedophile in US
history, said Amy Robach on a hot mic. Robach was livid after prison
authorities found Epstein dead in his prison cell.[9]

Epstein had been an abuser for years. In 2005 authorities arrested
him on the accusation that he paid a fourteen-year-old girl for sex. Dozens of others made similar accusations against him, but prosecutors allowed him to plead guilty to only one count. He served thirteen months
in a work release program.[10] The decision of the authorities allowed for
Epstein to continue his years of abuse.

7. Montanaro, "Hillary Clinton's 'Basket Of Deplorables.'"
8. Slack, "Clinton."
9. Royston, "Jeffrey Epstein."
10. Associated Press and Guardian Staff, "Who Was Jeffrey Epstein."

While he did lose some of his famous friends after his confession, Epstein largely continued his life. He made large amounts of money, courted famous friends, and abused more victims. Not only did Epstein abuse victims himself, but he also procured victims for his famous friends, including Prince Andrew, allegedly.

For years Robach had worked on a story about Epstein's sexual abuse. She had interviewed Virginia Roberts Giuffre and had gotten a detailed account of the abuse that occurred on Epstein's private island. When Giuffre was seventeen, she was one the young women recruited to Epstein's island. There she would serve as a masseuse, which often meant performing sexual favors.[11]

Robach had the story, she claimed. She had it years before Epstein's arrest and subsequent death. Why was it not released? ABC News would not release it. The decision, Robach claimed, was partially because of pressure from the royal family. The royals, deeply concerned about their reputation and Prince Andrew's reputation, threatened ABC's access to Prince William and Princess Kate.[12]

ABC was not the only organization to spike abuse accusations against Epstein. Vanity Fair did an expose on Epstein in 2003. The reporter of the story, Vicky Ward, had information that Epstein used Ghislaine Maxwell to lure girls for abuse. After Epstein pressured editor Gradon Carter, the story ran but did not include the allegations.[13] In other manipulative tactics by Epstein, Carter had found the severed head of a cat at his home, and a reporter received a $30,000 donation to his favorite charity.[14] Epstein kept the media at bay along with others who might be affected by the story.

Cynically speaking, the list of powerful names that Guffrie mentioned in public interviews would be intimidating enough for media organizations to consider spiking the story. On the other hand, it is the responsibility of journalists to tell the truth. In a more colloquial cliche of what journalism is, journalists are to "speak truth to power." ABC spiked a news story that did just that, as did Vanity Fair. They would not tell the truth; they would not speak what they knew because they wanted access to power and were intimidated by power. For, its part ABC News released

11. Associated Press and Guardian Staff, "Who Was Jeffrey Epstein."
12. Barr, "ABC's Amy Robach."
13. Folkenflik, "Dead Cat."
14. Folkenflik, "Dead Cat."

a denial of Robach's claims and explained its actions. That explanation, however, is not believable.

The Epstein scandal is not just about powerful men seeking sexual favors or even a powerful man blackmailing those for whom he had provided favors. The scandal is also a news media scandal. ABC News and Vanity Fair did not serve the public well.

It could be argued that the news media's regression has little to do with one scandal, but when scandals like this one emerge where the truth tellers protect their interests, the whole media enterprise is called into question.

EDUCATING CHILDREN OR PROTECTING BROKEN SYSTEMS

As a result of the No Child Left Behind Act from the Bush administration and the Race to the Top school grant program from the Obama administration, standardized testing is now an integral part of the public education enterprise. Despite pleas from educators who doubt the effectiveness of testing, federal administrators tied success on standardized tests to funding. Further, federal administrators used the tests not just to measure student performance but to measure the performance of teachers and schools.[15]

Atlanta Public Schools' "Journey to Excellence 2008–9" reports a stunning recovery in student performance on standardized testing. In 2007–8, only 47 percent of students met or exceeded standards in English and language arts, but by 2008–9, 90 percent of students met the standard.[16] The improvement made the Atlanta school district one of the highest-performing metropolitan districts in the country.[17]

For her "no-excuses" attitude and exemplary results, Superintendent Beverly Hall earned the 2009 Superintendent of the Year Award from the American Association of School Administrators. She also earned $500,000 in performance bonuses.[18]

The turnaround was so profound that an investigation commenced. In two schools, students went from being among the worst performers to

15. Strauss, "Remember."
16. Atlanta Public Schools, "Journey to Excellence."
17. Atlanta Public Schools, "Journey to Excellence."
18. Kasperkevic, "Georgia Cheating Scandal."

among the best in a single academic year. The chances of that happening were one in one billion.[19] In the system as a whole, there were 256,779 right to wrong erasures, where a student had initially written the wrong response and had changed it to the correct on statewide exams. The odds of that happening that often are one in one quadrillion, a one followed by fifteen zeroes.[20]

Beverly Hall had instituted a zero-excuses policy and placed extreme pressure on principals and teachers. The schools that performed well got bonuses, and the ones that did not faced closure, termination of principals, and termination of teachers. Under increased pressure, teachers and principals cheated. To make matters worse, teachers who reported cheating were fired, and teachers who cheated but met their targets were only suspended.[21] Hall's behavior was a message to the teachers: pass the tests at all costs. Even if the cost was one's integrity.

As a result of the investigation, twelve educators were convicted and twenty-one pleaded guilty to lesser charges.[22] In a disturbing title, Annie Murphy Paul writes, "Atlanta Teachers Were Offered Bonuses for Higher Test Scores. Of Course They Cheated."[23] This is, of course, the problem. There is always a benefit for cheating. If not, no one would do it. Whether it is a student who can get a better grade or a teacher who can get a bonus, cheating has a benefit. It is, however, unethical. It harms the cheater and the system.

Systematic cheating is also a symbol of a system that does not value learning. The whole point of the educational endeavor is to push back the tide of ignorance. Testing is, for all of its flaws, supposed to reveal where students are and if they are learning.

The Atlanta scandal is hardly the only educational scandal. Harvard University has its own cheating scandal. President Claudine Gay made enemies by her congressional testimony after the October 7, 2023 attacks against Israel. She failed to condemn antisemitism strongly and did not suggest her role was to protect college students from it.[24] After investigation, Gay's research was revealed to be plagiarized. Other Ivy League officials have been implicated in research scandalsas well. Harvard DEI

19. Perry, "Are Drastic Swings."
20. McCray, "Altered Test Scores."
21. Strauss, "How and Why."
22. McCray, "Altered Test Scores."
23. Paul, "Atlanta Teachers."
24. Beckett, "Ousted Harvard President."

officer Sherry Charleston has been implicated in plagiarism.[25] DEI officer at Harvard Extension School Shirley Greene plagiarized portions of her dissertation.[26]

Beyond plagiarism, some have falsified research. The Dana-Farber Cancer Center has retracted six studies and corrected thirty-one over "mishandled" data.[27] When university presidents plagiarize, their actions teach that educational attainment is not the highest good; the pursuit of truth and excellence is secondary to titles and positions. Academic scandals do grave harm to academic institutions.

Other academic scandals include Stanford President Marc Tessier-Lavigne's resignation after an investigation into research misconduct,[28] and UNC Chapel Hill's fake classes scandal. UNC's case is particularly distressing. For eighteen years, students artificially improved their GPAs by taking "paper classes."[29] Paper classes only existed on paper. Students registered for the classes and received no syllabus. There were no weekly meetings or readings. The only assignment was an end-of-semester paper, and the paper was never read.[30] While the classes were open to the student body at large, many who took the classes were athletes. The average grade for the class was a 3.6; nearly all of the students made an A or B.[31]

Yes, this was an athletic scandal as a good portion of the students involved were athletes. No one is surprised when an educational institution has athletes on its teams who are not the best students. Few are surprised that athletes get special consideration in grading. What is surprising is that a venerable university would allow an entire department to issue paper classes. The scandal undermines the purpose of the university. Is the purpose education, or is the purpose to provide credentials for students and student-athletes?

At least partially due to scandals, academia has lost the trust of the public.[32] Speaking to *Inside Higher Ed*, Michael Polikoff, president of the American Council of Trustees and Alumni, says, "The academy needs to restore public trust, and one of the ways they can do this is by taking all

25. Robinson and Shah, "Top Harvard Diversity Officer."
26. Rufo, "Harvard's Plagiarism Problem Multiplies."
27. Wosen and Chen, "Dana-Farber Expands Studies."
28. Moody, "When Presidents Plagiarize."
29. Chappell, "NCAA 'Could Not.'"
30. Nelson, "Inside UNC's Outrageous Academic Scandal."
31. Nelson, "Inside UNC's Outrageous Academic Scandal."
32. Schermele, "Public Trust in Higher Ed."

steps to ensure that its members—faculty and administrators—are operating at the highest ethical standards."[33]

SUFFER THE LITTLE CHILDREN

To join a religion is to take on oneself the ethical teachings and norms of the faith. It is hard to imagine someone becoming Buddhist without taking on the eightfold Noble Path. It is equally hard to imagine someone becoming a Muslim without practicing the Five Pillars of Islam. To convert to Judaism without an agreement to keep God's commands is nonsense.

The same phenomenon can be seen in Christianity. To become Christian is, at least partially, to put into practice the teachings of Jesus. The first term for the new religion of Jesus was not Christianity. It was "People of the Way." It was not until the people of Antioch labeled followers of Jesus "Christian" that the faith inherited its name. Even that term implies a way of life. "Christian" means "Christlike." The term referenced living like Jesus.

At Christianity's outset, individual believers were called "disciples." In a religious context, the term can often have a meaning foreign to how the earliest followers of Jesus used it. "Disciple" meant "pupil" or "student." A disciple was a student of Jesus. To follow Jesus was to learn his teachings and put them into practice. Jesus's ethics are simple to understand and difficult to practice. They are summarized by his command to love God with all of one's being and to love one's neighbor as one's self. Aquinas described the love Jesus taught as seeking the highest and best good for another and the desire to be unified with the other.[34]

To be Christian means, therefore, a belief in Jesus strong enough to compel a loving life. Christianity assumes that not all who believe will be able to follow Jesus's teachings fully at first, but over the course of one's life, a believer should become more and more Christlike.

Scandals of any sort become problematic for the church then. Nearly every scandal for the church is a violation of Jesus's ethics. As is the case with other institutions, though, scandals in the church only become destructive when they become systematic. If the institutions take responsibility and take appropriate action, the public can be quite

33. Moody, "When Presidents Plagiarize."
34. Stump, *Wandering in Darkness*, 91.

forgiving. When the evidence is that no responsibility has been taken, the public can be a harsh judge, perhaps rightly so.

Beginning in the early 1990s, reports began to emerge about pedophilia among Catholic priests. More than one hundred thirty people came forward with reports about priest John Geoghan.[35] By the time Geoghan was defrocked and convicted, church leaders had moved him from parish to parish while knowing of his record of abuse, leaving hundreds of abused victims in his wake, some as young as four.[36] Geoghan's record of abuse covers three decades back to his ordination in 1962. More disturbing is that his immediate supervisors knew of his predatory behavior toward children and moved him anyway.[37]

If Geohan's behavior were the end of the scandal, it would be horrid enough. The overall picture is much, much worse. The state of Illinois found that 450 Catholic priests abused nearly 2,000 children between 1950 and 2019.[38] One of the priests, Daniel McCormack, has 100 abuse claims against him, and despite recommendations from an archdiocese review board, Cardinal Francis George did not remove him.[39] In 2021 Cardinal McCormack was accused of assaulting a boy at a 1974 wedding reception.[40]

In 2007 the San Diego Diocese declared bankruptcy after facing over 100 lawsuits alleging abuse, and the Diocese of Los Angeles paid $660 million to settle abuse claims.[41] The abuse cases are not limited to the US, however. Accusations of abuse were made in Argentina, Australia, Chile, France, Germany, Ireland, Italy, and Vatican City.[42] The problem of abuse in the Roman Catholic Church is international, intercultural, and systemic.

Protestants have their own issues with sexual abuse. The largest Protestant denomination in the US, the SBC, has 750 cases of clergy sexual abuse documented by the Houston Chronicle. Further, an independent investigation also confirmed abuse. Even more recently, Paul Pressler has settled a lawsuit accusing him of abuse. With such documentation, it is odd that all of the candidates for SBC president in 2024 claimed there was no systemic sexual abuse issue in the denomination. Their reasoning

35. The Pulitzer Prizes, "*Boston Globe.*"
36. Flintoff, "Timeline."
37. The Pulitzer Prizes, "*Boston Globe.*"
38. Foody and Tarm, "Catholic Clergy."
39. Foody and Tarm, "Catholic Clergy."
40. Associated Press, "Wisconsin Sexual Abuse Case."
41. Flintoff, "Timeline."
42. Winfield, "Global Look."

is simple: individual Southern Baptists have committed abuse, but the denomination as a whole has not. It is not at all clear they are right. What is clear is that they want to move past the issue. Their refusal to admit the nature of the abuse keeps them from addressing their vulnerabilities in the ordination process.

To become an ordained SBC pastor, all one needs is the majority vote of an individual congregation. Since many congregations are small, all a predator would have to do is convince a handful of people in an individual congregation of his worthiness to serve as a pastor, and he could be ordained. There is no required process for ordination. In most instances, a group of local congregations called an association will convene a committee to interview a candidate for ministry. A local congregation, however, is free to ignore their advice.

In an even more difficult state of affairs, there is no process to defrock a minster. Once a minister is ordained, he is forever ordained regardless of post-ordination behavior. This loophole is born of Baptist theology. Baptists believe that each congregation is responsible for discerning the voice of God on matters of ordination. No outside body has the right to intervene. While born of its theology, it enables abusers to achieve ordination and have access to victims.

The scope of the problem has done great damage to the church. Not only has the scandal created an image problem, but people are actually leaving the church because of it. According to a recent poll, one in ten young Protestants have left the church over abuse.[43] The scandal of abuse and the response of leadership have left the impression that the gospel is not what the organization exists to preserve. It appears that protecting the institution is more important than protecting the innocent.

SEXUAL ABUSE IN THE CLASSROOM

Twenty-five-year-old McKenna Kindred, a teacher in Spokane Valley, Washington, pled guilty to sexual misconduct and communication with a minor for sexual purposes. Kindred and the student began a relationship over Instagram. Communication over Instagram became more lurid, and eventually, the two started a sexual relationship inside Kindred's home while her husband was away on a hunting trip.[44]

43. Shellnutt, "1 in 10 Young Protestants."
44. McEntyre, "Former Washington State High School Teacher."

The media report incidents like Kindred's frequently, as sexual abuse occurs with alarming regularity in the educational system. A 2023 study states that 11.7 percent of 2023 graduates experienced sexual misconduct by an educator.[45] Extrapolating that number to the whole population would indicate between 4–5 million children were abused in the school system.[46] While the abuse of one child is tragic, the abuse of millions of children is a systemic failure. Who is responsible to protect children from their teachers?

Educators are a beloved group in US society. They willingly take a low salary and work with impossible demands so that students can get the education they need. They are trusted. When a teacher violates trust, it not only damages the student: it damages the educational enterprise. With the number of cases of sexual misconduct students report, a systematic scandal is underway.

The public, however, has not noticed this, at least not to the same degree it has noticed sexual abuse in religious institutions. True, the public does see individual arrest reports and reads the details of individual cases of abuse with revulsion, but the public does not seem to get the widespread nature of the scandal.

In comparison to abuse in congregational settings, the public seems to believe abuse is much worse in churches than in schools or other institutions. That is simply not the case. By way of comparison, the SBC's sexual abuse scandal consisted of 700 victims over 20 years, a truly tragic number. If the SBC's abuse was worth noting, how much more is the abuse in the public school system? According to the Department of Education, there were 14,900 incidents of sexual violence in the public school system in the *2017–18 school year alone*.[47] That is 20 times the number of the SBS's scandal in just one year.

If prosecutors investigated sexual abuse in the public school system with the same tenacity they did with church abuse, there would be much more clarity, and the school system itself would face bankruptcy from all of the lawsuits.

45. Jeglic, "Educator Sexual Misconduct."

46. Jeglic, "Educator Sexual Misconduct."

47. NEA Today, "Sexual Violence in Schools."

PERSONALIZED CARE, CANCER, AND DUKE: SCIENTISTS BEHAVING BADLY

In 2005 Duke University announced a highly advanced experimental treatment for cancer. Scientists designed the treatment to match individual patients' genetic makeup with treatments that would work more effectively with their genetic makeup. The logic was simple: every person has an individual DNA, so a drug that was effective for one patient might not be effective for another.[48]

Researcher Anil Potti and his team published articles in prestigious journals like *Nature* and *The New England Journal of Medicine*,[49] reporting that certain gene expression signatures could predict a patient's response to chemotherapy.[50] A result like Potti claimed was met with excitement, and over one hundred cancer patients at Duke signed up for treatment.[51]

Unfortunately, Potti was not correct in his assertions. In fact, *Science* reports that his experiments were so badly designed that they were "useless."[52] Worse than being a mistake, it was a fraud. After the release of the data, other scientists expressed concerns that his results were not standing up to scrutiny. Potti rebutted those claims in additional articles.[53] The problems with his research, however, were not just found after publication. Third-year medical student Bradford Perez discovered problems with the research and made his concerns known to the university.[54]

In response to his concerns, Duke allowed Potti to investigate Perez, his student at the time, and even worked to convince Perez to present his findings as a disagreement between researchers.[55] Duke presented Perez's position to the funding organization as just that: a disagreement. Further, despite Perez's assertion that the research was fraudulent, Duke claimed that no such assertion was made.[56]

48. CBS News, "Deception at Duke."

49. National Academies of Sciences, Engineering, and Medicine et al., "Detailed Case Histories."

50. Kaiser, "Potti Found Guilty."

51. CBS News, "Deception at Duke."

52. Lowe, "Duke/Potti Scandal."

53. National Academies of Sciences, Engineering, and Medicine et al., "Detailed Case Histories."

54. Lowe, "Duke/Potti Scandal."

55. Lowe, "Duke/Potti Scandal."

56. Lowe, "Duke/Potti Scandal."

Finally, three years after complaints about the research were first made, Potti's supervisor looked carefully at the research. It is worth noting that examination of the research came only after Potti's résumé padding was revealed.[57] Finally, in 2010, Duke placed Potti on leave.[58] It was not until 2019 that Potti was found guilty of research misconduct.[59] A horrifying note to this story is that Duke told the patients in the trial that there was an 80 percent chance that they would get the right drug. That assertion was untrue.[60]

Potti's story is not the only story of scientific misconduct. A key 2006 Alzheimer's study had to be withdrawn in 2022.[61] The significance of the story is in part that the research has been cited 2,300 times in scientific literature.[62] Other scandals include Jan Schön's falsified physics at Bell Labs[63] and Tessier-Lavine's falsified research.[64]

Most scientists indeed commit themselves to doing good research. They are honest brokers seeking truth. Investigators at *The Guardian*, however, estimate that 100,000 papers should be withdrawn every year, and about 80 percent of those are due to fraud.[65] Whatever the scope of the problem, it is toxic for the reputation of science. As Karl Herrup, professor of neuroscience at the University of Pittsburg Brain Institute, put it, findings of fraud "are really bad for science. . . . It's never shameful to be wrong in science. . . . What is completely toxic for science is to be fraudulent."[66] With public doubts about science creeping upward, scandals only make the situation worse.

Modern institutions are regressing in part because all of them have scandals that call their aims into question. Media, education, religion, and science serve as examples. If one goes looking for evidence to distrust institutions, *the institutions themselves have given sufficient reason.*

57. National Academies of Sciences, Engineering, and Medicine et al., "Detailed Case Histories."

58. Kaiser, "Potti Found Guilty."

59. Kaiser, "Potti Found Guilty."

60. CBS News, "Deception at Duke."

61. CBS News, "Deception at Duke."

62. Grimes, "What an Alzheimer's Controversy Reveals."

63. Service, "Physicist Fired."

64. Ayana, "Stanford President Resigns."

65. Oransky and Marcus, "There's Far More Scientific Fraud."

66. Bendix and Chow, "Allegations of Fabricated Research."

13

Cause 4
The Collapse of Ethics

Winter is coming.

    —GEORGE R. R. MARTIN

It is not the brains that matter most—but
the character which guides them.

    —FYODOR DOSTOEVSKY

IF THE REGRESSION OF American institutions was simply a matter of process, then they would regress no more. Some enterprising researchers
would have created a solution already, and the ocean of leadership books
and the collected wisdom therein would have described an orderly process of renewal. No such solution awaits. A technical solution will not be
found because it cannot be found. *There is no technical solution to a moral
problem.* Institutional regression is partially a result of moral flounder-
ing. As the famed sociologist Robert Bellah argues, our problems are
not technical—they are moral.[1] American institutions are in regression
because of a moral and ethical collapse.

---

1. Bellah, *Good Society*, 393.

INSTITUTIONAL RESPONSES TO SCANDAL

Many institutional responses to scandals are ineffective. Typically, these responses only serve to quash responsibility and diffuse blame to systems instead of people. These solutions may be effective public relations strategies, and they may resolve anxiety, but they cannot fix the underlying issue.

Seldom do they hold individuals responsible. What tends to happen is an independent investigator or an internal review board will review the processes that led to the failure. After significant time has elapsed, the reviewers will propose changes to processes designed to prevent that failure or failures like it from happening in the first place. The problem is that no process can prevent ethical lapses. There are always methods for unethical people to get past processes.

In the aftermath of the Duke cancer scandal, the review board changed various processes to prevent incidents like it from happening in the future.[2] While certain processes could have been improved, no process can survive supervisors failing to do their work. Potti's supervisor, Nevins, did not review the data until years after the first accusation.[3] That is not a process problem: that is an individual failure, an ethical failure of leadership. When medical student Bradford Perez first reported significant issues with the research, the oversight board pressured him to change his story.[4] Worse, the oversight board presented his objections in a favorable light to the funding body. There is no set of processes that could prevent that.

ETHICAL CHOICES

Why would leaders at a prestigious medical institution make such poor choices? In one sense, it was the fallacy of confirmation bias. Duke wanted the research to be true, as any research institution would. Any research hospital would love to be among those making significant progress in the treatment of cancer. It would have helped fulfill the mission of Duke School of Medicine. It would also bring healing to many who suffer from the terrors of cancer. They had many good reasons to want to believe the research.

2. National Academies of Sciences, Engineering, and Medicine et al., "Detailed Case Histories."

3. National Academies of Sciences, Engineering, and Medicine et al., "Detailed Case Histories."

4. Lowe, "Duke/Potti Scandal."

More cynically, there were reasons connected to finances and image. If the research had proven to be true, it would have provided a financial windfall for Duke. More studies based on the research would be commissioned, and Duke would receive more research funding. Duke would also burnish its already stellar reputation as a provider of cancer care.

Just two years before Potti published his fraudulent research, Duke Hospital was embroiled in a significant controversy due to a grave medical mistake. On February 6, 2003, young patient Jesica Santillian had a heart and lung transplant procedure. Jesica's parents came into the country illegally in search of a cure for her restrictive cardiomyopathy.[5] A local builder started a charity to raise money for her procedure, and after three years of waiting, the procedure was scheduled.[6]

The procedure was going well until the surgeons had taken Jesica off the heart-lung machine and off bypass. They were getting ready to close when they received the call. The donor organs were of the wrong blood type.[7] It was a tragic, fatal mistake. Even though a second donor was found and a second surgery was performed, it was too late. Jesica died of brain damage.[8]

While it is impossible to know if the review board at Duke had Jesica in mind when looking at the questionable research, it would be human for them to think of her. A major medical mistake by Duke had ended the life of a seventeen-year-old. Duke's public perception had taken a hit. Worse, *The New England Journal of Medicine* published an article about the saga, the title of which had to sting: "A Death at Duke." Hoping to restore Duke's image would not be wrong. Failing to look carefully at research out of that desire would be wrong though. Whether honest or cynical, whether hopeful or reputation-burnishing, Duke had every reason to want to believe Potti, and it did.

While reviewing systems is an appropriate action, Duke already had all of the precautions in place that it needed to have effectively prevented the fiasco. Perez informed multiple administrators of the problem. Instead of hearing his complaints or verifying his research, they pushed him to violate his conscience and change his report. When presenting research to the funding body, they denied his claims were anything more than a disagreement among scholars. Further, Duke attempted to silence Perez.

5. Tanne, "When Jesica Died."
6. Kopp, "Anatomy of a Mistake."
7. Kopp, "Anatomy of a Mistake."
8. Tanne, "When Jesica Died."

Potti's supervisor had the opportunity to monitor his research and chose not to do so. It was only after Potti was caught padding his résumé that the investigation began, three years after the fact. When Potti was challenged on the validity of his research, he promised to present his data. It never happened. The missing research did not seem to be a problem.

Procedures are important, but ethics trump procedures. At multiple steps in the Potti saga, officials at Duke had the information and opportunity to stop the fraud. It chose not to. Worse, no one other than the original researcher suffered the consequences. Those who did not act in accordance with their role in the institution should have faced consequences as well. The Duke cancer scandal failure is not a failure of processes: it is a failure of ethics. *There is no procedural fix for an ethical problem.*

OF UNIVERSITIES AND COSTUMES

In 2015, Yale professor Nicholas Christakis faced the wrath of undergraduates at the prestigious Ivy League institution. Christakis, a sociologist and a physician, got into a confrontation with a horde of angry undergraduates over Halloween costumes, of all things.[9]

In the days before Halloween, the Intercultural Affairs Council at Yale sent an email to the student body, encouraging them to be inoffensive to their fellow students and not wear culturally insensitive costumes.[10] Christakis's wife Erika, who was also a faculty member at the time, sent a letter to the student body in opposition to the Council. Her point was that the students' free speech rights dictated they should be able to be provocative with their costumes and even should be able to be offensive.[11] She wrote:

> I don't actually trust myself to foist my Halloweenish standards and motives on others. I can't defend them anymore than you could yours. Why do we dress up on Halloween anyway? Should we start explaining that too?
>
> Even if we could agree on how to avoid taking offense— and I'll note that no one around campus seems overly concerned about the offense taken by religiously conservative folks to skin-revealing costumes—I wonder, and I am not trying to be provocative: Is there not room anymore for a child or a young

9. Gillespie et al., "Yale Professor."
10. Gillespie et al., "Yale Professor."
11. CBS News, "Yale Teacher Resigns."

person to be a little bit obnoxious . . . a little bit inappropriate or provocative or, yes, offensive? American universities were once a safe space not only for maturation but also for a certain regressive, or even transgressive, experience; increasingly, it seems, they have become places of censure and prohibition. . . . Have we lost faith in young people's capacity—in your capacity—to exercise self-censure, through social norming, and also in your capacity to ignore or reject things that trouble you?

What does this debate about Halloween costumes say about our view of young adults and the strength of their judgment?

In other words: Whose business is it to control the forms of costumes of young people? It's not mine, I know that.[12]

She added a note from her husband: "Nicholas says, if you don't like a costume someone is wearing, look away, or tell them you are offended. Talk to each other. Free speech and the ability to tolerate offence are the hallmarks of a free and open society."[13]

Her email led hundreds of students and professors to protest on campus. Many students were deeply offended by the email, and 740 of them signed an open letter criticizing the email because it minimized the "concerns of students of color."[14]

In a scene with a disturbing resemblance to Mao's "struggle sessions," the following Thursday, students attended a panel on free speech hosted by Nicholas Christakis to berate him for his position. Even with his great frustration, Nicholas endured four hours of impassioned diatribes against him and his wife. Many of those diatribes were recorded by a panel member.[15]

One student said, "As your position as master, it is your job to create a place of comfort and a home for the students that live in Stillman. You have not done that. By sending out that email, that goes against your position as master. Do you understand that?" When Nicholas did not agree, the student responded, "Then why the f*** did you accept the position? Who the f*** hired you?"[16]

12. Christakis, "'Dressing Yourselves.'"
13. Nelson, "Yale's Big Fight."
14. Nelson, "Yale's Big Fight."
15. Soave, "Watch Students Tell Yale."
16. Soave, "Watch Students Tell Yale." Censor mine.

Trying to restate his position, Nicholas responded and she interrupted him: "Then step down! If that is what you think about being a [inaudible] master, you should step down. It is not about creating an intellectual space! It is not! Do you understand that? It is about creating a home here! You are not doing that. You're going against that."[17]

Other students wanted both Erika and Nicholas Christakis fired because they allegedly failed to protect them from "possible psychic injury." In a four-hour meeting, students expressed great sorrow and anger over Yale's perceived lack of sensitivity to the issues facing minority students and the Christakis position over costumes. Even the president of Yale was "deeply disturbed" by the students' concerns.[18]

In a video, one hundred students insist that Nicholas resign for his wife's email. Nicholas gave in to the protesters by apologizing. He said, "First of all, I would like to apologize for hurting your feelings." The students found that phrase patronizing.[19] One particular student was angry because Nicholas did not know her name, even though he had five hundred students at the time. Refusing to call his wife racist was met with outrage as one student burst into tears and "left hysterically."[20]

One student said, "I'm going to live my life knowing that you're going to be the disgusting man you were twenty seconds ago, a minute ago, thirty minutes ago, an hour ago, a week ago, and onward."[21]

In response to the protests, Nicholas and Erika resigned from being faculty-in-residence at Stillman College at Yale, while Nicholas maintained his tenured position at the university.[22] Essentially, the couple was bullied into submission.

All of that reaction was for an email saying that students should be able to dress how they wanted on Halloween. The story ends well for Nicholas as Yale awarded him the Sterling Professorship, Yale's highest honor, three years later.[23]

Awards notwithstanding, what happened to the Christakises is a moral failure, an ethical failure. Nicholas wanted to communicate with the crowd of students trying to get him fired. Even though they were

17. Soave, "Watch Students Tell Yale."
18. Nelson, "Yale's Big Fight."
19. Becker, "Hysterical Yale Students Cry and Scream."
20. Becker, "Hysterical Yale Students Cry and Scream."
21. Becker, "Hysterical Yale Students Cry and Scream."
22. Friedersdorf, "Perils of Writing."
23. Gillespie et al., "Yale Professor."

chanting and screaming at him, he tried to reason with them. Reasoning with impassioned mobs seldom works, however. Mobs cannot be convinced or persuaded. The more impassioned they are, the more dangerous they are, and the less likely they are to listen. The mob taunting the Christakises had no intention of being placated. No apology or groveling would change their verdict. They would not be satisfied with anything short of the Christakises no longer being at Stillman College. Their moral failure is that in their herd mentality, they were unwilling to hear a position that challenged their victim status.

The second moral issue is the student's irrational expectations. They expected that the professors at a major research university would protect them from "psychic" injury. It is not entirely clear what a psychic injury is and how a student would sustain one. From the context, a psychic injury is the result of having to think that a professor would not be concerned about controversial Halloween costumes. If exposure to offensive Halloween costumes creates psychic damage, then no place is safe. Causes for offense are everywhere in a society of free people. It is a breakdown of both ethics and good sense to control another person's attire to protect one's sensibilities.

Another irrational expectation is that the university would be a "safe place." One student wrote about Nicholas Christakis's role at Stillman College, "His responsibility is to make it a place . . . where you can feel free to talk with them about your pain without worrying that the conversation will turn into an argument every single time."[24] The student continued, "I do not want to debate. I want to talk about my pain."[25]

A college professor is not employed to listen as someone endlessly talks about their pain. Yes, in some instances they can do that. Some might even do that well. That, however, is not their responsibility. Their responsibility is to teach and create an atmosphere where students learn. If a student needs to talk about his or her pain, the proper person to do that with is a therapist. Talking about one's pain may be helpful, but to insist that professors fulfill that role is born of an irrational expectation that the professor is there for the student to psychologically process what has happened to them.

Merely thinking about controversial costumes and having a professor support freedom of speech, including the freedom to wear whatever

24. Nelson, "Yale's Big Fight."
25. Nelson, "Yale's Big Fight."

costumes one wants, is enough to damage these students, or at least give these students reason to say they are harmed. There is no reasonable logic by which arguments about free speech and offensive Halloween costumes should reduce college-age students to tears. Giving that logic oxygen is a dangerous and preposterous notion. It emerges out of a belief that students should never be offended or see something offensive. It was an ethical failure on the part of the administration to grant hours for students to publicly vent their hurt. It did not help; it only exacerbated the situation.

It might be tempting to say that these students were fragile, that they were too weak to experience reality. That is not exactly the case. These students were using their feigned fragility to get their way. They were being manipulative. Their preposterous ideology and unhinged chants were successful as two highly respected professors resigned.

Another moral issue is the behavior of the administration regarding how the students treated the Christakises. Students treated these professors with contempt and with all the due process of a Soviet show trial, and there was no consequence. In fact, two of the most prominent abusers of the Christakises earned the Nakanishi Prize for "exhibiting exemplary leadership in enhancing race and or ethnic relations at Yale College."[26] A university cannot value free speech and allow abusive behavior toward professors over a Halloween letter. Yale, like every other university, is obligated to create an atmosphere for learning. The students' response to the email and their willful berating of a valued, well-respected professor are destructive to the values of learning and free speech.

Simply put, students who cannot endure a contrary opinion from a professor without devolving into tearful, angry emotional outbursts do not have the emotional maturity or the mental fortitude to study at an elite university. Administrators who do not recognize this fact do not have the character or the judgment necessary to lead one either. This situation is a collapse of ethics and character.

INABILITY TO DISCERN RIGHT FROM WRONG

On October 7, 2023, Hamas terrorists used parachutes and fans to overcome barriers from the Gaza Strip and gain access to Israel. Once inside Israel, the terrorists unleashed a reign of terror seldom seen in the modern world. One of Hamas's first targets was the Nova music festival. The

26. Nelson, "Yale's Big Fight."

attack on the festival was not accidental. It was a planned target. There Hamas terrorists raped women, sometimes beside the warm corpses of their friends. Hamas murdered 260 at the festival and raped countless more. As the day continued, Hamas went on a campaign of rape, kidnapping, and murder, often recording their atrocities. Hamas killed the elderly and burned whole families alive.

A decent human would easily denounce such atrocities. That kind of decency was often missing on college campuses. Tufts University students praised the creativity of Hamas terrorists as they went after the "colonizers." For these students, the Hamas terrorists were "freedom fighters."[27] At Yale, professor Zareena Grewal tweeted, "Settlers are not civilians."[28] What is preposterous about her statement is that even if the settlers were not civilians, prisoners of war should not be raped or dismembered. It is difficult to understand why a moral norm this obvious needs to be expressed. Further, her comment is an effort to give Hamas legitimacy for its horrendous actions. Morally, her comments are bankrupt.

In other institutions, Jewish students were taunted, genocidal chants echoed across campus centers, and Jews became targets. In fact, in New York, a Rabbi recommended that Jewish students leave campus. Despite pleas from Jewish students for their safety, many colleges did nothing to stop the harassment.

Shortly after the attacks unfolded, Claudine Gay, president of Harvard, wrote:

> At such a time, we want to emphasize our commitment to fostering an environment of dialogue and empathy, appealing to one another's thoughtfulness and goodwill in a time of unimaginable loss and sorrow.
>
> As many colleagues, classmates, and friends deal with pain and deep sorrow about the events in Israel and Gaza, we must all remember that we are one Harvard community, drawn together by a shared passion for learning, discovery, and the pursuit of truth in all its complexity, and held together by a commitment to mutual respect and support. At this moment of challenge, let us embody the care and compassion the world needs now.[29]

The response from Israel was appropriate indignation. The president of Hebrew University in Jerusalem responded:

27. Poleo, "Tufts University Students."
28. Lewis, "Progressives Who Flunked."
29. Gay, "War in the Middle East."

The Hamas leader's explicit statements, as well as their actions, provide a clear indication that the mass killing was committed with the intent to destroy Jews in Israel. One does not have to be an expert in international law to realize the extreme immorality of this crime of genocide. All that is needed is basic common sense and minimum integrity.

The statement of the leadership of Harvard University fails to reflect any of this. It is explicit in giving priority to one value, namely that of maintaining "one Harvard community," over the commitment to unequivocally condemn evil. You conclude your statement noting that "[a]t this moment of challenge, let us embody the care and compassion the world needs now." With all due respect, the world needs more than that from the lighthouse of wisdom. It needs you to show some moral courage, even if some members of "one Harvard community" hold immoral positions.[30]

The lack of moral courage the letter notes was a pervasive problem with Harvard at the time. In her testimony before Congress, then-Harvard President Claudine Gay would not describe calls for genocide of Jews harassment.[31] Testifying at the same time, then-President of the University of Pennsylvania Liz Magill would not describe calls for genocide as harassment either.[32]

One commonality in these cases is a lack of moral judgment, moral clarity. It would not have been difficult to condemn Hamas by name. It would not have been difficult to call for justice for the victims. What these university leaders did, however, was talk about the events in Israel and Gaza as if they were morally the same. In no sense was Israel's early response to the events of October 7 equivalent to what Hamas did.

Also lacking is the moral clarity of safety on campus. Neither professors nor students should face harassment on campus. University administrators have a duty to protect students from threats. Notice the contradiction. University administrators were very concerned about Halloween costumes but could not find the moral clarity to stop calls for genocide against the Jews. There is no technical solution to the problem. Creating task forces, listening sessions, and classes on cultural sensitivity will not repair the issue. They cannot because it is impossible for them to do so. The problem is not in a process. The problem is moral and ethical. Moral issues require moral solutions.

30. Cohen et al., "Letter to Harvard President."
31. Herszenhorn and Yuan, "'I Am Sorry.'"
32. Ma, "How the Presidents."

MORAL PROBLEMS AS SYSTEMIC

The issues with Duke, Harvard, Yale, and the University of Pennsylvania is that of a systemic moral failure. Moral failures come in various sizes. Fortunately, most of them feature one person choosing to do wrong. When it comes to institutions, though, seldom is just one person involved. Whether it is universities not being able to differentiate between right and wrong, institutions pushing faulty research, or football programs run amok, the common thread is a systemic collapse of character.

For a scandal to become systemic, multiple persons need to be involved. In the case of sexual abuse in the Baylor football program, multiple persons knew of the sexual assault happening to women on campus and did nothing. In the Pennsylvania State University scandal, the prosecutor's report claimed that it was essentially common knowledge on campus that Jerry Sandusky was a pedophile. Even armed with this knowledge, no one intervened. With the anti-Semitic chants on campus, videos abound of their vile bullying of Jews, yet few in charge have the moral clarity to bring it to an end.

Why the loss of moral clarity? Why the collapse of character? At the most basic level, the collapse of character is a result of disconnection from God. The great Russian writer Fyodor Dostoevsky says, "Without God, anything is possible."[33] By saying that, he is not indicating that something good can emerge without belief in God. Without God, his argument concludes that there is no consequence for any human behavior. Without such consequences, there are no longer moral brakes on human behavior.

What is left is the accumulation of pleasure and the avoidance of pain. This explains much of the systemic collapse of character. Without the belief that God will bring justice, fewer are willing to sacrifice to tell the truth.

Telling the truth might cost one benefits. In college athletic scandals, telling the truth could mean the team would lose games, the university could lose money, and the individual could lose employment. Without belief in God, those losses could provide a strong temptation to go along or try to find plausible deniability.

Telling the truth might actually cause a loss of connection. The most difficult lies to counter are the lies humans tell themselves. When people are enraptured with another or have a profound belief in another person,

---

33. Paraphrased from Dostoevsky, *Brothers Karamazov*, loc. 453 of 15308.

they are not likely to believe damaging information about them. Ignoring what they see, ignoring their deepest suspicions, becomes a habit. They cannot see the truth because they are invested in not seeing the truth. In ignoring one's instincts or one's suspicions, one can become part of a systemic character collapse.

In the case of Duke, it was not so much deliberate complicity. The collapse of character was in not doing due diligence. A simple background search combined with performing oversight as prescribed, as the program director should have, would have stopped the scandal. There was no good reason for the scandal to happen.

When other tactics fail, those caught in an individual scandal will often use threats to silence those who would speak out. Threats are quite effective, unfortunately. When faced with losing life or having someone harm a family member, many will go along.

In 2024, Boeing suffered significant safety issues in their airline division. A whistleblower, Sam Salehpour, testified that he made 1,400 reports of safety violations in the production of Boeing's 787 Dreamliner. Salehpour testified that a quality manager told him not to document the safety issues. Salehpour, who credits his continued employment to whistleblower protection laws, claims that he has received threats to his personal safety.[34] The medical student in the Duke cancer scandal was ordered to stand down. He ended up having to leave Duke and lost a year of residency. He could have easily bowed to threats. When systemic scandals emerge, it is worth knowing how many people succumb to threats and keep their silence.

SYSTEMIC FAILURES AND CHARACTER

Systematic failures and scandals are necessarily failures of character. Acting with character and responsibility would have prevented these instances from causing harm to the participants or to the institutions. Society would be much better off, the patients at Duke would be better served, and even the protesting students at Yale would be better prepared for society. When institutions collapse, it is often the result of systematic failures of character.

---

34. Rains, "Boeing Whistleblower."

14

Cause 5

Elitism and Anti-Elitism

> The more stupid one is, the closer one is to reality.
>
> —FYODOR DOSTOEVSKY

SOCIETY NEEDS EXPERTS

WITHOUT EXPERTS, BUILDINGS CANNOT be constructed, legal processes would descend into chaos, children would remain uneducated, and the sick remain untreated. Without experts, discoveries would be chance and advances would be rare. Without experts, wars could not be won and evil could freely prowl. Expertise is one of the most valuable commodities in a society.

The degenerating of the relationship between experts and ordinary people is a sign of a society in regression. For a society to be healthy, the relationship between ordinary people and experts should be one of mutual trust, understanding, and accountability.

EXPERTISE IN THE UNITED STATES

With perfectly manicured hair and polished nails, the news anchor interviews her guest expert. Although serious, deadly serious in demeanor, her eyes betray an excitement, an agreement with the expert already.

The questions betray not curiosity or skepticism but a desire to hear the banal opinions of her guest. Interviews like this one fill the time on the 24/7 news cycle. They do not often press for answers but serve as a communication device for public leaders, presumably experts, to state their positions.

What makes an expert? In academia, experts are often those who have earned PhDs in their fields. The PhD, however, is not earned by the accumulation of knowledge: it is earned by creating new information. The person who has mastered two thousand years of Christian thought is not a scholar of theological studies, necessarily. The scholar is the one who produces a novel thesis for a dissertation. Universities do not measure scholars by how much they know or how well they teach: they measure them by how often they can publish articles for peer-reviewed publications. The same is true in scientific fields. New studies, new cures, and new theories are what make for scholarship.

This path of expertise is helpful in many ways. Scholarship-producing knowledge advances fields of knowledge, but it does come with a set of problems. Scholars can become self-referential and submit to groupthink.

The term "groupthink" emerged after the infamous Bay of Pigs Invasion in 1961. In the buildup to the ill-fated invasion, the CIA trained Cuban exiles to return and overthrow Castro's oppressive government.[1] The plan was for the 1,400 exiles to have naval and air support for the invasion. The support never arrived. Two hundred Cuban exiles were killed, and 1,200 were taken prisoner. Not only did the invasion fail to topple Castro, it made him a national hero.[2] After the fiasco, a reflective JFK asked, "There were fifty or so of us, presumably the most experienced and smartest people we could get. But five minutes after it began to fall in, we all looked at each other and asked, 'How could we have been so stupid?'"[3] Kennedy was indeed surrounded by very intelligent people, and they all should have made a better decision. Many of them had reservations, but they did not voice them. The process by which a group comes to a decision and loses sight of its wisdom as it gets caught up in the power of group spirit is known as groupthink.[4]

1. Evans, "Groupthink."
2. NeuroLeadership Institute Staff, "How JFK Inspired."
3. NeuroLeadership Institute Staff, "How JFK Inspired."
4. NeuroLeadership Institute Staff, "How JFK Inspired."

Of course, politics is not the only place where such groupthink exists. It happens in the medical field, scientific endeavors, economics, and the social sciences. In economics, Thomas Piketty's *Capital* became a bestseller in the 2010s. Absorbed by thinkers and public policy experts, Piketty's thesis was that rising inequality was a problematic result of capitalism. As the title of his work suggests, Piketty's solution was from the Marxist lineage of governmental control of markets and redistribution of wealth. Piketty believed that rising inequality would create a society of uber-rich and desperately poor, and the rich would game the system for themselves. Inequality would keep the poor underfoot and cause democracy's collapse. Missing in his analysis is that global inequality is falling.[5] Also missing is that wealth is gained and lost. Many who were among the wealthiest 1 percent at the time of his work are now worth much less.

Nevertheless, social scientists, politicians, and thinkers touted his work as a solution to the problem, and scores of articles and public policies proposed solutions to reduce rising inequality.[6]

Following Piketty was a failed strategy from the beginning. His recommendation of high rates of taxation has been tried and failed in various nations since the advent of communism. Why follow him now? Why let a book whose title is an ode to Karl Marx influence public policy? It was a failure only an expert could make.

THE DERISION OF EXPERTS

The general public has become wary of experts and expertise. Experts in science, medicine, and economics, as well as government executives and journalists, have all lost some of the trust the public once invested in them.[7]

Some scholars note the origin of this distrust is part of the American experience.[8] Americans, egalitarian by nature, recoil at someone with higher status, even if that status was earned through great effort. Americans might recoil even more if the status was earned by academic degrees alone.

In his work, *The Death of Expertise*, Tom Nichols writes:

5. Delsol and Martin, *Anti-Piketty*, xix.
6. Schiavenza, "Obama Will Focus."
7. Jacobs, "Downfall (and Possible Salvation)."
8. Bruinius, "Who Made You an Expert?"

Citizens no longer understand democracy to mean a condition
of political equality, in which one person gets one vote, and every individual is no more and no less equal in the eyes of the
law. Rather, Americans now think of democracy as a state of
actual equality in which every opinion is as good as any other on
almost any subject under the sun. Feelings are more important
than facts.[9]

While one might see the causes of the problem differently than
Nichols, he has observed the problem rightly. There is a cultural sense in
which expertise is no longer valuable. People are just as likely to believe
a YouTube videographer looking at ancient Egypt as they are an Egyp-
tologist. The spiritually curious may find Stephen Furtrick's version of
Christianity more compelling than N. T. Wright's. Increasingly, some do
not care to notice the difference between them. Experts, then, are often
subject to derision.

HOW EXPERTS HAVE CONTRIBUTED
TO THE PROBLEM

In another sense, American experts have earned some of the derision
they receive. During the COVID-19 pandemic, public policy experts
made decisions for the health and safety of the public based on the best
evidence available to them. At least that is what they told the public.
Some of these decisions, however, were based on limited evidence, or
worse, contrary to the best evidence.

Nestled behind the park and recreation gym and beside the public
pool in a small eastern North Carolina town is a park. It has a circular
gravel walking trail surrounding an overgrown natural area. Eight laps
around the trail is just longer than a mile. The massive oak trees over-
looking the trail protect walkers from the blazing sun. Just to the right
of the trail is a gated playground. It has a swing set and a yellow sliding
board that twists in the middle. On most days parents from the declining mill village near the park can be seen taking their children to play.
Squeals of delight from toddlers and the occasional cry of "I don't want to
go home!" echo to the tennis court above. At least until COVID.

During the pandemic, the once-welcoming park was closed to children. Authorities kept the path open to walkers, but the children's park

9. Nichols, *Death of Expertise*, 232.

somehow caught the ire of officials. The park was closed. A sign posted on the locked chain-link gate deterred visitors, and yellow crime scene tape closed off the sliding board to children. Once filled with the laughter of children, the park was now a symbol of a disease running rampant. It was now illegal for little children to swing until their feet pointed to the sky or scale the ladder for the slide again and again.

This sight was not only common in rural North Carolina. In many cities, public parks and playgrounds were closed. In California, officials filled a skateboard park with sand.[10]

Closing playgrounds affected children the most. It took away normalcy and the kind of play that could make a pandemic tolerable for a small child, and it did nothing to prevent the spread of COVID.

Even at the time, scientists had said the best protection against COVID was sunlight and fresh air. Children were also the least likely to be affected by COVID. So, closing the park to protect the least likely victims and keeping them away from the least likely way of catching the disease was not productive. Closing a park not only served no positive purpose: it actually did emotional harm. Worse than that, keeping children away from these activities could have left them to remain at home indoors, where they were much more likely to catch the disease. Why would ordinary citizens trust experts who made decisions like that?

The inflation outburst from 2021–24 is another example of why Americans have lost trust in their experts. At the first whiff of inflation, Federal Reserve Chair Jerome Powell said, "It will turn out to be a one-time sort of bulge in prices, but it won't change prices going forward."[11]

At first, the Federal Reserve Chair Janet Yellen said the inflation was "transitory" as the inflation pressures mounted, rising to 5.3 percent,[12] double the Federal Reserve's target in August of 2021. Powell said, "History also teaches, however, that central banks cannot take for granted that inflation due to transitory factors will fade."[13] Inflation did not fade. By July 2022, inflation reached a forty-year high of 9.1 percent.[14]

Now expressing some regret at the term "transitory," Yellen suspects that citizens heard the term and suspected she meant that inflation would

10. Asmelash, "California City."

11. Schneider, "Fed's Stages."

12. Focus Economics, "Inflation Eases Slightly."

13. Schneider, "Fed's Stages."

14. Rugaber, "U.S. Inflation."

be tamed in a matter of months.[15] Inflation was not tamed quickly. It reached heights not seen since the stagflation era and decimated the finances of Americans. Forbes argues that it now takes $120 to make the same purchase $100 would have made in 2020.[16]

Why, then, would a nonexpert in economics feel compelled to listen to the experts at the Federal Reserve? It is not just that they were wrong: they were wrong spectacularly, and with damaging consequences to the purchasing power of Americans. Failing to thwart inflation has meant not only higher prices but also higher interest rates, making major purchases like homes out of the reach of ordinary citizens.

ETHICS, MISTAKES, AND EXPERTS

It is not just that experts can be wrong: they can sometimes be unethical. Nichols laments the clients of plumbers and electricians who followed them around, quizzing them with details about their work "despite an obvious inability to understand the answers."[17]

Nichols's wording here hints at an attitude that is pervasive in his text. The experts are smarter, better informed, and competent. They should not have to face the incessant questions of the less intelligent, those *without the ability to understand.*

Perhaps experts are more intelligent than the rest of the public. Perhaps, though, people follow plumbers and electricians around because they have been taken advantage of and their questions are an attempt to make sure the expert is not selling them something they do not need or billing them for hours not worked. Experts are not immune from the ethical lapses of nonexperts. Frequent-enough lapses would naturally generate a more skeptical response from an ordinary person.

Equally as important, experts are not always right. Doctors misdiagnose, lawyers misread the case law, and scientists misread data. Questioning experts is not a problem. It is important. Pity the patient at the hospital who is not able to question his medical team about his care.

15. Giorno, "Yellen Says She Regrets."
16. Tobey, "Federal Reserve's Folly."
17. Nichols, *Death of Expertise*, x.

PERSONALITIES

Himself an expert, Nichols is a bit baffled at why anyone would hold an expert in suspicion. Experts have, after all, contributed to the improved quality of life in the US. They have extended life through improved medical care and have created technology unimaginable one hundred years ago. For him, the experts are to be celebrated, and those who do not understand that are a problem.

Speculating about why ordinary Americans would hold such negative opinions about experts, he writes, "Let's confront the most painful possibility first. Perhaps experts and laypeople have problems communicating because the ordinary citizen is just unintelligent."[18] Some people, according to Nichols, are not that bright, think they are brighter than they are, do not care about the subject at hand, and lack metacognition.[19] What was hinted at in the preface is stated here boldly: experts are smarter than the rest of the public.

Unexamined in his work is the contempt in which the experts hold the public. Suppose an author wanted to write a tome about how the experts were ruining the world. Perhaps he would say, "Let's confront the most painful possibility first. Perhaps experts and laypeople have problems communicating because the so-called expert lacks common sense, often peddles nostrums, and has a demonstrated contempt for people he thinks are beneath them." I wonder how the expert class would hear that. Nichols puts the problem at the feet of the laypeople rather than noting the distinct problem among the elites. The cause of the distrust between experts and ordinary citizens is born in both groups.

In late 2023, RMG Research conducted a study of the "American elite." Their definition of "elite" was having at least one postgraduate degree, earning at least $150,000 per year, and living in a densely populated area.[20] The result presented a series of deep differences between the elites and the country at large. They did not suffer as much from inflation, favored rationing to combat climate change, trusted the government much more, and believed that educational professionals should decide what

18. Nichols, *Death of Expertise*, 42.
19. Nichols, *Death of Expertise*, 42–45.
20. Watson, "On the Elites."

children learn rather than parents.[21] Nearly 60 percent of the elites believe the US has too much freedom, and most would ban SUVs.[22]

These elites' attitudes and mindsets are very different from the rest of the nation. It is important to note that an expert is not necessarily part of this cultural elite, and being a part of the cultural elite does not mean one is an expert. The overlap between the two groups is significant. When the media wants to interview an expert, he or she will often come from this group.

These elites tend to live in densely populated areas. Most of that is in or near urban areas like New York City, San Francisco, Boston, Miami, Chicago, Philadelphia, Washington, DC, and Providence.[23] While all of these are interesting cities, they bear little resemblance to Charleston, South Carolina, or Waco, Texas. This isolation explains why the solutions they concoct bear little resemblance to the needs of great swaths of the country. Mass transport, for example, gets elite support, while in great swaths of the country, it is impracticable.

Elites think the public agrees with them more than they do, overestimating the public's support for positions they strongly support by 25 percent.[24] One is reminded of Pauline Keal's "Nobody I know voted for Nixon."[25]

The divide between the expert/elite class and the ordinary citizen is stark, and much of it has to do with class. The experts and elites are significantly wealthier and live in different locales than the common citizens. They are as different as Mississippi truck drivers and New York museum curators. Add to that mix some mutual loathing and distrust and the distinctions become even more pronounced.

Nichols notes increasing derision and anger directed at experts. He labels the anger "narcissism," a disdain for experts as a kind of self-actualization.[26] What he does not note, and sometimes practices in his book, is the easy contempt for the masses shared by experts and elites.

Contempt is easy to sense, and once sensed it ends communication. Why would laypeople listen to experts who hold them in contempt?

21. Watson, "On the Elites."

22. Watson, "On the Elites."

23. Watson, "On the Elites."

24. Niskanen Center, "Elites Misperceive the Public."

25. Podhoretz, "Actual Pauline Kael Quote." This is the oft-paraphrased version of his actual quote: "I live in a special world. I only know one person who voted for Nixon."

26. Nichols, *Death of Expertise*, xxii.

Nichols speaks of experts with reverence even when listing their many mistakes. He makes no effort to do the same for laypeople.

The only adequate term for this easy condescension is elitism. Only someone who himself derides a group of people would be willing to speak of them in these terms. Nichols' condescension is hardly alone, however. Michael Beller, former council at PBS said in an undercover video,

> Americans are so f*cking dumb. . . . You know, most people are dumb. It is good to live in a place [Washington, DC] where people are educated and know stuff. Could you imagine if you lived in one of these other towns or cities where everybody's just stupid?
>
> What's great is that COVID is spiking in all the red states right now. So that's great . . . a lot of them [red state voters] are sick and dying.[27]

The non-elites notice the condescension and receive it with great umbrage. In an article that could best be described as an angry screed, Armando Simón vents:

> A radical change has come over many elites: they have declared war on us. They hate us and they have contempt for us. And, although they may be occasionally reprimanded socially for doing so, they have been openly voicing their hatred and contempt.
>
> A consistent theme repeatedly voiced among the elites is that, intellectually, they are so much more superior than us peasants.[28]

After listing numerous incidents of elites' contempt and disuse for ordinary Americans, Simón discusses the possibility of a civil war in the United States and invites the elites to think through how badly it would go for them using graphic imagery.

While the article is incendiary, one wonders what kind of society has this level of animosity between its elites and ordinary citizens. These two groups live in a "perverse communion of mutual hate,"[29] to borrow a phrase from theologian Miroslav Volf.

In healthy societies, elites and ordinary citizens live in mutual trust and respect. Ordinary citizens listen critically to what experts have to

---

27. Olohan, "PBS Fires Former Employee."
28. Simón, "Elites Hate Us."
29. Volf, *Exclusion and Embrace*, 99.

say, and experts thoughtfully respond to criticism. Ordinary citizens are neither defiant nor gullible. The experts are neither eggheads nor gods.

WHEN EXPERTS CONTRADICT EACH OTHER

Laypeople are right to be dubious about nutrition experts when something as simple as the health value of eating an egg is a matter of prolonged contention or when given different directions about butter, margarine, and low-fat milk. Most recently, a study in the *Annals of Internal Medicine* concluded that lowering consumption of red meat had limited improvement on cardiovascular health.[30] If true, that means years of medical advice and countless nutritional guidelines are simply wrong.

With the blizzard of contradictory papers on health from serious scientists often providing contradictory information, how is the public supposed to discern what is healthy and what is not? How can the public trust experts under these circumstances?

It is true that science discovers new treatments, leaving the older ones to be discarded. One should welcome that. What is happening with nutrition, however, is that multiple competing claims get presented to the public as truth at the same time. The public, then, has no realistic way of deciding which expert to believe. No wonder the public is dubious about the venture of expertise itself.

FAILURE TO COMMUNICATE

One aspect of the struggle between experts and the public is communication. Experts should explain complicated concepts in ordinary terms without condescension. Allegedly, Albert Einstein once said, "If you can't explain it to a six-year-old, you don't understand it yourself." While the origin of the quote is a matter of some debate, there is a point. Every discipline has jargon and gobbledygook. Using it obscures the meaning, bores the listener, and gives the speaker an inflated sense of his expertise. Using the jargon does not demonstrate the intelligence of the speaker. Unfamiliarity does not expose a lack of intelligence.

A physician could get lost in the intricacies of the internal combustion engine or the inner workings of a pneumatic car lift. This is no lack of intelligence. A theologian could befuddle the most intelligent of

---

30. Johnston et al., "Unprocessed Red Meat."

laypersons by talking about the *eschatological* nature of the *kerygma*. Even well-educated pastors can get frustrated trying to grasp theological terms like *ousia, homoousias, homioousia, persona,* and *hypostatic.*

Every discipline has its jargon. English teachers have the bildungsroman, engineers have Nyquist, welders have brazing, and economists have asymmetric information. Using internal language to unfamiliar audiences is unhelpful, and they who tune out those who use it are not unintelligent.

Expertise, then, is not a matter of status or intelligence. It is a matter of subject. A brilliant surgeon could be a terrible farmer. A brilliant builder could be a terrible lawyer. Scientist Richard Feyman once said, "I believe that a scientist looking at nonscientific problems is just as dumb as the next guy—and when he talks about a nonscientific matter, he will sound as naive as anyone untrained in the matter."[31] Perhaps a more memorable way of saying it is Will Rogers's maxim: "For there is nothing as stupid as an educated man if you get him off the thing he that he was educated in."[32]

RESPECT

One of the hallmarks of a democratic society is respect for the wisdom of the common person. After all, democratic societies entrust ordinary citizens with governance. Respect for the ordinary person and understanding the source of her wisdom seems missing in *The Death of Expertise* and many responses of experts to criticism.

Elitism among experts is not exactly a new occurrence. It occurs when experts live in isolation from the rest of society and have few reasons to interact with people outside of their class. In describing why Charlie Chaplin was successful, Orwell writes:

> We live in a period in which democracy is almost everywhere in retreat, supermen in control of three-quarters of the world, liberty explained away by sleek professors, Jew-baiting defended by pacifists. And yet everywhere, under the surface, the common man sticks obstinately to the beliefs that he derives from the Christian culture. The common man is wiser than the intellectuals.

---

31. Feynman, "Value of Science."
32. Quoteresearch, "For There Is Nothing."

Any intellectual can make you out a splendid "case" for smashing the German Trade Unions and torturing the Jews. But the common man, who has no intellect, only instinct and tradition, knows that "it isn't right." . . . An education in Marxism and similar creeds consists largely in destroying your moral sense. . . . Chaplin's appeal lies in his power to reassert the fact . . . that *vox populi is vox Dei* and giants are vermin.[33]

Not to be outdone by Orwell's loathing of the intelligentsia, William Buckley once noted that he would rather be governed by the first two hundred names in a phone book than by the faculty of an Ivy League institution.

Why do sentiments like Orwell's and Buckley's exist? It is not just a "know nothing" ideology or an anti-science mentality. It is that Orwell and Buckley both noted the wisdom of ordinary citizens. Ordinary citizens are not experts on climate change or fiscal policy. They are not experts on trade imbalances or the sociology of crime. Many of them are, however, experts in their own fields. Having expertise close to home, they recognize when a so-called expert is not really an expert or when the expert class has come to a conclusion against common wisdom. They can also see when an expert is operating out of his or her field of expertise.

EXPERTS WHO ARE AGGRESSIVELY WRONG

Nichols writes that America has moved from being uninformed to misinformed to being aggressively wrong. He writes, "People don't just believe dumb things; they actively resist further learning rather than let go of those beliefs."[34]

Missing, however, is that the same problem exists among experts. Take, for example, communism. The ideology of communism has failed spectacularly every time it has been tried. Wherever it has been implemented, communism has produced poverty, starvation, misery, and death. Communists have killed approximately 250,000,000 of their own citizens since the takeover of Russia in 1917.

The nations who have implemented it have failed. Marx's predictions of ever-expanding poverty in non-communist nations have not come true. In fact, extreme poverty is decreasing worldwide with the notable exception of communist countries. When implemented, communism

33. Orwell, *All Art Is Propaganda*, 146–47.
34. Nichols, *Death of Expertise*, xx–xxi.

did not create a class-free society: only a ruling and ruled class. Marxism has failed everywhere it has been tried. Most persons looking at this data would reject communism outright.

Most people, that is, outside of the expert class. Experts in literature, philosophy, economics, sociology, race relations, government, and other ventures are quite willing to argue for Marxism. All the while, residents of Marxist nations flee when given the opportunity.

Orwell once said, "One has to belong to the intelligentsia to believe things like that: no ordinary man could be such a fool."[35] When it comes to Marxism, very few ordinary people believe it. Marxism is the platitude of the experts, the creed of the sophomoric, the opiate of the intellectuals. Its true believers are found mostly among university professors and indoctrinated undergraduates. To hold it, as many experts do, is to be aggressively wrong, blind to evidence.

Nichols is not wrong that many Americans are aggressively wrong; he just does not apply that to the class of experts. Many of them are just as aggressively wrong as the public. If a citizen notices an expert expressing something he thinks is wrong, the citizen may well be right.

EXPERTS AND IDEOLOGICAL BIASES

Another facet to this problem is ideological biases. While everyone has ideological biases, experts can get caught in theirs in a way their expertise should prevent. Part of the issue stems from the nature of expertise itself.

In describing the nature of expertise, Nichols writes:

> Another mark of true experts is their acceptance of evaluation and correction by other experts. Every professional group and expert community has watchdogs, boards, accreditors, and certification authorities whose job is to police its own members and ensure not only that they live up to the standards of their own specialty, but also that their arts are practiced only by people who know what they are doing.[36]

In one sense, the process Nichols describes is correct and healthy. Boards and authorities police most professional groups, assuring that the practice is protected. The bar for lawyers and the board of medicine for

35. Orwell, "Notes on Nationalism."
36. Nichols, *Death of Expertise*, 35.

doctors, for example, provide the public some assurance that their law-yers and doctors are not quacks.

The problem that can emerge from a process like this is groupthink. If the boards become invested in one way of thinking, then challenging that way of thinking can become problematic, especially if challenging a long-standing practice. This kind of policing can produce conformity in the name of excellence and rigidity in the name of quality.

Further, if each field polices itself, then the replication scandal should not have happened. Since most fields of scientific inquiry have organizations whose role is to ensure the integrity of the field, then the replication scandal should not have been possible.

DEATH BY EXPERTISE RESURRECTION
BY TORCHES AND PITCHFORKS

The problem of expertise even involves churches. Worship attendance is down in the US across regions and denominations. There is, however, one outlier: Pentecostals. While most mainline denominations are in a death spiral, only three times in the last forty years has the largest Pentecostal denomination, the Assemblies of God, failed to grow.[37] Worldwide, the number is even more striking. There are over 650 million Pentecostals, representing between 25–30 percent of global Christianity.[38]

Ed Stetzer, missiologist and dean of Talbot School of Theology, sug-gests that Pentecostal growth has multiple causes. Pentecostals tend to be more passionate in worship than their mainline counterparts. They tend to be more missional, and they tend to be more passionately involved in the life of their congregations. Pentecostal practice weeds out nominal attendees.[39]

While all of these reasons have merit, Pentecostals have accom-plished something most other denominations have not figured out. What Pentecostals have figured out is a way to communicate their faith to that group of people, at least in the US. Their ranks come from lower educated and lower income strata.

Also important to note is the educational data among Protestant clergy. Presbyterians have the most educated clergy, and Pentecostals

37. Stetzer, "Pentecostals."
38. Stetzer, "Pentecostals."
39. Stetzer, "Pentecostals."

have the least educated clergy. If education develops expertise, then one should find more expertise among the Presbyterian clergy. If so, then expertise has not saved Presbyterianism. Lacking expertise has not harmed Pentecostalism.

It might be better to put it this way. Pentecostalism and Pentecostal pastors have different kinds of expertise. They know better how to communicate the faith than their mainline counterparts. They certainly know better how to grow their communities of faith than their mainline counterparts. Perhaps the right question is not why expertise failed, but rather, who is really the expert? Bearing a graduate degree does not make one an expert.

WHAT EXPERTS NEED FROM ORDINARY CITIZENS

While it is true that experts have shown contempt for ordinary citizens, ordinary citizens do not always treat experts well either. Mockery and revulsion are not helpful responses to the work of experts.

The general public needs to remember that expertise is very valuable. Experts are necessary. Experts are not immune to groupthink, political partisanship, confirmation bias, false analogies, hasty generalizations, and other biases. These biases affect every discipline, and they affect the public as well. Acknowledgment of that fact by the public in interacting with experts would be helpful. The public does not need to revere experts. It just needs to believe it can trust them. Experts do not need to be worshiped; they do need critical engagement.

15

Cause 6

Institutions and the Acid of Time

HANK AARON, BASEBALL, FOOTBALL, AND A WORLD NO MORE

ON APRIL 28, 2023, a video emerged on X, formerly Twitter, of a plate appearance from Milwaukee Brave Henry Aaron during the 1957 World Series.[1] On the mound was Don Larsen, who threw the only perfect game in World Series history the season before, and behind the plate was the ever-quotable Hall-of-Famer Yogi Berra. The grainy video is black and white. Perhaps the quality of the video is why the game appears to move at a more relaxed pace than the modern game, even though there is less extraneous movement. No one is in a hurry, yet the game moves at a better pace than its modern counterpart.

Aaron, MLB's home run king, does not step out of the batter's box or unfasten and refasten his batting gloves; he does not appear to be wearing any. He does not spit while staring dramatically into the void. Don Larsen does not shake off signs endlessly either. Berra gives the sign quickly and Larson moves immediately into delivery. Although there is a runner on first, Larson does not seem overly worried that he might steal second. Missing are the endless throws over to first to keep the runner's lead to a minimum. The pitches do not seem to have the same velocity as in the modern game, but the movement on the pitches seems more pronounced.

1. BaseballHistoryNut (@nut_history), "Full at Bat."

The commentator notes how the camera distorts how the game looks. He notes how the sixty feet and six inches of distance between the pitcher's mound and home plate looks much smaller on TV. He is correct, of course, but those who have watched baseball on TV for generations would need no such reminder. While televised sports had been around for some time, TVs were just becoming common in American homes.

Larsen's first two pitches were outside, as if trying to stay away from Aaron's bat. The third pitch caught a little more of the plate, and Aaron fouled it off into the stands on the first-base side, a glancing blow. The right-hander was late with his swing. Pitch three was high for ball three. Perhaps Larsen was again avoiding giving anything near the plate for Aaron. The next pitch was high, but Aaron swung and made full contact. He blasted the ball to deep right-center, a home run. The whole at bat took two minutes and nine seconds.

The stands were filled that day. Bunting lined the fences going down the baseline, the outfield fence, and the stands, except for immediately behind the plate. The crowd was quiet but not hushed. One could speak in a normal inside voice and be heard. There was no melodrama from the announcer. The crowd was not in a state of delirium. It was a different game.

Beyond the differences in the game, the crowd looked very different than those who attend a modern game. In the most expensive seats, those behind the plate and down the baselines, men wore suits. Suits, ties, and hats were the attire even in the less expensive upper-deck seats of Milwaukee County Stadium. It was not only a different game; it was a different group of fans. Of course, that has to be the case. It was a different world. L. P. Hartley wrote, "The past is a different country."[2] Indeed. Seventy years ago, not only baseball was different, but almost everything was different.

The Civil Rights Movement had not blossomed. African Americans and others still lived in segregation's ghastly shadow. Rosa Parks had not refused to give up her bus seat yet. Martin Luther King Jr.'s "I Have a Dream Speech" was still seven years away. Many bathrooms were "white only." While many would come to cheer for Aaron, many others would not see him as an equal.

In 1957, the Korean War was an unfortunate memory. Still living in the afterglow of World War II victory, the stalemate of Korea was quickly becoming "the forgotten war." Americans still trusted the government

2. Córdova, "Thinking Through History."

with 73 percent believing it would do what is right about always or most of the time.[3] Kennedy had not been elected, and the terror of the Cuban Missile Crisis had not transpired. Kennedy's ill-fated ride in the back of the midnight-blue Lincoln Continental convertible was six years in the future.

1957 was *before*. It was Kennedy's election, JFK's and RFK's assassinations, before LBJ and Vietnam. 1957 was before the moon landing and the Ford Mustang. It was twenty years before Nixon said "I am not a crook." 1957 was before Woodstock. In 1957 Muhammed Ali was still Cassius Clay.

The world *looked* different because it *was* different. The world was different because the minds of the populace were different. For an adult in 1957, Michael Jackson's popularity, Beyoncé's cultural import, and the Obama Presidency would have been otherworldly. Baseball was built for a world that only exists in fading memories and grainy photographs.

A modern baseball game is technically the same game even with Major League Baseball's (MLB) best efforts to modernize. MLB has added a pitch clock, reduced the number of visits to the mound, and how often a pitcher can step off the rubber. The pace is faster, but the game is still very similar.

Compared with football, baseball is a relic. Jay Bilas, basketball analyst for ESPN, calls football a "sadistic land acquisition game."[4] If he traded the word "sadistic" for "violent," many football fans would readily agree with the description and relish it. Football is a violent game and one that fits American culture. In almost a religious frenzy, fans celebrate every big hit, broken tackle, touchdown, interception, and wild catch. Football is a spectacle, and Americans are captivated. As Hall-of-Famer Howie Long said, "While baseball is America's pastime, football is America's passion."[5]

Attending a baseball game leads to conversation over a hotdog and listening for the crack of the bat. The smell of popcorn welcomes the nostrils and assures fans all is as it should be. In some stadiums, fans will sing a communal ode to the game. "Sweet Caroline" and "Take Me Out to the Ballgame" are among the favorites.

3. Pew Research Center, "Public Trust in Government."
4. Bilas, "March Is Coming."
5. Grossman, "Why Has NFL Viewership."

Football appeals to a different set of sensibilities. Attending a football game is a series of rituals with a throng of people. Fans gather in the parking lot hours before the game for tailgating. When game time approaches, they assemble for the National Anthem, which is often accompanied by military jets flying over. Applauding the Anthem with a religious fervor, the crowd waits for kickoff, at which time they scream in glee. All of these rituals are a prelude to a collective, primal roar.

What MLB is trying to do and the NFL has accomplished is transition their games, their institutions, out of the culture into which they were born into a different one. Both MLB and the NFL know the culture is changing rapidly, and they work to change with it. This is not to say they are always successful. Both of them have made mistakes that have alienated their audiences in the past. At least, however, they understand how culture works. They know the culture into which they were born is gone, *and it is never coming back*. The distance from 1957 to now cannot be traversed in rewind.

INSTITUTIONS AND TIME

Many contemporary institutions have nineteenth-century origins. The Salvation Army was founded in 1845. Duke University traces its origin to 1838, and the University of Michigan originated in 1817. *The New York Times* dates to 1851. President James K. Polk signed the law authorizing the Smithsonian in 1846.[6] The modern Olympic Games began in 1896.

Like the 1800s, the 1900s birthed many institutions. Henry Ford founded the Ford Motor Company in the early 1900s, with General Motors being born shortly thereafter. The federal government created the FBI, CIA, NSA, Department of Labor, Department of Education, and GAO in the 1900s as well. The question is, can institutions built in previous centuries carry out their purpose in a world very different from the world of their birth?

Consider the Southern Baptist Convention. Born in 1845, the SBC emerged after a bitter dispute with Northern Baptists over whether or not slaveholders could serve as missionaries. At its formation, the SBC created two missionary organizations: the Foreign Missions Board and the Domestic Missions Board.[7] After the Civil War, the SBC reorganized its

6. Smithsonian, "Our History."

7. North American Mission Board Staff, "Brief History."

missionary activity and created the Home Missions Board as a successor to the Domestic Missions Board.[8]

The SBC is an American success story. Since its founding, the SBC has become the largest Protestant denomination in the US. The problem is, however, that denominational life is dying. With nearly every major denomination in the US declining, and many of them dying, it is fair to ask whether denominational Christianity itself is dying.

Denominations have benefits. Denominations fund seminaries for the training of future pastors and missionaries. Seminaries also serve as guardians of orthodoxy. Beyond seminaries, denominations help fund the work of the churches. Children's homes, hospitals, retirement homes, and social service organizations owe their origin to denominational entities.

Denominations also have benefits for local congregations even in free-church traditions. As part of a denomination clergy and non-clergy staff can gain retirement and health benefits unavailable to them if their church were independent. Congregations gain access to a network of clergy when they have an opening. Clergy gain a collection of congregations for when it is time to find a new place to serve.

Despite all of these benefits, denominational life is dying. The growing edge of the church is in freestanding, independent, evangelical congregations. Part of the issue is in the nature of denominations themselves.

Denominations are difficult to manage and maddening to lead. When it comes to Baptists, it would be easier to wrangle a flock of rabid wolverines than lead them. Methodists have much the same issue, and for years, protesters showed up to PCUSA meetings. Leading denominations is not an easy task.

Denominations can be full of well-meaning people who speak in a way that does not reflect well on the organization. Open mics at denominational meetings often lead to embarrassed leaders and observers.

Perhaps the most maddening part of denominational life is the cumbersome committee structure. When denominations want to change, or when someone recommends a change, the recommendations often get sent to a committee for study. Sometimes, sending the recommendations to a committee is a genuine effort to study the recommendation more thoroughly. Other times, sending it to a committee is an effort to bury it in organizational purgatory where only prayer and a hefty indulgence can

8. North American Mission Board Staff, "Brief History."

get it out. The ones who make the recommendation often have no clue which is the case.

In short, denominations often have a Byzantine structure that seems to actively prevent action from being taken, and that sounds a lot like Congress. Congress is notably loathed by the US public, whose approval of them is approaching single digits.[9] Prom night pimples and colonoscopies have more fans. Like Congress, the denominations are structured to move slowly and cautiously. By the time they can take action, it is too late.

Another reason denominations are in decline is their inability to change their approach, as is the case with the SBC. Its last reorganization, known as the Great Commission Resurgence, was a failure. It accomplished little and did not help the SBC reverse its decline.

The SBC has structures that no longer work. At the smallest level, the SBC had a unique organizing tactic at its founding. Each congregation was part of a local association, and each association had an Associational Missionary. This functioned differently than the similar structure in the Methodist church. In Methodism, the district superintendent appointed pastors to churches. In contrast, the Associational Missionary had no such authority. The purpose of the Associational Missionary was to create community among the local congregations, help congregations as they transitioned from pastors, and provide them with missions opportunities. It was a very effective strategy for more than a century.

Very few associations are effective in contemporary SBC life. Despite changing the title of the Associational Missionary and changing the parameters of the work, associational work remains underproductive. The reasons for the creation of associational Baptist work no longer exist. Churches can create their own partners for community and service, and the role of finding a pastor has shifted from an association-led process to an Internet-driven process. There are exceptions to this observation, but many associations have limited roles in their local congregations. While associations were a very effective tool at the beginning of the SBC, their relevance in the future is unknown. The circumstances that called for their birth no longer exist. Having structures that have outlived their usefulness is part of the reason denominations are clumsy.

It is not just structures of denominations that are ill-suited to contemporary culture. Denominations themselves struggle because their founding vision is for a world that no longer exists. The world of the

9. Jones, "Congress' Job Approval Drops."

eighteenth and nineteenth centuries no longer exists. The post-Civil War South which gave birth to the SBC is a terrible memory. Even the world of the SBC's zenith is gone.

The SBC does not seem to grasp its reality. Many of its leaders are fixated on purported "liberal drift" in its institutions. Believing that some SBC leaders are progressives, they are fixated on moving them out and getting back to principled conservatism. The conservative-liberal split in the SBC is over, however. Liberals and most moderates left years, if not decades, ago. Framing the SBC's struggle as a repeat of its past will not help it in the present.

The struggles the SBC faces over ideology are insignificant in comparison to their ineffective governance, strategy failures, and public image. The SBC's image problem is so severe that when the SBC starts a new congregation, it rarely uses the name "Baptist" in its name. The term "Baptist" and connections to the SBC have proven to be toxic to the greater public, and the SBC has no strategy to correct its image problem. The SBC's membership and attendance have been declining for years, and its leaders have no ready solution.

Repeating the denominational wars of the SBC's past may relieve anxiety. It might give SBC leaders and members somewhere to focus their angst, but it will not change the reality. The SBC was built in and for a world that no longer exists. Addressing that challenge is pressing.

WHAT IS THE DATE HERE?

Staying connected to the culture is a daunting task. Institutions can get frozen in time and become irrelevant. One of the best ways to understand an institution is to ask, "What is the date here?" The obvious answer is that the date in the institution is the same as everywhere else. When asking this question of an institution, however, more is meant than the obvious. When asking the date of the institution, one is asking what date their institutional clock is set to or what the date is of the culture the institution is trying to preserve.

Long before the mouth waters from the smell of freshly baked biscuits, Cracker Barrel is a feast for the senses. The restaurant chain with its many locations on US interstate highways is famous for its outdoor rocking chairs and ceiling fans. While waiting for a table, customers can sit in a rocker and play a game of checkers on the jumbo sets outside. Once indoors, customers can shop Cracker Barrel's wares, including cookware, nostalgic games, and quilts.[10]

The entire experience at Cracker Barrel is like a visit to the past. Antique decorations are Cracker Barrel's style. Painted metal advertisements for companies long vanished are on the walls. Gulf Oil, Texaco Gas, Crescent Gas, and others greet the customers seated at their tables. A fire crackles in the fireplace, inviting customers to set aside their worries and enjoy the food and atmosphere. All of the emphasis Cracker Barrel places on the atmosphere allows for a certain suspension of disbelief. For just a moment, diners are in a different, happier time.

Even a restaurant that is deliberately a throwback cannot survive without change, however. The chain is trying desperately to regain relevance as many of its customers have never returned after the COVID shutdown.[11]

If one were to ask what the date was inside a Cracker Barrel, or more precisely, what date Cracker Barrel is trying to project, one would say the mid-1950s to early 1960s. That date would feel like home to many of their customers who grew up in that time frame. Many of them would have happy memories of the companies and artifacts on Cracker Barrel's walls.

The customers, however, always knew this was a projection, a deliberate reminiscing. The more pertinent date is 1969, the date Cracker Barrel was founded.[12] That is the date the company's culture was trying to preserve. Selling a visit to an older time of hospitality and country food combined with an atmosphere of 1960s Americana was a winner for a while.

No longer a winner, the company is struggling and working on a corporate makeover. How does the company keep its customers who want a 1960s experience while attracting new customers for whom the feel of the restaurant is foreign?

Much like a quick visit to a home listing can give a prospective buyer an idea of when a home was built or when it was redecorated, a visit to an institution will often help discern the answer to the date question. It is often easier for a guest to see what the date of the institution is rather than someone who has a long history within the organization. That is why new leaders and even mystery shoppers can be helpful. Often the date can best

---

10. Cracker Barrel, "Retail Merchandise."
11. Wiener-Bronner, "Cracker Barrel."
12. Cracker Barrel, "Cracker Barrel History and Timeline"

be discerned intuitively. A quick walk through the breezeway, a glance at publications, a look at the furniture, or a study of the budgets reveal very quickly the date of the institution. If an organization remains stuck in a date, they have a limited future.

TECHNOLOGY

Before the advent of the personal computer and the Internet, before the advent of high-speed Wi-Fi and Twitter, a different world existed. Many, if not most, families had a ritual of sorts. The children would come home from school and do their homework, play, and do chores while waiting for their father to return from work. When the father would come home, they would greet him briefly and let him settle before family supper. Families gathered for supper, often dressing for the occasion. Discussing the events of their day over a home-cooked meal, they shared the events of their days.

After dinner, the father would go to his favorite chair, crack open the newspaper, and wait for the evening news at 6:30. The news would be followed by prime-time TV offerings from the big three networks beginning at 8:00 EST. While families were gathering in different homes, they were watching the same programs, on the same nights, at the same time.

TV became a staple of American family life for decades. *The Cosby Show, Family Ties, Cheers,* and *The Golden Girls* dominated the '80s. *Friends, Seinfeld, ER, Frazier,* and *Law & Order* were favorites from the '90s. Network TV had found magic. People wanted entertainment, the networks could provide it, and advertisers paid a premium for product commercials. It seemed like a party that would never end.

While the funeral is a way off, network TV is under hospice care. High-speed Internet and streaming services have delivered the fatal blow, even if the networks lumber in a zombie-like stupor for several more years. Netflix and streaming services like it destroyed Blockbuster Video first. Why rent a movie from a story when streaming saves time, avoids lines, and streaming services never run out of the newest releases? Why worry about a collection of DVDs when a digital collection cannot be lost or scratched?

The networks had nothing to fear from the streaming services at first. No, video rental companies were the first victims. Gradually, something happened, however. People began to eliminate cable. By 2010 cable had reached 90 percent of TV homes, and by 2013 it generated $10 billion in ad revenue.[13] As of 2023, however, only 45.6 percent of TV homes have cable, and projections are that number will further collapse to 34.9 percent by 2027.[14] Cable TV is collapsing faster than Keir Starmer's popularity. Cable is the primary delivery system for network TV. Its collapse portends ill for the networks.

Also contributing to the networks' decline is that paid streaming services now create their own programming. Netflix's *Stranger Things*, *Cobra Kai*, and *House of Cards* created buzz for the service and were much higher quality than most network shows.

Faced with sudden competition and a deteriorating share of the marketplace, the networks are now scrambling to join the streaming revolution. So far, however, their efforts have not stopped the decrease in viewers. Twenty-four percent of Americans do not watch any live TV.[15] Worse still for the networks, those who do watch TV spend less than 50 percent of their TV watching time watching broadcast networks or pay TV.[16]

The year is not 2012, and networks cannot put pages back on the calendar. The streaming revolution, along with social media, YouTube, and Tiktok, have changed the way people consume entertainment. No amount of wishing will change that.

TECHNOLOGY AND CHANGE

Technology has not just changed entertainment. Virtually every institution has to reckon with the changes technology brings. At the advent of the economic shutdown, churches and schools faced difficult challenges. In an effort to continue worship, many congregations began to livestream their service. Others recorded a service and broadcast it over social media. Schools used the Internet to have synchronous classes with mixed success.

The technological revolution has even affected Wall Street. Individual investors can access their accounts through trading platforms and execute trades without ever contacting a broker. Scarcely any American institution has remained unaffected by the technological revolution. There are even websites for Amish furniture.

13. Adgate, "Rise and Fall."
14. Clark, "Less than 50%."
15. Fitzgerald, "Americans Are Watching."
16. Rizzo, "Broadcast and Cable."

While declining institutions may blame technology, technology is a neutral actor. Like a hammer, technology can be used to build or destroy. Harnessing its power or adapting to the circumstances technology creates separates institutions that survive and thrive from those that do not. Seeing technology as the great destroyer of institutions is a grave mistake.

Institutions that learn how to employ technology in their mission find that it can significantly enhance their chances of success. Those who cannot adapt will face peril.

TECHNOLOGY AND CHARACTER

Technology can be an asset or a liability for society depending on how individuals and institutions use technology. For those whose character is formed by a search for the good, technology gives access to information and knowledge unimaginable for most of human history.

A student who wanted to improve her SAT or ACT scores could learn calculus or trigonometry by watching a YouTube video or by seeking instruction at Kahn Academy's website. A person devoted to learning can find videos or instruction on virtually any subject online.

Those who want to learn a skill can find that online too. From woodworking to how to change brake pads, from how to play Eddie Van Halen's rock masterpiece "Eruption" to studying a Bach concerto, if it exists, someone is explaining it online. The technological revolution makes any skill easier to master.

As surely as it makes any field of knowledge more accessible and any skill easier to learn, technology enables human bad behavior. The Internet not only makes viewing images of Michelangelo's *David* easier. It makes viewing any image easier, including pornography. While getting accurate information is very difficult, two recent studies estimate that 13 percent of web searches and 20 percent of mobile searches are of pornographic material. Just as technology enables those who want to learn, technology enables the 87 percent of US men and 28.5 percent of US women 18–35 who view pornography weekly to do so from their office, their home computer, or their mobile device.

The Dark Web enables the purchase of illegal weapons, human trafficking, backdoor entry into websites, and a whole slew of disturbing activities. Whatever one wants to do to feed his or her ego, one can find there.

UTILITY AND SELF-GRATIFICATION

When one's character is given to self-gratification, the predominant value is utility. When one sees other people as only an object, their primary value is in what they can provide. In extreme cases like narcissism, people become fungible assets. They are quickly found and quickly replaced. The moment a person stops catering to the narcissist's needs, they are quickly discarded.

It is not only narcissists who use people as objects, though. Ordinary people so involved in their own experiences can cease to see others as people. Self-gratification is partially a process and partially a character trait. All people are, at one time or another, wholly focused on their own needs and desires. A person rushing to the hospital should be forgiven if they fail to give a turn signal or cut off someone in traffic. Even in less dramatic moments, people can become self-focused. A parent can get frustrated with a child for playing loudly while he or she is watching social media. A small child can get very upset when a parent says no to his impassioned request for ice cream. Becoming self-focused happens because people are people, and most people do not remain focused on self-gratification for long.

The problem is that self-gratification, like other human behaviors, becomes normative. The repeated practice of self-gratification can lead to the character of self-gratification. When it becomes the tenor of a personality, self-gratification becomes cruel.

Pornography trades on abuses, and often, the women involved are underage. Even though the pernicious nature of pornographic production is well known, users continue at a brisk pace. The abuse of the women involved is of little relevance to them.

Famously, Harvey Weinstein abused women. His "casting couch" was well known in Hollywood, yet no one cared. As long as he produced hit films, he was free to abuse. That is, until the "Me Too" movement.

In the Arbinger Institute's *Leadership and Self Deception* and the follow-up text *The Anatomy of Peace*, the institute argues the single most important characteristic of long-term success in relationships is the capacity to see others as individuals and not objects. An object can be cussed at, yelled at, and fired summarily. A person is an individual with wants, needs, and aspirations. Seeing each individual as a person takes constant effort as the desire to arrange one's world around the self is strong. The effort is worth it though. It makes for better personal and professional relationships.

Napoleon Bonaparte, at least as far as the legends go, treated every one of his soldiers as a person. They were not cannon fodder; they were not there for Bonaparte's grand plans. Every night before a battle, Bonaparte would walk through the soldiers' camp and greet the soldiers. With his vast intellect and impressive memory, he would remember details about their lives and families. Asking about their wives and children and genuinely concerned about their wellbeing, Bonaparte earned unmatched loyalty among his troops.[17]

Seeing others as a person inspires gratitude and makes for connection. Seeing others as objects leads to contempt. No one likes to be thought of as disposable.

Self-gratification does much the same thing to inanimate objects as well. For a person who is focused on self-gratification, objects themselves are only of value so much as they have immediate utility. Truth, goodness, and beauty are not their concern.

Utility, however, is a declining value. What has utility today has less tomorrow, and still less the day after. Eventually, even the most useful objects are useless piles of rubble. They must be disposed of before they become liabilities. Investing in utility must be at a minimum to keep the long-term costs down.

Nothing, whether a tool, home, or person, can withstand being measured as an object. Utility is the death of all things.

No institution can survive a populace addicted to self-gratification. Institutions, by their nature, exist to preserve a society of self-giving. Education exists to instruct the next generation. Religion exists to enlighten humanity. The military exists to protect civilization from the darkness. A self-gratifying society, however, turns all institutions for the self and ruins them.

To save institutions, then, requires nothing short of a spiritual revolution. Inversely, institutions can lead such a revolution if they remain connected to their core values and the culture around them.

17. Pascal, "Napoleon."

THE ACID OF TIME

Waiting on events to slow down or for traumas to become less frequent before facing a changing world is an ineffective strategy. The traumas continue. The last twenty-four years of US history were filled with trauma and drama. Beginning in November 2000 with the contested election of President Bush, the nation has faced a series of traumatic events. In April 2001, China took twenty-four US service members hostage after an in-air collision.[18] Five months later, the horror of 9/11 forever changed those who lived through it. 9/11 was followed by the war in Afghanistan, the Global War on Terror, the Second Persian Gulf War, Abu Ghraib, the economic meltdown of 2008–9, the COVID pandemic, race riots in the aftermath of George Floyd's killing, the 2020 election, the events of January 6, 2021, the catastrophic withdrawal from Afghanistan, the October 7 Hamas attacks against Israel, the assassination attempt against former President Trump, and President Biden's withdrawal from the 2024 election. Institutions and individuals cannot wait for calm before retooling. Calm might not come. Change, however, is a certainty.

18. "EP-3 Collision."

16

Where to Find Hope 1
Reconnecting to Transcendental Values

What is the truth, but a lie agreed upon.

—Friedrich Nietzsche

[The British are] modern barbarians camped out in the relics of an older and superior civilization to whose beauties they are oblivious.

—Roger Scruton

BLEAK HOUSE

A HEALTHY SOCIETY CREATES healthy institutions, and healthy institutions lead to healthy societies. Noting regression across institutions is a bleak, dark process. Sometimes it feels like shouting "Get off my lawn!" into the void. There are few listeners for the shouting. Cursing at the decline while watching the decline accelerate makes one feel as if society itself is dying and wants nothing more and nothing else. Only let the society have its fill of pleasure on its way to oblivion.

All is not lost, however. Hope can be found in reconnection to values. The traditions and institutions on which Western society was founded can themselves be connected to what philosophers often call the "transcendentals": the good, the true, and the beautiful. It is by reconnecting to these three values that society and its institutions can survive, and maybe one day thrive again.

Regression can only be stopped then by a spiritual renewal. The philosophical and sociological analysis of the empires of dust can be helpful. The willingness to put institutions on a firm foundation of values and differentiation can have some success. For the society as a whole, however, nothing short of a spiritual renewal can restore it.

Resources for the renewal, however, are contained in wisdom Western society already possesses. Western civilization, whatever its faults, stands on the pillars of the ancient Greeks, the Christian theological tradition, the Judeo-Christian tradition, and the Enlightenment. The wisdom contained there is enough for renewal.

TRANSCENDENTALS

The concept of the transcendentals emerges from the philosophy of Plotinus, and Aquinas adopts them into the Christian tradition. The transcendentals are the good, the true, and the beautiful. Notoriously difficult to define, the good, the true, and the beautiful are categories of being and are of ultimate value.[1]

In one sense, they are different items. The good is both a characteristic of quality and a moral characteristic. The true is the correct description of reality. The smaller truths humans speak are true as they are part of that which is the truth. The beautiful, perhaps the most difficult to define, yields the power to create desire within the observer. These distinctions among these three are merely on the surface, and they are finally connected in God. For Plotinus, they are attributes of God himself.[2]

TRUTH DISMISSED

From modern journalists and philosophical theorists to ancient strongmen, the concept of truth has limited supporters. Pontius Pilate infamously interrogated Jesus with the question, "What is truth?" For Pilate, there was only one truth: the power of Caesar. Theologian Miroslav Volf notes about Jesus's trial, "For both the accuser and the judge, the truth is

1. Scruton, *Beauty*, 2.
2. Scruton, *Beauty*, 2.

irrelevant because it works at cross-purposes to their hold on power."[3] Jesus alone was interested in truth, and "it was the accused who raised the issue of truth by subtly reminding the judge of his highest obligation—find out the truth."[4] Truth becomes irrelevant when the only value is power.

Perhaps the connection between truth and power is ever-present. All truth claims are power claims in disguise, the postmodern philosophers teach. Perhaps they have a point. If there is a truth, then truth is the most valuable commodity. A person who could understand truth and teach the truth would rightly be the one to rule.

Of course, truth is contested. When there are multiple competing truth claims, the question of power necessarily emerges: who gets to decide what truth is? In the American legal system, the Supreme Court gets to decide what the Constitution means. Their power is not that they are always right. They have been famously wrong on several issues, slavery among them. Their power is that they are final. All legal claims could theoretically come before them, and they have the power to decide which reading of the law is the right one.

Truth, in its absolute sense, is quite slippery. Christian believers might suggest that the Bible is the truth. Who, however, gets to decide what the Bible means? Among believers there are numerous mutually exclusive readings of the ancient text. Which of these is the correct one? At least with the medieval Catholic Church, the church decided which interpretation was correct.

That, perhaps, was its downfall. With its ability to decide what was true, the Roman Catholic Church gained for itself power, prestige, and fortune. It could make or break kings and empires. It could bestow honor and inflict shame. King Henry IV walked barefoot in the snow in humiliation seeking Pope Gregory VII's forgiveness.

The Protestant Reformers placed the Bible as the final arbiter of truth. The problem, however, became whose interpretation of the Bible was the correct one. The Reformers differed among themselves and had their own struggles with heretics.

Philosophers, at least modern philosophers, believed that truth could be understood by any rational mind. Their goal was to describe reality in a way where any objective mind would come to the same

3. Volf, *Exclusion and Embrace*, 266.
4. Volf, *Exclusion and Embrace*, 266.

conclusion. Not only did they see the power of reason as a descriptor of reality, they thought the same of ethics too. They wanted to create a system of knowledge and ethics that was true for everyone everywhere. Even God would be subject to ethics just as God is subject to the laws of mathematics, they concluded. Of course, this project failed. It failed because there is no way for any one person to be completely objective.

At the height of belief in the power of reason, the scientific revolution was born. No longer bound by the traditions of the past, the scientific method would lead humans to the truth. The scientific method, however, cannot do that. It can only follow its own logic. The great questions of life cannot be answered by it, necessarily. Science is the discipline of discovering physical reality. The most important questions of life transcend physical reality.

Truth is not, then, easily defined or found. It is a transcendent value. It transcends sense experience. Facts and the truthfulness of a particular event can be determined, but the truth itself transcends ordinary experience.

Jesus says, "I am the way, the truth, and the life." For Jesus, truth is bound up in the character of God. To say that Jesus is truth or God is truth is not merely to say that God always truthful. The Christian tradition is emphatic on this point: what God has, God is. Better to say it this way: in God, all accidents are substances. If God has truthfulness, God is truth itself.

It is in proximity to God that truth becomes knowable. It is perhaps the case that those without a belief in God might disagree. Notice, however, the gleam in the eye of a mathematician whose formulas point to a reality undiscovered. Even notice a militant atheist like Richard Dawkins who speaks of the majestic nature of the universe. He even suggests that the universe might be worthy of worship. In his looking at the facts of biology, even if he does not grant that the processes are created by God, he sees in them a truth worthy of deep admiration of worship. As he approaches truth, he finds an identity worthy of worship.

If there is no God, then truth is probably impossible. The only thing left is the miserable search for meaning in a meaningless universe. Truth is, then, only the lie everyone agrees on at the moment. It is tied to power, and those in power insist that what benefits them is true.

It is only in God and God's revealing of the truth that humans have any access to truth. Atheists and skeptics might demur, understandably. Is truth impossible for them? What if they wanted truth and remained committed to a worldview that excludes God? Perhaps they could find solace in contemporary Platonists and others who define the truth as transcendental without making divine claims.

PERSONALIZED TRUTH

Instead of searching for the truth, modern society seems obsessed with personalized truth, "your truth" or "my truth." These, however, are not even pale imitations of the truth. They celebrate subjectivity, absolutize personal experience, and rely on fleeting emotions. They exist on the notion that human experience is the arbiter of individual truth. Human experience, however, is not reliable. Psychologists have long noted that humans are not reliable narrators of their own experience.

In sessions with clients, therapists encourage the retelling of personal stories. This retelling is not fanciful. It is the therapist seeing something in the story that the client has missed. The client has missed his or her power in their own stories sometimes. Other times they have missed their own culpability. Retelling and seeing their own story differently has healing power.

How is this kind of therapy possible? People do not always narrate their stories well. If people cannot narrate their own stories well, then personalized notions of truth are simply momentary preferences of the narrator within their personal story. When people discover that their personal narratives—their truths—are no longer helpful, they can rewrite the story. This new vision is now their new truth. One does not have to be an absolutist to recognize that this is not anything like truth; it is barely an impression of it.

Personalized truth is neither personalized nor truth. It is the preference of the moment based on something quite slippery like personal memory. Since memories change every time humans recall them, as psychologists suggest, then the memory has no permanence in the person and is quite separate from who he or she is. The truth of experience cannot be the truth of the person because the memory of the truth changes. It is not personal (that is, if by "personal," one means a permanent characteristic of a person who observes the memory).

Further, since personalized truth changes by necessity, it is not truth. Truth, if it is truth, cannot change. Truth exists beyond experience. It is the descriptor of all experience. That necessarily cannot change.

Truth cannot be owned in an individual's subjectivity. "My truth" cannot exist, for if it is truth, it belongs to the transcendent. If it can be owned by a person, it is necessarily shaped by that person. Truth, however, exists independently of the observer.

What has become difficult for society to manage is that these personalized truths have emotive power. Challenging someone's truth is tantamount to challenging someone's existence. If personal truth is the story of one's existence, the story of the "I," then challenging it is tantamount to saying that one's existence is a lie. It is not hard to see why one would recoil against having their personal truth challenged.

In *A Failure of Nerve*, Edwin Friedman recounts a story about a presentation he made on Christopher Columbus. The great explorer was a hero of Friedman's because of how he escaped the emotional system of medieval Europe. The continent was stuck emotionally. Islamic armies were pushing into Europe, Christianity was in an incoherent mess, and it was stuck.

Columbus thought differently than the herd. He began to think of a way beyond all of the warring factions toward the New World. Columbus was wrong about the size of the earth. What he expected to find when he discovered the New World was India. Despite his mistake, he discovered a new continent and brought Europe out of the Middle Ages.

In telling this story, Friedman provoked the ire of one of his listeners. "This was one of the most boring presentations I have ever heard, and I am deeply hurt by your ethnocentric bias,"[5] the listener responded.

Friedman, however, would not give in to his suggestions: "I told him directly that I couldn't care less about his feelings and that I was trying to present universal, challenging ideas about the orientations of stuck civilizations."[6] Freidman continued:

> It seems to me that any artist has no choice but to express himself in the medium of his own background. . . . My views may not always be correct . . . but if anyone in the audience is having trouble getting in touch with the universal themes of human existence that I am trying to portray because of the cultural context in which I have drawn my metaphor, then it seems to me that there is some serious question to be raised about whose ethnocentricity is getting in the way.[7]

5. Friedman, *Failure of Nerve*, 132.
6. Friedman, *Failure of Nerve*, 132.
7. Friedman, *Failure of Nerve*, 132–33.

Many listening to the lecture were offended. "You are still avoiding his feelings," one listener responded. Freidman was undeterred: "Dialogue is only possible when we can learn to distinguish feelings from opinions and recognize that the background or personality of a person is totally irrelevant to the validity of what he or she is saying."[8]

Friedman quickly made a distinction between being harmed and being upset. The listener was not harmed in any way. Hurt feelings are not the same as harm. The listener was upset. His being upset, however, had nothing to do with whether what Friedman said was true or not.

What Freidman calls the "fallacy of empathy" emerges when truth is personalized and feelings around personalized truth get wrapped up in emotional sensitivity. When truth becomes "my truth," it must be protected. The one protecting is easily offended and often expects acknowledgment of hurt feelings to stop any questioning about the truth of their experience.

INVENTING THE UGLY

It set tongues to wagging and the Internet on fire, as it was supposed to. The opening ceremony of the 2024 Olympic Games was a spectacle unlike any other in the modern games. It is difficult to say exactly what the director of the opening ceremony, Thomas Jolly, was trying to create.

At first glance, it looked to many casual observers like a visual reference to DaVinci's *Last Supper*. To other observers, it looked more like the image of *The Wedding at Cana*. Housed at the Louvre, *The Wedding at Cana* is the largest painting in France. Unconfirmed reports said that the Olympic promotional material called the performance "Le Cène, Sur La Scène, Sur La Seine," an obvious reference to the *Last Supper*. Unconfirmed reports state that one of the artists called the scene a "New Gay Testament."

After sensing outrage, Jolly and the International Olympic Committee began to issue denials. It was not intended to be a parody of a Christian image, they protested. It was a feast to Dionysus. The similarity to Christian images existed only in the eyes of believers, many of whom were taking offense where none was intended. It is very difficult to believe that images which bore striking similarities to famous Christian art were not intended to be parodies of that art, however.

8. Friedman, *Failure of Nerve*, 133.

Missing in the religious nature of the discussion was the aesthetic issue. Unlike most opening ceremonies in the Olympic Games, the ceremony was ugly, gaudy. At the center of the image was performer Barbara Butch, who calls herself a "fat, Jewish, queer lesbian." Sporting several tattoos and wearing a blue dress and a headpiece resembling a halo, Butch's character was the focal point of the ceremony. Making her hands into the shape of a heart, Butch claims she was intending to create love and unity. Oddly enough, beauty would have created the unity Butch claimed she wanted. There was no beauty to be had in this performance, however.

To her left was a tall transgender man in a revealing blue teddy complete with thigh stockings and boots. The dancer gyrated provocatively to the intense dance music. Also to her left was another transgender man wearing a sequin-covered, candy-apple red evening gown and matching gloves. Wearing a platinum blond wig, his dark skin stood out all the more. Between them was a woman wearing bright red dress. Flowers jutted out of her dress and called attention to her unnaturally red hair. Almost clownish in her makeup, she looked like a toddler had attacked her with rouge.

More transgender individuals were to Butch's right. One wore a reflective dress that shined like tin foil. Beside him was a young girl, not quite a teenager, or so it appears. Further along the parade of horribles was a series of male dancers wearing only very short black shorts and a black evening coat. One of the dancers had his genitals partially exposed.

During the ceremony, one of the dancers carried the underage girl away in what could be taken as an ode to pedophilia. In another scene, three lovers make their way to a room in a reference to a ménage à trois. As the show progressed, the character Dionysus appeared. Nearly naked and painted in glittering blue, he gyrates at a feast in his honor.

This Dionysus looked little like his ancient Greek namesake. The ancient deity of that name was a figure of beauty. The Greeks viewed him as remarkably handsome with a young appearance. With a perfect physique, he rode the back of a panther and was the representative of drunken orgies. This Dionysus was not handsome, nor was he intended to be. He had limited muscular tone and a potbelly. Looking more like a naked Smurf or a blue version of Guy Diamond from the *Trolls* movie series, Dionysus feasted with his guests. The only similarity to the ancient god was the drunken revelry. This Dionysus was the god of the drunken orgy, the feast of oddity.

The opening ceremonies were an ode to the ugly, a representation of the vile, a celebration of the revolting. Even without religious representation, the show was shocking, deliberately so.

French culture can be strange to outsiders and shock sensibilities. So perhaps surprise ought to be muted. Surprised or not, revulsion is the natural response of such images. Ugliness is repellent to the eye and revulsive to the intuition. Only those who have viewed ugly images until their sensitivity to them has been fatigued would not intuitively respond with loathing.

When artists and others celebrate the ugly, their goal is not only shock: it is to desecrate what society finds beautiful. The point of the ceremony, then, was to desecrate the beauty of France and its Catholic tradition with the ugly emerging from Jolly's imagination. It was to introduce a new version of an old deity and celebrate his debauchery. Even if not intended, this new Dionysus was very effective in his role. This ceremony was both a desecration and a profanation of the Olympics and, most likely, Christianity.[9] The ugliness was the point.

UGLINESS AND THE SOUL

Ugliness is heavy for the soul. Living in ugly houses or apartments depresses one's emotions. Working in ugly offices makes one feel like a worthless cog in a merciless machine. One need only look at the living quarters in communist and former communist nations to notice how ugliness and oppression go together. Broken windows, graffiti, trash, unmaintained facilities, and empty buildings are the bane of urban existence. The ugliness creates a feeling of unease, a lack of safety, lack of belonging, and a lack of power.

In the US, unfortunately, ugliness abounds. Automakers excel at creating cars distinguishable only by their badges. They are copies of copies of copies. A Corvette from the 1950s, a 1957 Bel Air, and a 1965 Mustang are all in beautiful different ways. A 2024 Mustang Mach-E or a 2024 Kia Forte, however, have no beauty in them. Their designers exhibit no desire for them to be beautiful. They are practical with limited aesthetic value; this is no accident. An ugly car, however expensive, is a disposable car. One might purchase a modern subcompact car every six years. One will not, however, become enchanted with it. It is as disposable as a paper

9. Scruton, *Beauty*, 151.

towel, only longer lasting. Very few contemporary cars exhibit any sort of beauty.

From McMansions littering suburban landscapes to horrid apartment buildings creating misery in the middle city, housing itself has lost beauty as well. Many modern residential structures have no beauty in them. These eyesores are oppressive to the soul.

Modern office spaces are so bereft of beauty that many of them actively communicate disdain for those who work there. After all, if the primary object is utility and price, those who work there are not worth the expenditure.

Ugliness even affects attire, and when it does, communicates poor self-esteem. Wearing pajamas to Walmart hardly communicates self-value. A person who cannot be bothered to get out of bedclothes before emerging in public communicates a lack of self-respect and a lack of the capacity to be embarrassed. What kind of grown man parades around a superstore in pajamas and Crocs?

The absence of beauty is connected to destructive forces. Lack of self-esteem, lack of value for others, and lack of permanence, among many other ideas, get communicated when beauty is missing. It does not take long for those values to radiate through the culture. Ugliness distorts life.

BEAUTY

The human eye responds to beauty. It is designed to do that. Human attraction to beauty explains why humans love koala bears even though they are execrable. It explains why humans loathe opossums even though they are useful in keeping pest populations under control. Humans like raccoons even though they are menaces. Why? Because they are beautiful.

The propensity for humans to value beauty can even show up in parenting. Provocative studies indicate that parents give preference to their more physically beautiful children.[10] While disturbing, especially for those who have beautiful siblings, studies like this remind their readers of the power of beauty.

The power of beauty is easily recognizable. It is why companies hire beautiful people to sell their products. The model's beauty causes the viewer to pay attention when they might not have otherwise. Beauty does

---

10. University of Alberta, "Researchers Show Parents."

not have to have an alluring face or physique to have power either. Beauty in nature, of music, or composition compels attention.

When gazing at the purple and pink tapestry of a summer sunset, beholding the Grand Canyon with mouth agape, or staring into the heavens on a cloudless night, it is easy to say something is beautiful. It would be a delusional denial of reality to describe any of these wonders as less than beautiful.

Describing something as beautiful and defining beauty itself are two different things, however. Artists like Albrecht Dürer and theologians like Thomas Aquinas have attempted to define beauty. Dürer tried to define beauty by seeking a mathematical basis and Aquinas attempted it by giving definitions. Both, however, were without success. Beauty defies definition. Perhaps the best way to describe beauty is that a beautiful object participates in the transcendental quality of beauty, and as much as it participates in that reality, it is beautiful.

Plotinus and the Christian thinkers who borrowed from his philosophy argued that beauty, truth, and goodness eventually were the same reality. If one comprehends the good, one sees beauty in it. If one can discern the truth, one sees it as beautiful. Beauty, then, would necessarily lead to truth.

The late British philosopher Roger Scruton disagrees. For Scruton, beauty is subversive. "Someone charmed by a myth may be tempted to believe it: and in this case beauty is the enemy of truth,"[11] he asserts. "Goodness and truth never compete, we assume, and the pursuit of the one is always compatible with a proper respect for the other. The pursuit of beauty, however, is far more questionable."[12]

While one might grant lies cover themselves in beauty and that wickedness might dawn a beautiful facade, that is a misuse of beauty and not beauty itself. These examples are of evil disguising itself in beauty. That disguise, however, is no more a condemnation of beauty than the Inquisition is of the incarnation.

Evil always disguises itself in light. That does not make it less dark. Further, even if evil disguises itself as beauty, it gets exposed, eventually. The beautiful prose of the Marxist writer can only temporarily cover for the Gulag. The beautiful rhetoric of the demagogue only conceals the will

11. Scruton, *Beauty*, 2.

12. Scruton, *Beauty*, 2–3.

for domination in part. Wagner concerts in Berlin can only cover for the camps when one is swept away in the music. Ugly eventually surfaces.

Why do demagogues and tyrants, sociopaths, and monsters use beauty? They use beauty much the same way they use truth. They use just enough of it to deceive. Once deception is complete, they do not need to continue its use.

It is for this reason, among others, that movies and other artistic expressions portray the good as beautiful and the evil as ugly. This observation is true in fine art and even pop movies. Dostoevsky's villains were usually monstrous in appearance. In the popular *Star Wars* saga, Princess Leia was beautiful and Jabba the Hut was a gelatinous, slime-covered slug. In old western movies, heroes wore white hats. In artistic representations, the darker and more unattractive one's dress usually means the more morally ambivalent a character is.

In reality, however, the world of artistic representation fails us. Heroes can be physically unappealing and monsters can be quite attractive. This observation is rather banal. It also does nothing to divorce beauty from truth and goodness. An attractive monster is no more than a person whose ugliness remains undiscovered. The monster is only using one of the transcendentals to convince his victims that he is good and truthful.

For Scruton, beauty can be the enemy of truth. This, however, is to focus on beauty's use, not beauty itself. Beauty, transcendent in its nature, mesmerizes the viewer as it participates in a truth beyond the medium. "The tenebrous canvases of Rembrandt are beautiful, while the shrill daubs of Thomas Kinkade, with all their sugary glitter, are repellant,"[13] writes David Bentley Hart. While one does not have to agree with Hart (and judging by Kinkade's sales figures, many do not), Hart points to a reality. What makes Rembrandt beautiful and Kinkade distasteful is not necessarily skill, but rather, Rembrandt's work participates in the transcendent in a way that Kinkade does not. Beauty is not in skill, or in use of color, or expertise in the medium. Beauty exists in connection to the transcendent.

Beauty calls its viewer beyond the world of sense experience. It "is also the startling reminder, even for persons sunk in the superstitions of materialism, that those who see reality in purely mechanistic terms do

---

13. Hart, *Experience of God*, 279.

not see the real world at all, but only its shadow."[14] No attempt to divorce beauty from truth and goodness can, therefore, be successful.

WHAT IS GOOD?

For the ancient Greeks, to know the good was to make the good the highest value of one's life. One who lived in unethical ways had a very simple problem: he or she did not understand the good.

The good, or goodness itself, is transcendent in the same way that beauty and truth are. Doing what is good is the practice of participating in the good. To construct the good life, the ancient Greeks argued, was to participate in the good habitually.

For them, habit is not something as trivial as which shoe one puts on first. By habits, they had in view the kind of moral formation by which one chooses the good by force of character. The great Protestant Reformer Martin Luther at the Diet of Worms was invited to recant his views. With the real possibility of death, Luther said, "Here I stand, I can do none other. God help me."[15] What made Luther able to resist the temptation to recant his views? His moral habits.

The signers of the Declaration of Independence had much the same habits. Pledging their "lives, fortunes, and sacred honor" in support of independence, they knew the British would try them for treason had the revolution failed. Their commitment to the good meant that they were willing to suffer for it.

Civil Rights leader Martin Luther King Jr. taught his listeners that even suffering could be part of the good. In his "I Have a Dream" speech, King said unmerited suffering is redemptive. If that is the case, such suffering is not to be avoided. While unpleasant and painful, unmerited suffering helps to bring about the redemption of society. While it is not something King stated directly, consistent with his thought is that unmerited suffering is redemptive in that it brings about a society more connected to the good. In this case, part of the good is the equality of every person before the law.

That kind of commitment to the good is a result of character formation. Doing what is good once gives one the power to do it again.

---

14. Hart, *Experience of God*, 284.

15. Luther, as quoted in Smith Jr., "'Here I Stand.'"

Eventually, the practice of doing the good transforms the character so that one does the good without having to think through it.

The Greeks were also insistent that doing the good yielded the good life. The good life was not a life of mindless pleasure pursuit. That kind of life could not even create happiness. Temporary pleasure is only as valuable as eating pie. It is tasty in the moment. Anything lasting beyond the moment the sensation from the taste buds ceases is a net negative. The good life was more. It was a life spent with the good as its aim and practice, a life of character. A life of wealth and comfort, if it was not connected to the good, was not the good life.

WHAT WOULD SOCRATES SAY ABOUT A CARJACKING?

In 2023, a rash of carjackings hit the residents of Washington, DC.[16] Not only did the number of carjackings spiral, but other crimes increased as well. Residents of DC were under siege as the city experienced one carjacking per day on average.

Carjacking is a particularly violent crime. The criminals find a car and wait for a victim to emerge. Once the victim approaches his or her car, the carjackers leap from their hiding spot. Often brandishing a gun, the carjackers will hold the gun to the victim's head and demand the keys.

Carjackers trade on terror. Holding a victim at gunpoint, often forcing them on the ground, forces compliance. The victim trades compliance for the hope of survival. As if the act of violence was not enough, carjackers often scream insults at their victims, taunting them. The destructive force of a carjacking is not limited to the event. Carjacking makes victims frightened and creates in them a terror that is not easy to deconstruct.

What would the Greeks say about such a thing? Those who commit a carjacking have exchanged the good for something else. For some it is the financial gain of stealing a car. Perhaps for others it is the status they gain among their peers for being successful in their dubious venture. It could be that some do it for the perverse thrill of it all.

For whatever reason, they have traded the good for something else. They have become the misbegotten children of a lesser good. Longing for what cannot satisfy, they steal and abuse. Trading character for irrational desire, they have malformed their character. They do not know the good.

16. Oberg et al., "MPD Carjacking Task Force."

Perhaps the more pressing question is, how is it possible for a city to have enough people in it to have a carjacking every day? One could argue the problem is a lack of police, although one would suspect the ancient Greeks would approach the problem differently.

They would presumably talk about education, though not in the sense of education in the US. They would talk about moral education. For the Greeks, education was not to teach a set of facts or skills for a well-educated job force. They would have thought the primary occupation of an educator was to teach the good. In other words, in a city full of carjackers, the ancient Greeks would have seen a collapse of moral education. They would ask, "How is it possible to have a society with so many who do not understand the good?"

TRANSCENDENTALS AND LIFE

Reconnecting to transcendental values would have the effect of lifting the spirit of the culture, reenergizing its institutions, creating shared expectations of individuals, lifting the self-esteem of individual persons, and reducing maladaptive behaviors.

The good, the true, and the beautiful, then, are not quaint values of a bygone era. They are essential aspects of any healthy society. If a society wants a good populace, forgetting the transcendental values that would create a good populace is an odd practice.

17

Where to Find Hope 2
Making Institutions Faithful and Flexible

FAITHFUL AND FLEXIBLE

ONE OF THE MOST pressing struggles institutions encounter is rigidity. They become fixed on their processes and cannot change to meet the changing climate. An institution that cannot change its processes without changing its goals is bound to regress.

If intelligence is the ability to adapt to change, then many institutions have an intelligence problem. More likely, however, the inability to adapt to change is not about intelligence but about emotional regulation.

Sears was a leader in catalog sales. Every year, Sears's Christmas catalogs inspired visions of sugarplums on Christmas Eve. Children would happily stare at the catalogs, circle their favorite items, and their parents would get a good look at what their children really wanted for Christmas. Sears was a colossus. From 1950–90, Sears was the leading retailer in the US.[1] As of 2024, Sears is practically gone.

The transition from catalog sales to Internet sales should have been seamless. They function much the same way. With catalog sales, a customer sees the item, orders it, and waits for delivery. Sometimes, the customer could pick up the item at a local store. Online sales simply move the catalog to a website and the payment from phone to online processing. All that would have been necessary was to invest fully in the

---

1. Thomas, "Sears Was the Amazon."

online ordering business. How was it possible that Amazon became the worldwide leader in online sales?

The problem was Sears's mindset. Not recognizing the declining value of their brand was problematic. While Sears's stores did carry competitive merchandise, the in-person store experience was not on par with their competitors, and because of the Internet, they were losing their competitive edge in convenience.[2] Customers stopped thinking of Sears as the venerable brand that had served them for over one hundred years and as a middling competitor with middling merchandise and a store experience that was not nearly as good as other retailers. The brand was dying.

Not recognizing the death of the brand and not being able to capitalize on the new digital market, Sears entered a death spiral. They made poor business decisions and merged with a dying retailer.

> In reality, Sears's failure to innovate was its failure to innovate its psychology. Much of Sears' woes over the last two decades can be traced to the company's indifference toward adopting the mindset of a modern, digitally driven enterprise, one that uses its considerable brand, resources, and massive supply chain in a leveraged way, as a differentiator to win and retain yet another generation of loyal customers.[3]

The lesson from Sears is important: in a time of rapid and accelerating change, institutions that cannot adapt to the new environment will certainly fail. It is Darwinian. The smartest, strongest, best-suited institutions are not the ones who succeed. The ones who succeed are the ones who can adapt to the changing environment. The ones who can adapt quickly to change have the best chance of survival.

While some institutions adapt to change slowly because of emotional resistance, other institutions are change-resistant by design. Some institutions' role in society is to preserve a way of life or a set of beliefs. Institutions whose role is preservation or those with similar roles cannot change quickly or adapt to changing situations quickly because that would be dangerous to their purpose.

The architects of the US Constitution deliberately made it very difficult to change. Amending it requires two-thirds of each House and three-fourths of the state legislatures. Since the passage of the Bill of Rights in 1791, there have only been seventeen amendments. The Constitution has

2. Davis, "How Sears Failed."
3. Keeports, "Blog: The Slow Burn."

a change process, but it is deliberately slow because the Constitution exists to define the relationship of the individual to the state and to protect the rights of the individual. Changing it without deep deliberation and slow processes could be dangerous to liberty.

Other institutions tasked with preservation change slowly as well. Churches change slowly by design. Governed by local congregational rules, *Robert's Rules of Order*, and denominational requirements, they resist sudden change because one task of the church is to preserve the faith. Of course this can be maddening when dealing with an emergent situation. Most congregations are ill-prepared to do that.

Society, however, is in a state of constant flux. In the last forty years, the change in society and societal norms accelerated with the force of a muscle car. Melting rubber as it breaks traction, society has reversed itself on a range of issues, leaving those unable to cope frustrated and bumfuzzled.

Over about forty years, society has reversed itself on gay marriage and has lost its negative posture toward premarital sex and cohabitation. Many states have legalized marijuana usage. Euthanasia has gained significant support and is now legal in several states. Most of these changes were unthinkable in the recent past.

Because society is changing and the pace of change is accelerating, institutions have to be able to change. Their change, however, is not a change in mission or of values. If institutions change their mission or values, they are devolving even if they are unaware. Eventually, changing values or their mission to change along with society will create institutions that die as sacrifices to the cult of relevancy. For institutions to survive, they have to be fast and flexible. They have to be able to sort through societal change while maintaining their values. The first step of this process is knowing and stating institutional values.

THE CURIOUS CASE OF CAMPBELL UNIVERSITY

Born in the aftermath of the conservative-moderate schism in Southern Baptist life, Campbell University Divinity School (CUDS) promised a theological education that was connected to a growing university in Eastern North Carolina. Immersed in Campbell's one-hundred-year history, CUDS catered to centrist Baptists in North Carolina. Those who wanted a much more conservative theological education could attend

Southeastern Baptist Theological Seminary or another one of the six major seminaries of the Southern Baptist Convention. Those who wanted a progressive theological education could pursue that at Duke Divinity or the now-closed Baptist Theological Seminary at Richmond.

On a muggy September day in the aftermath of Hurricane Fran, thirty-five students gathered at Memorial Baptist church in Buies Creek, North Carolina, for the initial convocation. The next year, CUDS declared its charter class with eighty-four students.[4]

The founding dean of Campbell University, Dr. Mike Cogdill, was a well-known and respected North Carolina Baptist leader. The associate dean, Dr. Bruce Powers, was a well-respected Christian educator whose books on church leadership and administration were quite influential.

CUDS's founding mission statement was easily remembered: "Christ-centered, Bible-based, ministry-focused." Students not only memorized it; they often accepted it as their personal mission statement. The mission statement was to preclude denominational drift and help CUDS to remain connected to its founding vision.

Something happened between 1996 and 2023, however. While there were some rumblings of a theological shift in the divinity school after Cogdill's retirement, most of those could be attributed to rumors, whispers fomenting suspicion. Yes, there were some professors more clearly aligned with the theological left, but the perception among the congregations CUDS served was that it was staying within the original parameters.

The Spring 2023 edition of *Campbell Magazine*, however, shocked many Campbell supporters and alumni. In it was a picture of a 2013 divinity graduate, who was an associate minister of a North Carolina Baptist church, on her wedding day.[5] The picture features her and her lesbian spouse leaving the church after exchanging their vows. Both dressed in white gowns, they held bouquets in their outside hands and clasped hands as they recessed from the renowned sanctuary.

Controversy erupted with the force of Mount St. Helens. Campbell tired to put down the controversy by maintaining it remain committed to its founding values. There is no sense that the founders of Campbell University would have accepted gay marriage, however. To suggest they would have been anything other than incensed is dishonest. The

---

4. Campbell University, "History."
5. Campbell University, "*Campbell Magazine*."

acquiescence to gay marriage betrayed by the image was a betrayal of
their values, not the implementation of them.

To suggest that taking a position on controversial issues is not the
role of an educational institution is also a nonstarter. Campbell takes
positions on controversial issues with regularity. For example, Campbell
University still has an alcohol policy forbidding its use in official university functions and on campus. According to the 2022–23 Student
Handbook:

> Main campus students are prohibited from possessing, consum-
> ing, or distributing alcoholic beverages on-campus or at any
> Campbell-sponsored event, which includes, but is not limited to
> academic, athletic, extracurricular, social, administrative, work-
> related by a university department, director, or group including
> travel that takes place off-campus and is sponsored by the uni-
> versity. Alcohol discovered in a common room or common space
> of an on-campus residential facility will result in all residents as-
> signed to that apartment/suite/hall being written up.[6]

To suggest that Campbell does not take a position on topics where
people of like faith could disagree is nonsense. Christians of all stripes
come to varied positions on alcohol usage. To ban its consumption at
university functions and in university housing is to take a position that
alcohol usage is unacceptable.

It is striking that Campbell would take no position on this controversial issue when CUDS is open in its support for women in ministry.
Few issues among CUDS's constituent congregations were more controversial at its founding than women pastors. From women in ministry
to alcohol usage, Campbell has taken positions on controversial issues,
continues to do so, and is right to do so.

More directly to Campbell's position on gay marriage, non-oppo-
sition is tacit support. If Campbell found gay marriage disqualifying, it
would say so. CUDS's tacit support for LGBTQ ministers became more
overt in February of 2024 when it invited the same minister whose nup-
tial pictures were published in the magazine to preach in the divinity
school chapel. The minister, now a Doctor of Ministry student at CUDS,
was the first openly gay student to preach in the chapel and celebrated
that fact on social media.

6. Office of Student Life and Christian Mission, "Undergraduate Student Handbook," 30.

Preaching in a divinity school chapel at CUDS is an opportunity not given to every student or graduate. It is an honor. It is also a statement of the core values of the institution. Who gets to speak from the pulpit is a statement of what is acceptable in the pulpit. CUDS leaders would disagree, but there is no sense in which CUDS is not a fully affirming LG-BTQ seminary. If a student gains acceptance to the divinity school with the knowledge of her sexuality, has the support of her professors, gets to speak at a divinity school chapel service, and presumably gets scholarships, then there is no lack of affirmation. CUDS is then an LGBTQ-affirming divinity school, if only tacitly.

In the fall of 1996, an LGBTQ minister speaking in the divinity school chapel service would have been seen as anathema. CUDS's early critics accused CUDS of enabling "denominational drift," the process by which orthodox institutions often morph into progressive institutions. Now with LGBTQ acceptance in divinity school, their accusations seem prescient.

Surprising in this episode is the unwillingness of CUDS leaders or leaders of Campbell as a whole to articulate a position. Failure to take a position is a failure of self-definition and creates anxiety.

Campbell's leaders could have said, "While we honor all of our students, we affirm biblical statements on sexuality." Conversely, they could have said, "We affirm LGBTQ inclusion in ministerial roles." They did not have the courage to take either position. They live, however, in tacit acceptance.

Tacit positions are the refuge of the fainthearted, the liquid courage of the spinally challenged. They allow an institution to act in a way contrary to their stated values while having access to their stated values to protect themselves in a pinch. Tacit positions allow the institution to say, "We are committed to those same values" when it is obvious it is not.

A leader who creates such systems is usually, in the words of the late Edwin Friedman,

> a highly anxious risk-avoider, someone who is more concerned with good feelings than with progress, someone whose life revolves around the axis of consensus, a "middler," someone who is so incapable of taking well-defined stands that his "disability" seems to be genetic, someone who treats conflict or anxiety like mustard gas—one whiff, on goes the emotional gas mask, and he flits.[7]

7. Friedman, *Failure of Nerve*, 13–14.

INSTITUTIONAL MISSION

Successful institutions are not those without challenges, for none of those exist. Successful institutions are those that can remain faithful to the mission while adapting to their changing environment. They are led by people who commit to the mission and articulate it well.

The mission of the institution functions much like self-differentiation in a person. When an individual is well self-differentiated, he or she knows and respects the personal boundaries of others. They do not impose their views on others and are content to allow others to think differently. They are also unwilling to have others impose their views on them.

Self-differentiated people are content to allow others to experience their own pain without attempts to mask it. Self-differentiated people can tolerate the pain of others and thereby increase the other's ability to tolerate it.[8] Poorly defined people rush in to soothe another's pain, preventing their growth. In a society controlled by anxiety and an overemphasized sense of empathy,[9] self-differentiated persons are difficult to find. Frightened by confrontation and painful emotional states, most leaders want to soothe. Well-differentiated people know that the quicker they are to alleviate others' pain, the less real change they can bring to the system.[10]

Self-differentiation is the ability to define the self and remain in contact with others. It requires taking responsibility for the self and being responsive to others. Equally as difficult, self-differentiation requires maintaining one's integrity and wellbeing without violating others' boundaries. Self-differentiated people are not saddened by the growth of others and can allow that without feeling a sense of loss. Perhaps the most difficult skill to master that self-differentiated people posses is the ability to have a personal relationship with another without losing their sense of self.[11]

What well-differentiated people have is deep self-knowledge. They know what they believe and why, and they can articulate those beliefs under duress. Never quick to stand down, they have courage born of an unwillingness to violate their values.

These same skills are necessary for healthy institutions. Without them, institutions trample on the boundaries of other institutions or

8. Friedman, *Generation to Generation*, 47.

9. Friedman, *Failure of Nerve*, 132.

10. Friedman, *Generation to Generation*, 236–37.

11. Steinke, *How Your Church Family Works*, 11.

people. They can lose sight of their mission and responsibilities without these skills.

One way to measure differentiation in an institution and a person is by noting the level of gossip: the more gossip, the less differentiation. Those who gossip are usually triangulating. In family systems theory, triangulation is the art of dealing with personal discomfort by bringing another person into the relationship. Triangulation puts another person in the middle of the emotional discomfort to manage the anxiety.

With institutions, the presence of gossip at a large scale is evidence of emotional dysregulation:

> Gossip in the work system is a good barometer of emotional reactivity in the system. A person is either part of that process or defines himself as outside that process. One reason such self-definition is important is that it takes energy to participate in the gossip, energy that is not available for productive work.[12]

More than that, gossip demonstrates who is not regulated emotionally and how much the institution tolerates it. An institution whose members are caught up in gossip and office politics does not have the self-differentiation or emotional stability necessary to remain effective. It is a destructive cultural norm where tolerated.

THE CULTURE OF AN INSTITUTION

When people create institutions, necessarily an institutional character develops. Institutional culture is hard to notice from the inside as many of the parts of the culture are subconscious and often not even articulated.[13] The institution's culture, however, is powerful. It shapes behaviors by censure and blessing. Culture can make an institution resistant to leadership or inviting of leadership. Institutional culture contains:

1. The observed behavioral norms of the group.

2. The dominant attitudes of the group.

3. The processes of the group.

4. The climate of the group.[14]

12. Wiseman, "Emotional Process in Organizations," loc. 704.

13. Stevens and Collins, *Equipping Pastor*, 48.

14. Stevens and Collins, *Equipping Pastor*, 48.

If an institution's culture expects self-differentiated functioning, it will not tolerate poorly differentiated leadership or toxic behaviors from its members. Gossip, for example, would get to the point that it is a minor problem because participants formed by the culture would not willingly participate and shun those who did. Most other inappropriate behaviors would get quashed without a word because they are outside the norm.

Poorly differentiated institutions, however, function like poorly differentiated people. They have no boundaries and need to regulate anxiety. It is the inability to regulate anxiety that is the root of most toxic work behaviors.

MISSION CREEP

Mission creep is a temptation for all institutions. Mission creep is similar but distinct from ideological repurposing. In ideological repurposing, leaders transform institutions from their organizing principles to work toward revamping society or toward another ideological end. Most of this repurposing comes in the form of leftward ideologues using an institution for a political end, although that does happen in reverse. The conservative mindset is to protect institutions from harm, so repurposing them does not happen as often, and when it does, it is often more subtle.

Mission creep is different. Mission creep is the steady drift of an institution to becoming what its founders never intended it to be. This often happens when religious organizations get involved in partisan politics or when partisans gain control over religious institutions. Eventually, the religion of the institution gets squeezed out and only the politics remain. It is not so much an ideological repurposing but a loss of the particular mission of the institution.

Not only are educational institutions vulnerable to mission creep, but nonprofit institutions are vulnerable as well. In 1967, in the aftermath of the Detroit riots, William Cunningham and Eleanor Josaitis started Focus: HOPE. The organization began in an effort to combat racism, poverty, and injustice. Their focus was social services and job training. Quite successful in its mission, Focus: HOPE employed two hundred people and had a budget of $30 million by 2020.[15]

In the fifty years of its existence, however, Focus: HOPE had become a very large venture with extensive activities beyond its initial mission.

15. Rosenthal, "Mission Creep."

By the 1980s, it had expanded its anti-poverty initiatives into educational and training institutes. In the early 2000s, it started real estate acquisitions for community redevelopment.[16]

Mission creep was not the result of outside influences or repurposing. Focus: HOPE saw needs in their community and expanded their programming to meet those needs. While each step along the way was well-intended and often led to positive results, they pulled further resources away from the primary mission and could have overwhelmed it.

What the board of directors at Focus: HOPE noticed was some of the pitfalls of mission creep. It can cause an organization to experience financial stress. Additional activities require additional staffing, and additional staffing requires additional funding. Additional activities also require additional oversight.[17]

All of these additions have the potential to reduce the quality of the services the organization already provides. A slip in quality can lead to angry disappointed donors, and disappointed donors may give less to the organization. Reduced quality can affect funding.[18]

Taking on activities outside the mission also adds layers of complexity.[19] Suddenly, those who were well-qualified to lead in the previous works of the organization do not have the requisite expertise to lead. A person who has expertise in guiding work-training programs may not have any experience, much less expertise, in housing acquisition.

By 2018, Focus: HOPE's programming was very broad. Its financial statement showed "the result of a long-standing, carefully-thought-out, and well-meaning expansion. It also shows a classic example of mission creep."[20]

Mission creep can be seen in the Worldwide Anti-Doping Agency, even affecting its legitimacy.[21] Mission creep has been found in military operations, corporate ventures, centralized banking,[22] the Department of Homeland Security,[23] and countless other organizations. Mission creep occurs every time an institution fails to keep its mission central in its activities.

16. Rosenthal, "Mission Creep."
17. Rosenthal, "Mission Creep."
18. Rosenthal, "Mission Creep."
19. Rosenthal, "Mission Creep."
20. Rosenthal, "Mission Creep."
21. Read et al., "Balancing Mission Creep."
22. Webb, "Central Banks."
23. Shelley, "Mission Creep."

LOSS OF FOUNDING VISION

Often due to mission creep, institutions can lose their founding vision. In *The Death of Expertise*, Tom Nichols bemoans the change in the attitude of students to their educational institutions. Students are now clients. Losing their mission as institutions of higher learning, colleges "are now marketed like multiyear vacation packages, rather than a contract with an institution and its faculty for a course of educational study."[24] Nichols continues: "Younger people barely out of high school are pandered to both materially and intellectually, reinforcing some of the worst tendencies in students who have not learned the self-discipline that once was essential to the pursuit of higher education."[25]

Imagine a scenario where the student body is a clientele. When a client skips class all semester and does not do the work, the school might ask its instructors to fill out his withdrawal paperwork for him in order to prevent him from getting the F he earned. Not even expecting the minimum of responsibility, the student does not even have to fill out the paperwork to be dropped from the class. The institution expects the instructors to coddle him and prevent him from getting the consequences he has earned. This prevention does the student no good. It does not teach him there are consequences for bad behavior or that there are successes to be had with hard work. It only softens the blow. It keeps the client coming back. It makes the client happy. The job of any representative of a company with clients is to keep the client happy. Keeping the client happy, however, is anathema to an educational process.

Education is not supposed to be easy, and it is supposed to force students to face uncomfortable ideas and uncomfortable realities. When education becomes client-driven, it does actual harm to the students, to the institution, and to the educational process itself. "Unearned praise and hollow successes build a fragile arrogance in students."[26] University officials get swamped with students who need client services,[27] and professors lose any sense of authority or expertise.[28]

The mission creep was simple. At first, it was to protect students from stressors that could cause them psychological harm. The process

24. Nichols, *Death of Expertise*, 72–73.
25. Nichols, *Death of Expertise*, 72.
26. Nichols, *Death of Expertise*, 84.
27. Nichols, *Death of Expertise*, 84.
28. Nichols, *Death of Expertise*, 86.

continued, however. Students were now the center of the educational enterprise rather than the content of the education. Universities bloated both their staffs and budgets with nonteaching staff whose focus was student experience. Managing the psychological wellbeing of students became a high priority. Finally, with the enrollment cliff, students became prized commodities. "What would we treat students like if we thought of them as our customers?," an administrator might ask.

This is not to suggest that caring for the wellbeing of students is unimportant. It is to state that caring for their wellbeing should include faithfulness to the educational endeavor and the institution's mission. Sometimes, the long-term wellbeing of a student is compromised by protecting them from short-term consequences.

Failure to adhere to the mission and values of the institution inevitably leads to regression. If regression is the devolving of an institution, then losing sight of the mission is act one of the production.

THE INVERSION

When the founding vision is lost, organizations often experience what social theorists call a "means-ends" inversion. A means-ends inversion is when the institution becomes more committed to its processes than to its mission. Often completely losing sight of its mission, institutions can become entranced with their processes.

Congregations are often the worst offenders with means-ends inversions. For example, many congregations will continue programs long after they have ceased to be effective. Rather than dismantling the programs and starting new ones directed at the same goals, congregations will spend human and financial resources trying to rehabilitate them. What the congregation needs to do is evaluate their programs in light of the mission. "Is this program helping us to achieve our mission?" is the most pertinent question.

HOW TO REFOCUS

The mission of an institution is its organizing power. Focus on the mission can prevent mission creep, but it can also redirect the organization when it has lost its way.

Focus: HOPE came to a realization. Their success as an organization was imperiled by the many activities they were supporting. The board of directors recognized the issue and refocused on the organization's mission statement. They spun off their community redevelopment work into a new 501(c)(3) organization. The new organization not only could do the work better under its own power, it allowed Focus: HOPE to refocus its energies on its core mission.[29]

SPEED

In 1993, Rudy Giuliani won the election to serve as New York City's mayor, promising to bring down crime. As a former prosecutor of organized crime, Giuliani had significant credibility on the issue. Between 1989 and 1993, New York City residents experienced 9,000–10,000 felonies per year. Worse, there were between 1,800 and 2,000 murders per year.[30]

Writing about the pre-Giuliani era, Senior Fellow at the Manhattan Institute George L. Kelling writes:

> New York City was racked with crime: murders, burglaries, drug deals, car thefts, thefts from cars. . . . Unlike many cities' crime problems, New York's were not limited to a few inner-city neighborhoods that could be avoided. Bryant Park, in the heart of midtown and adjacent to the New York Public Library, was an open-air drug market; Grand Central Terminal, a gigantic flophouse; the Port Authority Bus Terminal, "a grim gauntlet for bus passengers dodging beggars, drunks, thieves, and destitute drug addicts," as the New York Times put it in 1992.[31]

The drop in the crime rate was historic. By 1994, the murder rate fell by 17.9 percent and robbery fell by 15.5 percent. Crime continued to plunge. From 1993 to 1996, rapes decreased by 17 percent and murders fell by 49 percent.[32] By 2010, violent crime dropped 75 percent from its peak in the early '90s.[33]

Because of his involvement with Donald Trump and the 2020 election aftermath, it is not fashionable to speak of Giuliani with praise. It

29. Rosenthal, "Mission Creep."
30. Giuliani and Kurson, *Leadership*, 71.
31. Kelling, "How New York Became Safe."
32. Drum, "America's Real Criminal Element."
33. Drum, "America's Real Criminal Element."

takes a while searching through articles before one can find a full description of his successes. Before 2020, however, his reputation was quite solid.

Despite conspiracy theories and unfortunate accusations, Giuliani did something quite remarkable. He made New York City safe. What he attributes the success to is CompStat. CompStat combined two techniques. It collected crime data and created indicators to measure if the NYPD was meeting its goals.[34]

CompStat began having meetings twice per week. These meetings brought accountability to law enforcement officials. Officials knew that they would have to stand before their peers and give an account of their performance, encouraging them to improve. The meetings also served as sessions where police could share information and methods.[35] With more information at their disposal and with shared learning, police were able to shift from reacting to crime to preventing crime. The police were smarter and faster.

For most institutions, change is anathema, and Giuliani's work in New York City suffered significant opposition. In response to New York City's crime epidemic, it would have been tempting to give up. When institutions believe they cannot affect reality, they become content to endure it. Endurance, however, does not help. It only leaves a broken institution and the public scrambling to figure out what to do in its place. Struggling institutions also face the temptation to study the situation into oblivion. Taking difficult actions can be buried under mounds of reports. Change awaits until enough information has been gathered. Information, however, is no replacement for change. Studying a problem infinitely will not create a new vision, and it will not create success. It will only multiply committees. Struggling institutions often create new institutions to do their work. Giuliani could have created a new law enforcement team bypassing the existing structure. If he had, the existing structure would have actively fought against him and any reform he attempted. Endless turf wars would have emerged. The genius of CompStat was that it employed the existing structure and gave it the resources to create change. New York City's police were suddenly fast and flexible. As a result, they were successful.

34. Giuliani and Kurson, *Leadership*, 72–73.
35. Giuliani and Kurson, *Leadership*, 76–77.

18

Where to Find Hope 3
Ethical Renewal

We are what we repeatedly do.

—ARISTOTLE

THE ROLE OF EDUCATION IN ETHICAL RENEWAL

EDUCATION IS ONE OF the most powerful tools humans posses. With education, one can liberate generations from poverty, expand the mind to novel and challenging ideals, understand the mysteries of the cosmos and the caterpillar, learn to harness the power of critical thinking, and develop a passion for beauty.

A weekend venture to a college campus in mid-fall is enough to convince many that education is the solution to all of man's ills. Strolling into the library and looking at the myriads of tomes, one can easily ascribe Godlike powers to the enterprise. The smell of the library and the wonderful cacophony of voices in lecture halls are powerful sensations. Education is, however, limited. It can only teach; it cannot transform. No, transforming the human psyche is in the realm of God.

The enterprise, however, can help in society's current sickness if tooled correctly. A significant step society could take toward the renewal of its institutions is a renewal of individual virtue. Since scandals are one

of the chief enemies of our institutions, renewing them will require a renewal of character. Renewal of character will, however, require a change
in ethics education.

In his venerable text *After Virtue*, ethicist Alasdair MacIntyre writes:

> Imagine that the natural sciences were to suffer the effects of
> a catastrophe. A series of environmental disasters are blamed
> by the general public on the scientists. Widespread riots oc-
> cur, laboratories are burnt down, physicists are lynched, books
> and instruments are destroyed. Finally, a Know-Nothing po-
> litical movement takes power and successfully abolishes science
> teaching in schools and universities, imprisoning and executing
> the remaining scientists. Later still there is a reaction against
> this destructive movement and enlightened people seek to re-
> ceive science, although they have largely forgotten what it was.
> But all they possess are fragments: a knowledge of experiments
> detached from any knowledge of the theoretical context which
> gave them significance. . . . Nonetheless, all these fragments are
> reembodied in a set of practices which go under the revived
> names of physics, chemistry, and biology.[1]
>
> In such a culture men would use expressions such as "neu-
> trino," "mass," "specific gravity," "atomic gravity" in systematic
> and often interrelated ways which would resemble in lesser or
> greater degrees the ways in which such expressions had been
> used in earlier times before scientific knowledge had been so
> largely lost.
>
> The hypothesis I want to advance is that in the actual
> world which we inhabit the language of morality is in the same
> state of grave disorder as the language of natural science in the
> imaginary world which I described.[2]

ETHICS EDUCATION

If MacIntyre is right, the teaching of ethics as a subject matter is part of
the problem. That observation is likely to draw guffaws and moans from
university and college administrators who insist on ethics as a part of the
curriculum for nearly every discipline. The state of ethics as MacIntyre
describes is evidence that the current structure of teaching ethics is as
effective as attacking a tiger with a marshmallow gun.

1. MacIntyre, *After Virtue*, 1.
2. MacIntyre, *After Virtue*, 3.

Part of the problem is that the study of ethics is, invariably, a study of ethical systems. In a typical sixteen-week semester on ethics, college students learn about Kant and deontological ethics, feminist ethics, religious ethics, ethics of the New Atheist movement, utilitarian ethics, environmental ethics, Karl Marx, Adam Smith, Plato, Aristotle, Darwin, Huxley, and many others.

By the end of that semester, students may have a good grasp of what each ethicist taught and a good grasp of multiple ethical systems. What they cannot have gained is the character needed to be ethical persons. It takes longer than sixteen weeks to forge character. More importantly, ethics are about habits, and ethical habits cannot be gained by reading dusty tomes of philosophical scholarship. Even if it were possible, educators do not design courses on ethics to create ethical people: they design the courses so the student can understand ethics in an academic sense.

Students who have success in ethics classes may easily recount the differences between Kant and Mill and may readily write two-thousand-word essays on capital punishment, but that is not indicative of them becoming ethical persons. Without significant character training, students are left to themselves to discern what is right and wrong based on their critical reasoning skills and their preferences among the various ethical systems. Of course, this cannot work. If anything, knowledge of a diversity of ethical systems and their divergent viewpoints on many ethical issues permits students to find an ethical system that allows them to do what they are already inclined to do on a case-by-case basis. If their favored ethical system proscribes a behavior they want to participate in, they only need to think of another system and adopt it for the issue.

ETHICS IN THE IVY LEAGUE

In an article that seems almost quaint by contemporary standards, Robert Coles of Harvard recounts a narrative about a young woman who was attending Harvard and was having great difficulty enduring the abuse of her classmates. He writes:

> A few years ago, a sophomore student of mine came to see me in great anguish. She had arrived at Harvard from a Midwestern, working-class background. She was trying hard to work her way through college, and, in doing so, cleaned the rooms of some of her fellow students. Again and again, she encountered classmates who apparently had forgotten the meaning of *please*,

of *thank you*—no matter how high their Scholastic Assessment Test scores—students did not hesitate to be rude, even crude toward her.

One day she was not so subtly propositioned by a young man she knew to be a very bright, successful pre-med student and already an accomplished journalist. This was not the first time he had made such an overture, but now she had reached a breaking point. She had quit her job and was preparing to quit college.

At one point she observed of the student who had propositioned her: "That guy gets all A's. He tells people he's in Group 1 (the top academic category). I've taken two moral-reasoning courses with him, and I'm sure he's gotten A's in both of them—and look at how he behaves with me, and I'm sure with others."

"I've been taking all these philosophy courses, and we talk about what's true, what's important, what's *good*. Well, how do you teach people to *be* good? What's the point of *knowing* good if you don't keep trying to become a good person?"[3]

From his perspective, Coles stated the obvious: colleges do not take responsibility for the moral values of their students. Flummoxed at her resulting anger, Coles tried to explain that there is only so much anyone can do to affect the behavior of others. The question naturally arises, "Who, exactly, takes responsibility for the teaching of morals?"

Stating the problem with higher education well, Dallas Willard, the late Christian philosopher at the University of Southern California, writes:

> There is now not a single moral conclusion about behavior or character traits that a teacher could base a student's grade on— not even those most dear to educators, concerning fairness and diversity. If you lowered a student's grade just for saying on a test that discrimination is morally acceptable, for example, the student could contest that grade to the administration. And if that position on the moral acceptability of discrimination were the only point at issue, the student would win.[4]

The field of ethics, at least the academic study of ethics, is no longer about forming character, as it was among the ancient Greeks. It is now about imparting information, and the results are predictable.

---

3. Coles, "Disparity Between Intellect and Character." Emphasis original.

4. Willard, *Divine Conspiracy*, 3.

ETHICS IN SHAMBLES

Part of the evidence MacIntyre uses for his claim that the field of ethics is in shambles is the inconclusive nature of the debate about morals. Moral debates, MacIntyre argues, are interminable with no rational way of concluding them.[5] Society has no way of resolving moral disputes.

Of course, many moral debates end up in the Supreme Court for that very reason. Supreme Court decisions, however, are not final because they are correct. They are correct because they are final. Moral debates in the country might rage for generations even after the Court has rendered a verdict. The abortion debate was not decided by Roe and has not been settled by Dobbs.

Conservative political theorists once believed that Roe was controversial because, in part, the court made the decision, not the political process. It is hard to imagine, however, any political process that would conclude a divisive issue such as abortion in a way where the losing side would simply accept defeat. In the gay marriage debate, many states voted to ban the practice. That ban, however, did not settle the debate, nor for that matter did the Obergefell decision. While the debate has quieted, vast swaths of the public disagree with the Court passionately. They are quiet, but a quiet public is not tantamount to agreement on the issue.

The problem MacIntyre observes is that there is now no rational criteria for securing rational agreement on moral issues in society. The Enlightenment project of a source of knowledge available to every person regardless of external characteristics, knowable through reason, and binding on all persons failed. Its project of moving logically from rationality to a binding system of ethics also failed. The Enlightenment project could not have succeeded in principle.

In its place, however, came the revolution of emotivism, MacIntyre argues. In emotivism, all ethical perspectives are only judgments about preference.[6] Emotivism not only makes all perspectives about feeling and renders them unsolvable, it also makes the debates harsher.

Here is an important connection between MacIntyre and Edwin Friedman. Whatever their other differences, they share the argument that emotionality is harming society. MacIntryre argues it prevents solving ethical disputes. Friedman argues it prevents leadership. MacIntyre argues it makes arguments harsher. Freidman argues the shrill nature of

---

5. MacIntyre, *After Virtue*, 6.

6. MacIntyre, *After Virtue*, 11–12.

arguments is an example of emotional immaturity where people cannot imagine another person having a position differing from theirs. Shrill arguments and emotional intensity are manipulation tactics for him. For MacIntyre, these tactics work by bludgeoning people into agreement or silence. For Friedman, they work by enforcing the herd's norms on the individual.

In the wake of the death of Enlightenment ethics, Jeremy Bentham proposed utilitarianism. Utilitarianism advances a new purpose for human life. Life is no longer spent developing virtue in search of the good; life is the process of maximizing pleasure and minimizing pain. Utilitarianism had some noteworthy flaws, though, and John Stewart Mill refined the theory to account for higher and lower pleasures. As MacIntyre observes, though, happiness varies from person to person. There is not one single happiness with multiple avenues to achieve it.[7] If happiness is that subjective, then the process of creating it cannot be an end. Utilitarianism, then, has an Achilles's heel.

PETER SINGER

If MacIntyre is correct about the collapse of ethics, then one would note a collapse of ethical behaviors among ethical theorists and leaders working on ethical issues. Peter Singer is, perhaps, the most well-known living ethicist. From his perch in utilitarianism, Singer knows the field of ethics and is steeped in multiple branches of it. Despite his great knowledge of the field, Peter Singer has an ethical problem.

In a lawsuit against Singer, Karen Dawn accused Singer of using his power and prestige to lure her and other women into sexual relationships with him. In 2002, all of the women with whom Singer worked had either been in a sexual relationship with him or were those with whom he wanted a sexual relationship. Dawn believed that there would be rewards for maintaining a sexual relationship with Singer. So, despite her reservations, she maintained one. Singer's threat and reward system helped him procure a relationship with Dawn.[8]

In 2002, while working on an article for the Los Angeles Times, Dawn agreed to be part of Singer's "harem" as long as she was the favorite. At that time, Dawn was considering having a child with her partner.

7. Sweeden, "Review of *After Virtue*."
8. Trellis Law, "Motion-Secondary."

Singer, however, reminded her of the negative effects on her appearance and that it would negatively affect their affair. She, therefore, choose to delay motherhood.[9]

In 2003, Singer informed Dawn that while he still wanted her to be in his "harem," a new, younger woman had gained his attention. The woman was married, and Singer knew of the risk to the woman's marriage. As a result of being displaced, Dawn had cosmetic surgery to look younger than her forty-one years. There were complications with the surgery and Dawn was sick for weeks. Finally, Dawn shared the news of her affair with her partner of four years. They delayed their planned wedding. In light of the damage the affair caused, they ended their relationship.[10]

In her blog, Dawn states that Singer slept with thirty women in the animal rights movement.[11] With what Dawn shared in court, it is most likely the case that Singer has used his position and the power of publicizing work to gain favors. Of course, with Singer's belief in polyamorous relationships as the more rational way to relate, having multiple partners is unsurprising.[12] Having as many partners as he had, however, is a shock to the senses.

What also is surprising is that a person renowned for his ethical thinking would abuse his prestige and power in the most unethical ways. Simply put, there is no ethical way to exchange academic favors for sexual favors. The exchange breaks the link between sexuality, personhood, and affection. In Singer's case, sexuality was simply an exchange disconnected from any final end. His end was his pleasure, and harm followed him. Even if he did not harm members of his "harem," a dubious proposition, other deserving women did not get the benefit of his support because they were unwilling to sleep with him. They were harmed because of his pleasure-seeking and their virtue.

FRANCESCA GINO

Until the fall of 2021, Harvard professor Francesca Gino had an outsized reputation for her academic work. She was a bestselling author and was honored as one of the top forty professors under forty and as one of the

9. Trellis Law, "Motion-Secondary."
10. Trellis Law, "Motion-Secondary."
11. Dawn, "Peter Singer."
12. Alter, "Effective Altruism."

fifty most influential management thinkers.[13] Her most important work was her study of dishonesty.[14]

Four of Gino's papers have come under scrutiny, each of them showing signs of data manipulation.[15] While Gino denies the charges, Harvard completed an investigation resulting in a 1,300-page report. Although the investigators could not prove Gino was the source of it, they concluded there was manipulation of data in her work. Gino argued that someone else must have manipulated the data. She was innocent. In short, Gino claims she was framed.[16] Her claims are quite implausible as it would have required someone with extensive access to her work over several years. It would have also required someone to know the various security measures she employed over time. In short, the idea someone else manipulated her data is as plausible as O. J. Simpson's claim that someone else was the "real killer." Her claim should not be taken seriously.

What both Gino's and Singer's actions demonstrate is that knowledge of ethics does not necessarily yield ethical behavior. Singer's knowledge of ethics is formidable. Gino researched honesty and dishonesty. Neither of them behaved ethically.

Of course, they are not alone in their misdeeds. Many noteworthy thinkers before them have behaved in unethical ways. Karl Barth, perhaps the greatest theologian of the twentieth century, had a long-running affair with Charlotte von Kirschbaum, his assistant. Despite being warned by his friends and the damage his affair was doing to his wife and children, Barth persisted. He even eventually moved Kirschbaum into the family home. The recent discovery of their correspondence shows his awareness of the pain their affair was causing. Kirschbaum should not be absolved either. She was not an intellectual lightweight, a victim of Barth's prowess. She was a key contributor to Barth's theology, helping compose much of Barth's mammoth *Church Dogmatics*. She was party to this affair. She knew Barth was a married man. She also knew the damage they were doing to his family and his children. She persisted as well.

Misdeeds among academics and ethicists who know better continue apace. Google has fired two AI ethics researchers after violating company

---

13. Gino, "About."

14. Kim, "Harvard Professor Who Studies Dishonesty Is Accused of Falsifying Data."

15. Piper, "Francesca Gino Lawsuit."

16. Piper, "Francesca Gino Lawsuit."

ethics standards.[17] The State University of New York at Fredonia fired Stephen Kershnar for presenting arguments for adult-minor relationships—pedophilia—in two philosophy podcasts.[18]

Criminology Professor at Florida State University (FSU) Eric Stewart stands accused of falsifying data to make whites look more racist, specifically arguing that whites want longer sentences for crimes by blacks or Latinos.[19] Further, Stewart was on FSU's Academic Honor Policy Hearing Committee.[20] Louisiana State University fired professor David Sobeck under allegations he had an affair with a student and got her help to research the use of critical race theory among his peers, even using her to gain information on his estranged wife's scholarship at FSU.[21]

Of course, one could argue that these examples are a small number of incidents not indicative of the behavior of large swaths of ethics professors, professors researching ethical issues, or academia in general. Perhaps true, but it could also be true that their behavior is a direct outgrowth of the absence of training in virtue. Training in ethics tends to be based on information. *There is, however, no informational fix for a behavioral problem.* If the absence of virtue training has left professors without ethical restraint, why would students of ethics be any different?

Instead of teaching college students a series of systems and theories about ethics, society would be better served by instilling character at an early age. One way of looking at it is by comparison to educational systems, community groups, and others that teach young people the value of liberty. The concept comes up early in development and students internalize it well.

It would be odd to find a young person who did not believe in the right to self-determination, human freedom, or democracy. There are some examples of those who do not, but they are the minority. Society does not flinch from teaching this value, and it is effective at doing so.

In a recent ethics class I was teaching, we were discussing Augustine's just war theory. Augustine famously argues, among other concepts, that a just war requires a reasonable chance of success. In comparing Augustine's thought to the events in Ukraine, I asked, "Aren't there things worth fighting for until the last man?" Without hesitation, one of my

17. Schiffer, "Google Fires."
18. Blake, "SUNY Fredonia Fights."
19. *Daily Mail*, "Florida State University."
20. Schlott, "Professor Fired."
21. Quinn, "Fired LSU Professor."

students replied, "Freedom." That is a classic American answer. Raised on Nathan Hale's "My only regret is that I have but one life to lose for my country" and Patrick Henry's "Give me liberty or give me death," the student had internalized the values of the American Revolution. Life is not as dear as liberty.

Society reinforces that sentiment at every opportunity. From William Wallace's cry of "They may take our lives, but they will never take our freedom" in *Braveheart*, to the film *The Patriot*, to the postmodern patriotism expressed in Lin Manuel-Miranda's portrayal of Alexander Hamilton and George Washington in his Tony Award-winning *Hamilton*, the values of freedom, democracy, liberty, and self-determination are commonly expressed and given credence in our culture.

Even movies that question government and the military appeal to liberty and self-determination as the core of the plot. In Tom Cruise's *A Few Good Men*, it is not the ideals of liberty and the cost of those ideals that are on trial. Rather, it is the abuse of an individual in support of those ideals that is on trial. The message of the film is that even in protecting the liberty of the whole, the rights of an individual should not be abused.

For most freshmen college students, liberty is a core value worth protecting at all costs. If society can inculcate the value of human liberty, which itself is based on the concept of the value of every human life, then surely it can teach the virtues necessary for human flourishing. If society desires people of character, it would do well to start teaching character early and with repeated exposure to the idea.

ETHICS AND THE ANCIENT GREEKS

For the ancient Greeks, ethics were the way to have the good life, *eudaimonia*, they called it. In their system of ethics, one was to be instructed in the good. While the concept of the good can be a bit nebulous, the Greeks believed if one knew the good, one would make it the goal of life. To know the good was to make it the goal and focus of existence. Meaning in life is found only in connection with knowing the good.

Robin DiAngelo's work *White Fragility* was a seminal work in anti-racism in the US. In it, DiAngelo argues that conversations about race in the US are made much more difficult because whites are defensive, particularly when they are implicated in white supremacy.[22] Her book became a number-one bestseller, selling 1.6 million copies.[23]

It has come to light that parts of *White Fragility* were apparently plagiarized. Worse, it appears DiAngelo plagiarized two minority professors.[24] Why would DiAngelo plagiarize other authors? Since her plagiarism appears in her dissertation, completing her course of work could be her motivation. In using plagiarized work in her bestselling book, DiAngelo might have been trying to bolster her own reputation as a scholar. Whatever her motivation, though, it was not motivated by the good.

One motivated by the good would not trade in deliberate deception because truth is part of the good. It is the case that people make mistakes, and one should tread carefully about authors and their work. Sometimes well-meaning authors do make mistakes. Academics would refer to these mistakes as sloppy work. Even there, though, one motivated by the good would pursue excellence in her work and would be very unlikely to plagiarize someone else's ideas.

Often those who fail to do the good are motivated by pleasure. While pleasure is an important part of the good life, it is not the good itself. Confusing pleasure with the good makes someone the slave of pleasure. Pleasure, it must be said, comes to an end. All pleasures work themselves toward boredom. Having the same pleasure repeatedly only leads to it becoming common. If pleasure is the highest good, then it must be chased, but catching it only leads to diminishing returns.

In the original *Game of Thrones*, the Bible recounts the sad narrative of Israel's third king, Solomon. He was, Scripture teaches, incredibly wise. Arising to the throne after the reign of his legendary father David, Solomon naturally trembled at the responsibility before him. God provided wisdom. In his wisdom, Solomon was able to lead Israel to the highest point of prosperity and safety in this tiny nation's history. This success came at great cost, however. The once-enslaved people whom God liberated from the murderous clutches of Pharaoh now practiced slavery themselves. Further, to secure political alliances with neighboring nation-states, Solomon had seven hundred wives and three hundred concubines. For his wives, Solomon built places of worship for foreign gods, sowing the poisonous seeds of idolatry and pagan practices that destroyed his nation.

22. Waldman, "Sociologist Examines."
23. Braswell, "Why the Focus."
24. Reinl, "Anti-Racism Scholar."

In his wealth and luxury, Solomon devoted his life to gaining plea-sure. In a striking section of Ecclesiastes, he notes that he had acquired singers (Eccl 2:8). In a world where one has continuous access to music, his words lack punch. Thousands of years before iPhones gave humans access to a vast library of music for $0.99 a song, though, his words had power. Music has long been a great gift to humanity, and for most of human history, it was only available by live performance. Few had access to great musicians. Most only got to hear the greatest musical offerings of their culture once or twice in a lifetime. Solomon, however, had music on demand.

It was not only music. Solomon had access to whatever pleasure he wanted, whenever he wanted it. At the end of all of his seeking, what he found was that his pleasure was meaningless. He called it "vanity," meaning absurd. Solomon learned after a life of seeking what the Greeks learned a few hundred years later: pleasure is not the highest good. At its best, pleasure can point to the good, and can remind the seeker what the good is. Pleasure, however, cannot replace the good.

As David Bentley Hart puts it, "No finite intelligible object is suf-ficient for human happiness because the only final end of natural human desire is the real knowledge of God.[25] . . . There are, moreover, only two possible ways of pursuing a purpose: either as an end in itself or as a provisional end pursued for the sake of an end beyond itself.[26] . . . A finite object . . . can never constitute an end *in itself*."[27] No finite object can serve as a final end or *telos*. A life spent pursuing pleasure or any other finite object as a final end is a life spent in final meaninglessness. It is absurd, or to use Solomon's word, vanity.

The good, the Greeks would argue, leads to a full life and a life of doing the right thing. Looking back at Singer and Gino, the Greeks would argue that they misapprehended the good as well. Singer replaced the good with pleasure, Gino with academic success. In both cases, misap-prehending the good led to a disruption in their wellbeing. It also led, particularly in Singer's case, to a disruption in the wellbeing of others.

25. Hart, *You Are Gods*, 6.

26. Hart, *You Are Gods*, 14.

27. Hart, *You Are Gods*, 14. Emphasis original.

HABITS

The ancient Greeks, led by Aristotle, also believed in the power of habits. They would encourage young people to put into practice what is good until it becomes part of their makeup. They practiced doing the good until it was an automatic response. With people who believe in the notion of the good and who practiced doing good until it became habitual, there would be few ethical problems.

Aristotle believed that one is what one repeatedly does. In modern writing about excellence in a field, thinkers suggest that excellence in any field requires 10,000 hours of training. Although there is no guarantee, there is a correlation between consistent training and success. If a person aims to become a master piano player, he or she needs to invest hours in practice. One becomes a pianist by playing the piano. One becomes a master pianist by practicing regularly.

In human behavior, the same is true. One becomes what one practices. If a person acts irresponsibly routinely, they will become irresponsible in character. The same is true in reverse. If a person behaves responsibly, over time the habit makes them responsible. Behavior is a choice. The choices people make shape their character.

HOW TO TEACH ETHICS

Teaching ethics should not be based on an understanding of ethical systems. Instead of fluency in multiple ethical systems, ethical education for the young should be based on teaching virtue. If virtue can be put into practice, by the time one has the intellectual and emotional maturity to think through ethical systems, one can learn them without misusing them.

Of course, if society is going to teach character traits and virtue, it would be helpful to have a common understanding of which character traits are good and which virtues should be practiced. A commonly accepted view of right and wrong based entirely on reason and available to every reasonable person who thought about it is an Enlightenment fantasy. Cultures vary about what is right and wrong among each other and within themselves. While it would be good to objectively ascertain which culture had it right, objectivity is very difficult to achieve, if not impossible. Even if objectivity were possible, enforcing agreement among people who disagree can lead to a kind of tyranny.

Rather than focus on specific moral issues on which agreement might be limited or instruct in the values of the majority, why not teach virtues? The Greeks assumed five virtues: courage, wisdom, moderation, justice, and piety. Western virtues based on the Judeo-Christian tradition are Christian virtues: wisdom, courage, moderation, and justice. While the latter are connected to religious tenets, educators could easily teach them without the religious context. Looking at the virtues as a whole, virtue ethics have the advantage of being nonsectarian, have precursor ethical systems across the globe, and may be practiced by a follower of any or no religion.

Society and educational systems teach the value of liberty and the value of every person regardless of race or socio-economic status with excellence. Why would teaching virtues be any more difficult? Why would it meet with any less success?

Bibliography

9/11 Memorial. "Revealed: The Hunt for Bin Laden." 9/11 Memorial and Museum. https://www.911memorial.org/learn/resources/digital-exhibitions/digital-exhibition-revealed-hunt-bin-laden.

Abandoned. "St. Joseph's Church." October 4, 2018. https://abandonedonline.net/location/st-josephs-church/.

Abingdon Press. *The United Methodist Book of Worship Pastors Pocket Edition*. Nashville, TN: United Methodist, 1992.

Adams, Lisa, and Thao Nguyen. "Most United Methodist Church Disaffiliations Are in the South: Final Report Outlines Latest in Ongoing Split." *USA Today*. https://www.usatoday.com/story/news/nation/2024/01/23/methodist-church-rift-disaffiliations-report/72319658007/.

Adgate, Brad. "The Rise And Fall of Cable Television." Forbes, November 2, 2020. https://www.forbes.com/sites/bradadgate/2020/11/02/the-rise-and-fall-of-cable-television/.

Air Force Historical Support Division. "1980—Operation Eagle Claw." Accessed August 21, 2024. https://www.afhistory.af.mil/FAQs/Fact-Sheets/Article/458949/1980-operation-eagle-claw/.

Allen, E. L. *The Sovereignty of God and the Word of God: A Guide to the Thought of Karl Barth*. London: Hodder & Stoughton, 1950.

Alper, Becka A., et al. "Spirituality Among Americans." Pew Research Center, December 7, 2023. https://www.pewresearch.org/wp-content/uploads/sites/20/2023/12/PR_2023.12.7_spirituality_REPORT.pdf.

Alter, Charlotte. "Effective Altruism Promises to Do Good Better. These Women Say It Has a Toxic Culture of Sexual Harassment and Abuse." *Time*, February 3, 2023. https://time.com/6252617/effective-altruism-sexual-harassment/.

American Association of Colleges and Universities. "Campus Challenges and Strategic Priorities in a Time of Change." https://www.aacu.org/research/campus-challenges-and-strategic-priorities-in-a-time-of-change.

AP Wire. "University of Kansas Faces $120 Million Budget Shortfall, Chancellor Says." FOX 4, May 22, 2020. https://fox4kc.com/news/university-of-kansas-faces-120-million-budget-shortfall-chancellor-says/.

Asmelash, Leah. "A California City Filled Its Skate Park with Sand to Deter Skateboarders. Then the Dirt Bikes Showed Up." CNN, April 22, 2020. https://www.cnn.com/2020/04/22/us/skate-park-sand-venice-san-clemente-trnd/index.html.

Associated Press. "Financial Crisis, Controversy Deepen at West Virginia University."
    The Journal Record, September 12, 2023. https://journalrecord.com/2023/09/
    financial-crisis-controversy-deepen-at-west-virginia-university/.
———. "New Oregon Law Suspends Graduation Testing Requirement." August
    13, 2021. https://apnews.com/article/health-oregon-education-coronavirus-
    pandemic-graduation-1ac30980c9e2d26b288a5341464efde8.
———. "Wisconsin Sexual Abuse Case Against Defrocked Cardinal McCarrick
    Suspended." January 10, 2024. https://apnews.com/article/cardinal-mccarrick-
    wisconsin-clergy-sex-abuse-charges-d7e42351254fd214bc0b225b76ca0538.
Associated Press and *Guardian* Staff. "Who Was Jeffrey Epstein and What Are the Court
    Documents About?" *The Guardian*, January 3, 2024. https://www.theguardian.
    com/us-news/2024/jan/03/who-is-jeffrey-epstein-list-court-documents-
    explained.
Atkinson, Brianna. "UNC Board of Governors Unanimously Approves Program Cuts
    at UNC Asheville, UNC Greensboro." WUNC, July 24, 2024. https://www.wunc.
    org/education/2024-07-24/unc-board-governors-approve-program-cuts-unc-
    asheville-greensboro.
Atkinson, Emma. "New DU Study Highlights Risks of Living Together Before
    Engagement." DU College of Arts, Humanities and Social Sciences. University of
    Denver, April 26, 2023. https://liberalarts.du.edu/news-events/all-articles/new-
    du-study-highlights-risks-living-together-engagement.
Atlanta Pubic Schools. "Journey to Excellence 2008–9: Report on Atlanta Public
    Schools." https://www.atlantapublicschools.us/cms/lib/GA01000924/Centricity/
    ModuleInstance/1089/APSannualreport-08-13-09-online.pdf.
Ayana, Archie. "Stanford President Resigns after Fallout from Falsified Data in His
    Research." NPR, July 20, 2023. https://www.npr.org/2023/07/19/1188828810/
    stanford-university-president-resigns.
Baker, Monya. "1,500 Scientists Lift the Lid on Reproducibility." *Nature* 533 (2016)
    452–54. https://doi.org/10.1038/533452a.
Bala, Nicholas. "The Debates About Same-Sex Marriage in Canada and the United
    States: Controversy Over the Evolution of a Fundamental Social Institution." *BYU
    Journal of Public Law* 20.2 (2006) 195–231. https://digitalcommons.law.byu.edu/
    jpl/vol20/iss2/2/.
Barr, Jeremy. "ABC's Amy Robach Says She Made Jeffrey Epstein Comments in 'Private
    Moment of Frustration.'" The Hollywood Reporter, November 5, 2019. https://
    www.hollywoodreporter.com/tv/tv-news/abcs-amy-robach-made-jeffrey-
    epstein-comments-private-moment-frustration-1252410/.
Barshay, Jill. "Dual Enrollment Has Exploded. But It's Hard to Tell if It's Helping More
    Kids Get a College Degree." The Hechinger Report, October 28, 2024. https://
    hechingerreport.org/proof-points-dual-enrollment-national-analysis/.
———. "How Dual Enrollment Is Changing the Face of Community Colleges."
    FutureEd, July 24, 2023. https://www.future-ed.org/how-dual-enrollment-is-
    changing-the-face-of-community-colleges/.
Barth, Karl. *The Word of God and the Word of Man*. Gloucester, MA: Peter Smith, 1978.
Barth, Karl, et al. *The Doctrine of the Word of God*. Vol. 1.1 of *Church Dogmatics*.
    London: T. & T. Clark, 2004.
BaseballHistoryNut (@nut_history). "A Full at Bat Involving Hank Aaron. You Don't
    See These Pop up Very Often. Enjoy Https://T.Co/9j24CC3Sio." X, post, April 28,
    2023. https://x.com/nut_history/status/1652095841287503872.

Baucom, Erin. "What Is It that Binds Us to This Speech? Charles Kuralt's 1993 UNC Bicentennial Address." For the Record (blog), January 26, 2016. https://blogs. lib.unc.edu/uarms/2016/01/26/what-is-it-that-binds-us-to-this-speech-charles-kuralts-1993-unc-bicentennial-address/.

Beauchamp, Zack. "The World's Victory over Extreme Poverty, in One Chart." Vox, December 14, 2014. https://www.vox.com/2014/12/14/7384515/extreme-poverty-decline.

Becker, Carlin. "Hysterical Yale Students Cry and Scream at Their 'Racist' Professor [Video]." Washington Examiner, September 15, 2016. https://www. washingtonexaminer.com/red-alert-politics/1077428/hysterical-yale-students-cry-and-scream-at-their-racist-professor-video/.

Beckett, Lois. "Ousted Harvard President Claudine Gay Warns of 'a Broader War' in Op-Ed." The Guardian, January 4, 2024. https://www.theguardian.com/education/2024/jan/03/claudine-gay-harvard-president-resignation-new-york-times-op-ed.

Bellah, Robert N., ed. The Good Society. New York: Vintage, 1992.

Bendix, Aria, and Denise Chow. "Allegations of Fabricated Research Undermine Key Alzheimer's Theory." NBC News, July 25, 2022. https://www.nbcnews.com/science/science-news/alzheimers-theory-undermined-accusations-fabricated-research-rcna39843.

Bennet, James. "When the New York Times Lost Its Way." The Economist, December 16, 2023. https://www.economist.com/1843/2023/12/14/when-the-new-york-times-lost-its-way.

Berliner, Uri. "I've Been at NPR for 25 Years. Here's How We Lost America's Trust." The Free Press, April 9, 2024. https://www.thefp.com/p/npr-editor-how-npr-lost-americas-trust.

Better Explained. "How to Develop a Sense of Scale." https://betterexplained.com/articles/how-to-develop-a-sense-of-scale/.

Biden, Joseph. "Remarks by President Biden on the Drawdown of U.S. Forces in Afghanistan." The White House, July 8, 2021. https://bidenwhitehouse.archives.gov/briefing-room/speeches-remarks/2021/07/08/remarks-by-president-biden-on-the-drawdown-of-u-s-forces-in-afghanistan/.

Bilas, Jay. "March is Coming, so It's Time to Get Some Things Straight." ESPN, February 7, 2017. https://www.espn.co.uk/mens-college-basketball/insider/story/_/id/18638889/the-bilas-index-sets-record-straight-march-approaches.

Binkley, Collin, and Associated Press. "The Labor Shortage Is Pushing American Colleges into Crisis, with the Plunge in Enrollment the Worst Ever Recorded." Fortune, March 9, 2023. https://fortune.com/2023/03/09/american-skipping-college-huge-numbers-pandemic-turned-them-off-education/.

Blake, Jessica. "American Confidence in Higher Ed Hits Historic Low." Inside Higher Ed, July 11, 2023. https://www.insidehighered.com/news/business/financial-health/2023/07/11/american-confidence-higher-ed-hits-historic-low.

———. "SUNY Fredoinia Fights to Keep Controversial Professor Off Campus." Inside Higher Ed, August 18, 2023. https://www.insidehighered.com/news/faculty-issues/academic-freedom/2023/08/18/suny-fredonia-fights-keep-professor-campus

Bolman, Lee G., and Terrence E. Deal. Reframing Organizations: Artistry, Choice, and Leadership. 7th ed. Hoboken, NJ: Jossey-Bass, 2021.

Bond, Shannon. "A Major Disinformation Research Team's Future Is Uncertain after Political Attacks." NPR, June 14, 2024. https://www.npr.org/2024/06/14/g-s1-4570/a-major-disinformation-research-teams-future-is-uncertain-after-political-attacks.

———. "What It Means for the Election that the Government Can Talk to Tech Companies." Texas Public Radio, June 26, 2024. https://www.tpr.org/2024-06-26/what-it-means-for-the-election-that-the-government-can-talk-to-tech-companies.

Booth, Alison. "The 'Public' Elite." North Eastern University Political Review, March 4, 2021. https://nupoliticalreview.org/2021/03/04/the-public-elite/.

Boston University. "Guide Star and Values." Wheelock College of Education and Human Development. https://www.bu.edu/wheelock/about/guide-star-values/.

Bowman, Rachel. "DHS Officials Created a 'Disinformation Group' at Stanford University to Help Censor Americans' Speech on Social Media Ahead of the 2020 Election, Bombshell Emails Reveal." Daily Mail, November 7, 2023. https://www.dailymail.co.uk/news/article-12719021/DHS-disinformation-group-Stanford-2020-election-emails.html.

Brady, Michael. "California Unveils 7 Guaranteed Income Pilot Projects." Smart Cities Dive, November 29, 2022. https://www.smartcitiesdive.com/news/california-guaranteed-income-pilot-projects/637502/.

Braswell, Porter. "Why the Focus on 'White Fragility' Is a Distraction." Fast Company, August 3, 2022. https://www.fastcompany.com/90774869/why-the-focus-on-white-fragility-is-a-distraction/.

Brenan, Megan. "Americans' Confidence in Higher Education Down Sharply." Gallup, July 11, 2023. https://news.gallup.com/poll/508352/americans-confidence-higher-education-down-sharply.aspx.

———. "Media Confidence in U.S. Matches 2016 Record Low." Gallup, October 19, 2023. https://news.gallup.com/poll/512861/media-confidence-matches-2016-record-low.aspx.

The Bridgespan Group. "Faith-Inspired Nonprofits Provide 40 Percent of Social Safety Net Spending but Can Still Be Overlooked by Donors, According to New Bridgespan Group Research." January 28, 2021. https://www.bridgespan.org/press-releases/faith-inspired-nonprofits-provide-40-percent-of-social-safety-net-spending-but-can-still-be-overlook.

Brown, Jenny, and Lauren Errington, eds. Bowen Family Systems Theory in Christian Ministry. Neutral Bay, NSW: The Family Systems Practice and Institute, 2019.

Brown, Lee. "Shocking Video Shows Black Kids Attack, Force White Kids to Say 'Black Lives Matter' at Ohio School: Cops." New York Post, March 3, 2023. https://nypost.com/2023/03/03/black-kids-forced-white-kids-to-say-black-lives-matter-cops/.

Brown, Matthew. "A Timeline of the US Withdrawal and Taliban Recapture of Afghanistan." USA Today, August 15, 2021. https://www.usatoday.com/story/news/politics/2021/08/15/timeline-afghanistans-history-and-us-involvement/8143131002/.

Bruinius, Harry. "Who Made You an Expert? Is America's Distrust of 'Elites' Becoming More Toxic?" The Christian Science Monitor, August 27, 2018. https://www.csmonitor.com/USA/Politics/2018/0827/Who-made-you-an-expert-Is-America-s-distrust-of-elites-becoming-more-toxic.

Buchanan, Cecilia. "Universities Facing Financial Ticking Time Bomb." Fierce Network, June 12, 2023. https://www.fiercetelecom.com/leadership/universities-facing-financial-ticking-time-bomb.

Burge, Ryan. "Dropping Out of Everything." Graphs About Religion, April 22, 2024. https://www.graphsaboutreligion.com/p/dropping-out-of-everything.

———. "Religion Has Become a Luxury Good for the Middle Class, Married College Graduate With Children." Religion Unplugged, July 12, 2023. https://religionunplugged.com/news/2023/7/3/religion-has-become-a-luxury-good-for-the-middle-class-married-college-graduate-with-children.

Burke, Lilah. "Marietta College to Cut 3 Dozen Administrators and Faculty." Higher Ed Dive, February 13, 2024. https://www.highereddive.com/news/marietta-college-to-cut-3-dozen-administrators-and-faculty/707303/.

Burris, Devan. "Why More and More Colleges Are Closing Down Across the U.S." CNBC, June 17, 2023. https://www.cnbc.com/2023/06/17/why-more-and-more-colleges-are-closing-down-across-the-us.html.

Bushard, Brian. "ACT College Admission Test Scores Drop To Thirty-Year Low As Effects Of Covid-Era Online Learning Play Out." Forbes, October 12, 2022. https://www.forbes.com/sites/brianbushard/2022/10/12/act-college-admission-test-scores-drop-to-30-year-low-as-effects-of-covid-era-online-learning-play-out/.

Butler, Judith. "A 'Bad Writer' Bites Back." The New York Times, March 20, 1999. https://query.nytimes.com/gst/fullpage.html?res=950CE5D61531F933A15750C0A96F958260.

Butrymowicz, Sarah. "A Crisis Is Looming for U.S. Colleges—and Not Just Because of the Pandemic." NBC News, August 4, 2020. https://www.nbcnews.com/news/education/crisis-looming-u-s-colleges-not-just-because-pandemic-n1235338.

Cadwallader, Mervyn. "Marriage as a Wretched Institution." The Atlantic, November 1966. https://www.theatlantic.com/magazine/archive/1966/11/marriage-as-a-wretched-institution/306668/.

Calhoun, John C. 1848. "Speech on the Oregon Bill." Transcript of speech delivered at the Senate of the United States, Washington, DC, June 27, 1848. https://teachingamericanhistory.org/document/speech-on-the-oregon-bill-3/.

Calisher, Charles, et al. "Statement in Support of the Scientists, Public Health Professionals, and Medical Professionals of China Combatting COVID-19." The Lancet 395.10226 (2020) e42–43. https://www.thelancet.com/journals/lancet/article/PIIS0140-6736(20)30418-9/fulltext.

Campbell University. "Campbell Magazine | Spring 2023." April 25, 2023. https://issuu.com/campbelluniversity/docs/spring-23-campbellumag-final.

———. "History." https://divinity.campbell.edu/about/history/.

Caputo, John D. What Would Jesus Deconstruct? The Good News of Postmodernism for the Church. Grand Rapids: Baker Academic, 2007.

The Carolina Story: A Virtual Museum of University History. "The Old Well." https://museum.unc.edu/exhibits/show/water/the-old-well.

Caruso, Justin. "Yale Honors Students Who Mobbed Prof over Costume Controversy." Campus Reform, May 30, 2017. https://campusreform.org/article/yale-honors-students-mobbed-prof-costume-controversy/9238.

Carvalhaes, Cláudio. "Why I Created a Chapel Service Where People Confess to Plants." Sojourners, September 26, 2019. https://sojo.net/articles/why-i-created-chapel-service-where-people-confess-plants.

CBS News. "Deception at Duke: Fraud in Cancer Care?" March 5, 2012. https://www.
    cbsnews.com/news/deception-at-duke-fraud-in-cancer-care/.
———. "Yale Teacher Resigns over Halloween Costume Controversy." December 7,
    2015.   https://www.cbsnews.com/news/yale-teacher-resigns-over-halloween-
    costume-controversy/.
Cha, Ariana Eunjung. "Cruel Twist of Fate for Single Woman Who Froze Her Eggs in
    Her Late Thirties to 'Free Her Career.'" *National Post*, January 29, 2018. https://
    nationalpost.com/news/world/i-was-sad-i-was-angry-i-was-ashamed-inside-the-
    struggle-to-conceive-with-frozen-eggs.
Chadwick, Jonathan. "Eating Just One Egg a Day Increases Your Risk of Diabetes by 60
    Per Cent, Study Warns." *Daily Mail*, November 19, 2020. https://www.dailymail.
    co.uk/sciencetech/article-8954561/One-egg-day-increases-risk-developing-
    diabetes-60-study-warns.html.
Chambers, Clare. "Against Marriage." Aeon, April 17, 2018. https://aeon.co/essays/
    why-marriage-is-both-anachronistic-and-discriminatory.
———. *Against Marriage: An Egalitarian Defence of the Marriage-Free State*. Oxford:
    Oxford University Press, 2017.
Channel Islands University. "What Is a 'Social Justice Framework'?" School of
    Education. https://education.csuci.edu/about/justice-conference/faq.htm.
Chappell, Bill. "NCAA 'Could Not Conclude Academic Violations' in UNC Athletics
    Scandal." NPR, October 13, 2017. https://www.npr.org/sections/thetwo-
    way/2017/10/13/557581005/ncaa-could-not-conclude-academic-violations-in-
    unc-athletics-scandal.
———. "The Pentagon Has Never Passed an Audit. Some Senators Want to Change
    That." NPR, May 19, 2021. https://www.npr.org/2021/05/19/997961646/the-
    pentagon-has-never-passed-an-audit-some-senators-want-to-change-that.
Chernikoff, Sara. "1 in 5 Americans Have Low-Literacy Skills: These Charts Explain
    Reading Levels in the US." *USA Today*, September 9, 2023. https://www.usatoday.
    com/story/news/education/2023/09/09/literacy-levels-in-the-us/70799429007/.
Chicago Tribune. "Turner Backtracks on Religion." August 22, 2021. https://www.
    chicagotribune.com/2008/04/02/turner-backtracks-on-religion/.
Christakis, Erika. "'Dressing Yourselves,' Email to Silliman College (Yale) Students
    on Halloween Costumes." Genius, October 30, 2015. https://genius.com/Erika-
    christakis-dressing-yourselves-email-to-silliman-college-yale-students-on-
    halloween-costumes-annotated.
Clark, Christine. "A New Replication Crisis: Research that Is Less Likely to Be True Is
    Cited More." UC San Diego Today, May 21, 2021. https://today.ucsd.edu/story/a-
    new-replication-crisis-research-that-is-less-likely-be-true-is-cited-more.
Clark, Douglas. "Less Than 50% of US Households Now Subscribe to Pay TV, as Cord-
    Cutting Jumps More Than Expected." EMarketer, March 7, 2023. https://www.
    emarketer.com/press-releases/less-than-50-of-us-households-now-subscribe-to-
    pay-tv-as-cord-cutting-jumps-more-than-expected/.
CNN Editorial Research. "Osama Bin Laden Fast Facts." CNN, revised April 27, 2021.
    https://www.cnn.com/2013/08/30/world/osama-bin-laden-fast-facts/index.html.
Cogan, Michael F. "Exploring Academic Outcomes of Homeschooled Students." *Journal
    of College Admission* 208 (2010) 18–25. https://eric.ed.gov/?id=EJ893891.
Cohen, Asher, et al. "Letter to Harvard President from HU Management." Office of the
    Rector. The Hebrew University of Jerusalem, October 11, 2023. https://en.rector.
    huji.ac.il/news/harvard-response-israel-war-october-23.

Coles, Robert. "The Disparity Intellect and Character." *The Chronicle of Higher Education*, September 22, 1995. https://www.chronicle.com/article/the-disparity-between-intellect-and-character/.

Collins, Gary. "GW President Says School Needs Help from DC Police as Protesters Call for Beheadings." NBC15 News, May 6, 2024. https://mynbc15.com/news/nation-world/gw-president-pleads-for-police-intervention-as-protesters-call-for-beheadings-george-washington-university-ellen-granberg-washington-dc-metropolitan-police-department-mpd-dc-columbia-israel-palestine-gaza-strip-ceasefire.

Collins, Leah. "Job Unhappiness Is at a Staggering All-Time High, According to Gallup." CNBC, August 12, 2022. https://www.cnbc.com/2022/08/12/job-unhappiness-is-at-a-staggering-all-time-high-according-to-gallup.html.

Consolmango, Guy, and Christopher M. Graney. "What the Story of Galileo Gets Wrong About the Church and Science." America, September 18, 2020. https://www.americamagazine.org/arts-culture/2020/09/18/what-story-galileo-gets-wrong-about-church-and-science.

Córdova, Andrés L. "Thinking Through History: The Past Is a Foreign Country." *The Hill*, July 7, 2020. https://thehill.com/opinion/civil-rights/506232-facing-our-history-the-past-is-a-foreign-country/.

Cracker Barrel. "Cracker Barrel History and Timeline." https://www.crackerbarrel.com/about/Historical-Timeline.

———. "Retail Merchandise." https://www.crackerbarrel.com/newsroom/photos/gift-shop-items.

Curl, Joseph. "Expecting People to Be Promptly on Time Is Part of 'White Supremacy Culture,' Duke Medical School Claims." *The New York Sun*, July 9, 2024. https://www.nysun.com/article/expecting-people-to-be-promptly-on-time-is-part-of-white-supremacy-culture-duke-medical-school-claims.

Dabrowski, Ted, and John Klinger. "Illinois Education 2022: Not a Single Student Can Do Math at Grade Level in 53 Schools. For Reading, It's 30 Schools." Wirepoints, February 14, 2023. https://wirepoints.org/not-a-single-student-can-do-math-at-grade-level-in-53-illinois-schools-for-reading-its-30-schools-wirepoints/.

Daily Mail. "Florida State University Professor Abruptly Left his $190,000-a-Year Role After Being Accused of Faking Data to Make Racism Seem More Common that [*sic*] It Is and Having Six of His Research Papers Retracted." October 23, 2023. https://www.dailymail.co.uk/news/article-11963421/Florida-State-University-criminology-professor-leaves-accused-falsifying-data.html.

Darcy, Oliver. "News Outlets Are Collapsing as Advertisers Flock to Social Media Platforms. It Has Major Implications for Society." CNN, February 28, 2024. https://www.cnn.com/2024/02/28/media/news-outlets-collapse-advertisers-flock-to-social-media/index.html.

Davis, Don. "How Sears Failed in the E-Commerce Era Even as It Innovated Online." Digital Commerce 360, October 19, 2018. https://www.digitalcommerce360.com/2018/10/19/how-sears-failed-in-the-e-commerce-era-even-as-it-innovated-online/.

Davis, Maggie. "Average Car Payment and Auto Loan Statistics: 2025." LendingTree, December 17, 2024. https://www.lendingtree.com/auto/debt-statistics/.

Dawkins, Richard. "Postmodernism Disrobed." https://richarddawkins.com/articles/article/postmodernism-disrobed.

Dawn, Karen. "Peter Singer Is Not Animal Liberation Now." Dawn Watch. https://dawnwatch.com/petersingeressay/.

Delsol, Jean-Philippe, and Emmanuel Martin, eds. *Anti-Piketty: Capital for the 21st Century*. Washington, DC: Cato Institute, 2017.

DePaul University. "University Mission Statement." Division of Mission and Ministry. https://offices.depaul.edu/mission-ministry/about/Pages/mission.aspx.

De Graaf, Mia. "One Egg a Day 'Lowers Your Risk of Type 2 Diabetes:' Controversial Study Says It Promotes Fatty Acids that Protect You from the Disease." *Daily Mail*, January 3, 2019. https://www.dailymail.co.uk/health/article-6555491/One-egg-day-LOWERS-risk-type-2-diabetes.html.

Diamond, Dan. "In the Pandemic, We Were Told to Keep Six Feet Apart. There's No Science to Support That." The *Washington Post*, June 2, 2024. https://www.washingtonpost.com/health/2024/06/02/six-foot-rule-covid-no-science/.

Dickens, Charles. *A Christmas Carol*. Philadelphia: Lippincott, 1915.

Dickler, Jessica, and Ana Teresa Solá. "'NEETS' and 'New Unemployables'—Why Some Young Adults Aren't Working." CNBC, July 1, 2024. https://www.cnbc.com/2024/07/01/neets-and-new-unemployables-why-fewer-young-adults-are-working.html.

Divorce Lawyers for Men (blog). "Facts About Child Custody For Fathers in the US." https://www.divorcelawyersformen.com/blog/the-true-facts-of-child-custody-for-men/.

Dokoupil, Tony, and Martin Finn. "Millions of Men Have Dropped Out of the Workforce, Leaving Companies Struggling to Fill Jobs: It's 'A Matter of Our National Identity.'" CBS News, January 26, 2023. https://www.cbsnews.com/news/men-workforce-work-companies-struggle-fill-jobs-manufacturing/.

Dong, Junzhi, et al. "Re-Evaluating the Role of Partnership-Related Perceptions in Women's Preferences for Men with Masculine Face Shapes." *Evolutionary Psychology* 22.2 (2024). https://doi.org/10.1177/14747049241262712.

Dostoevsky, Fyodor. *The Brothers Karamazov*. Waxkeep, 2013. Kindle.

Douglass, Frederick. "Frederick Douglass's 'Fourth of July' Speech (1852)." San Diego State University. https://loveman.sdsu.edu/docs/1852FrederickDouglass.pdf.

Douthat, Ross. "Douthat: Why Liberal Academia Needs Republican Friends." *The Mercury News*, November 7, 2023. https://www.mercurynews.com/2023/11/07/douthat-why-liberal-academia-needs-republican-friends/.

Drum, Kevin. "America's Real Criminal Element Is Lead." Mother Jones, February 2016. https://www.motherjones.com/environment/2016/02/lead-exposure-gasoline-crime-increase-children-health/.

Duke Divinity Live. "Service of Word." YouTube, April 24, 2022. Video. https://web.archive.org/web/20220412080007/https://www.youtube.com/watch?v=WDktgNcUY3k.

Earls, Aaron. "Protestant Church Closures Outpace Openings in U.S." Lifeway Research, May 25, 2021. https://lifewayresearch.com/2021/05/25/protestant-church-closures-outpace-openings-in-u-s/.

———. "Public Trust of Pastors Hits New Record Low." Lifeway Research, January 24, 2024. https://research.lifeway.com/2024/01/24/public-trust-of-pastors-hits-new-record-low/.

Eberstadt, Nicholas. *Men Without Work: Post-Pandemic Edition*. West Conshohocken, PA: Templeton, 2022.

Elliott, Philip. "'Major American Failure': A Political Scientist on Why the U.S. Lost in Afghanistan." *Time*, August 18, 2021. https://time.com/6091183/afghanistan-war-failure-interview/.

"EP-3 Collision, Crew Detainment, Release, and Homecoming." Naval History and Heritage Command, October 10, 2024. https://www.history.navy.mil/research/archives/Collections/ncdu-det-206/2001/ep-3-collision--crew-detainment-and-homecoming.html.

Evans, Kyle. "Groupthink—Understanding and Avoiding It." Prodity: Product Thinking (blog), November 30, 2020. https://www.productthinking.cc/p/groupthink-understanding-and-avoiding.

Federal Reserve Bank of St. Louis. "Median Sales Price of Houses Sold for the United States." January 27, 2025. https://fred.stlouisfed.org/series/MSPUS.

Feynman, Richard. "The Value of Science." Thejesh GN, March 6, 2011. https://thejeshgn.com/wiki/great-speeches/the-value-of-science-richard-feynman/.

Fitzgerald, Toni. "Americans Are Watching Less TV as Prices Rise, Study Suggests." Forbes, July 16, 2024. https://www.forbes.com/sites/tonifitzgerald/2024/07/16/study-americans-are-watching-less-and-less-tv-heres-why/.

Fleck, Anna. "Americans Are Getting Married Older Than Ever." Statistia, December 15, 2023. https://www.statista.com/chart/7031/americans-are-tying-the-knot-older-than-ever.

Flintoff, Corey. "Timeline: Priest Abuse Claims Date Back Decades." NPR, April 26, 2010. https://www.npr.org/2010/04/26/126160853/timeline-priest-abuse-claims-date-back-decades.

FocusEconomics. "Inflation Eases Slightly in August." FocusEconomics, September 14, 2021. https://www.focus-economics.com/countries/united-states/news/inflation/inflation-eases-slightly-in-august/.

Folkenflik, David. "A Dead Cat, A Lawyer's Call and a 5-Figure Donation: How Media Fell Short On Epstein." NPR, August 22, 2019. https://www.npr.org/2019/08/22/753390385/a-dead-cat-a-lawyers-call-and-a-5-figure-donation-how-media-fell-short-on-epstei.

Foody, Kathleen, and Michael Tarm. "Catholic Clergy Sexually Abused Illinois Kids Far More Often than Church Acknowledged, State Finds." AP News, May 23, 2023. https://apnews.com/article/catholic-clergy-sexual-abuse-illinois-investigation-a298133cec9486c2e51172316bfe7b4b.

Forbes. "#278 University of Massachusetts Boston." https://www.forbes.com/colleges/university-of-massachusetts-boston/.

Foster, Sarah. "Inflation Accelerated Again Last Month—Here Are the Prices Rising Most." Bankrate, February 12, 2025. https://www.bankrate.com/banking/federal-reserve/latest-inflation-statistics/.

Freile, Victoria E. "SUNY Fredonia to Cut 13 Majors. See What Programs Are Being Eliminated." *Democrat and Chronicle*, March 19, 2024. https://www.democratandchronicle.com/story/news/2024/03/19/suny-fredonia-to-cut-majors-see-what-programs-are-being-eliminated/72970865007/.

Friedman, Edwin H. *A Failure of Nerve: Leadership in the Age of the Quick Fix*. New York: Seabury, 2007.

———. *Generation to Generation: Family Process in Church and Synagogue*. Vol. 9 of *The Guilford Family Therapy Series*. New York: Guilford, 1985.

Friedersdorf, Conor. "The Perils of Writing a Provocative Email at Yale." *The Atlantic*, May 26, 2016. https://www.theatlantic.com/politics/archive/2016/05/the-peril-of-writing-a-provocative-email-at-yale/484418/.

Fry, Hannah. "A 'Failure to Launch': Why Young People Are Having Less Sex." *Los Angeles Times*, August 3, 2023. https://www.latimes.com/california/story/2023-08-03/young-adults-less-sex-gen-z-millennials-generations-parents-grandparents#:~:text=For%20what%20researchers%20say%20is,'%20and%20grandparents'%20generations%20did.

Gabbat, Adam. "Losing Their Religion: Why US Churches Are on the Decline." *The Guardian*, January 22, 2023. https://www.theguardian.com/us-news/2023/jan/22/us-churches-closing-religion-covid-christianity?utm_term=Autofeed&CMP=twt_gu&utm_medium&utm_source=Twitter#Echobox=1674380529.

Gaskins, Kayla. "White House Pressed Meta to Censor COVID-19 Posts on Lab Leak Theory and Vaccine Hesitancy, Internal Emails Show." ABC News 4, July 31, 2023. https://abcnews4.com/news/nation-world/white-house-pressed-meta-to-censor-covid-19-posts-on-lab-leak-theory-and-vaccine-hesitancy-internal-emails-show-coronavirus-pandemic-president-joe-biden-facebook-social-media-mark-zuckerburg.

Gay, Claudine. "War in the Middle East." Harvard University, October 12, 2023. https://www.harvard.edu/president/news-gay/2023/war-in-the-middle-east/.

Geller, Patty-Jane, and Jack Kraemer. "40 Years After Reagan, Neglected U.S. Missile Defense Is Dangerously Obsolete." The Heritage Foundation, March 23, 2023. https://www.heritage.org/missile-defense/commentary/40-years-after-reagan-neglected-us-missile-defense-dangerously-obsolete.

Gelles-Watnick, Risa. "For Valentine's Day, 5 Facts about Single Americans." Pew Research Center, February 8, 2023. https://www.pewresearch.org/short-reads/2023/02/08/for-valentines-day-5-facts-about-single-americans/.

Generes, Wendy. "Recession, Unemployment, and Drug Addiction: What's the Link?" American Addiction Centers, July 19, 2024. https://americanaddictioncenters.org/blog/recession-unemployment-and-drug-addiction-whats-the-link.

Germino, Elizabeth. "Documents Reveal Bin Laden's Bid for American Support." CBS News, April 24, 2022. https://www.cbsnews.com/news/osama-bin-laden-documents-american-support-60-minutes-2022-04-24/.

Gilbert, Roberta M. *The Eight Concepts of Bowen Theory: A New Way of Thinking About The Individual and the Group*. Lake Frederick, VA: Leading Systems, 2006.

Gillespie, Nick, et al. "The Yale Professor Attacked by Angry Students over Halloween Costumes Believes Evolution Wants Us to Get Along." Reason, April 5, 2019. https://reason.com/video/2019/04/05/the-yale-professor-attacked-by-angry-stu/.

Giorno, Taylor. "Yellen Says She Regrets Saying Inflation Was 'Transitory.'" *The Hill*, March 13, 2024. https://thehill.com/business/4529787-yellen-regrets-saying-inflation-transitory/.

Gino, Francesca. "About." Francescagino.com. https://francescagino.com/about.

Giuliani, Rudolph W., and Ken Kurson. *Leadership*. New York: Hyperion, 2002.

Godwin, Janet. "Average ACT Score for the High School Class of 2022 Declines to Lowest Level in More than 30 Years." ACT Newsroom and Blog. ACT.org, October 11, 2022. https://leadershipblog.act.org/2022/10/GradClassRelease2022.html.

Goldberg, David E. "Boat Luxury Tax Drives an Industry Aground." *The New York Times*, January 3, 1991. https://www.nytimes.com/1991/01/03/opinion/l-boat-luxury-tax-drives-an-industry-aground-926091.html.

Grace, Molly, and Aly J. Yale. "What Is the Average Mortgage Payment?" Business Insider, August 26, 2024. https://www.businessinsider.com/personal-finance/mortgages/average-mortgage-payment.

Greene, Robert. *The Daily Laws: 366 Meditations on Power, Seduction, Mastery, Strategy, and Human Nature.* New York: Viking, 2021.

———. *The Laws of Human Nature.* New York: Viking, 2018.

Greenleaf Robert K. *Servant Leadership: A Journey into the Nature of Legitimate Power and Greatness.* Mahwah, NJ: Paulist, 2002.

Griffith, Keith. "Damning Report Reveals There Are NO Students Proficient in Either Math or Reading at 60 Different Public Schools in Illinois: Lawmaker Slams Pandemic Policies for 'Serious' Academic Decline." *Daily Mail*, February 20, 2023. https://www.dailymail.co.uk/news/article-11774133/Report-reveals-no-students-proficient-math-reading-60-Illinois-schools.html.

Grillo, Ian. "It Was Once the Richest Country in Latin America. Now It's Falling Apart." *Time*. https://time.com/venezuela-brink/.

Grimes, David Robert. "What an Alzheimer's Controversy Reveals About the Pressures of Academia." *The Atlantic*, July 29, 2022. https://www.theatlantic.com/science/archive/2022/07/alzheimers-disease-data-fraud-sylvain-lesne/670995/.

Grindon, Lucy. "Clarkson Announces Plan to Phase Out Majors in Humanities, Communications." NCPR, December 22, 2023. https://www.northcountrypublicradio.org/news/story/49014/20231222/clarkson-announces-plan-to-phase-out-majors-in-humanities-communications.

Grossman, Dan. "Why Has NFL Viewership Surged over the Decades?" Scripps News, February 7, 2024. https://www.scrippsnews.com/sports/why-has-nfl-viewership-surged-over-the-decades.

Gryboski, Michael. "Southern Baptist Convention Lost over 1,200 Churches in 2022, Data Shows." *The Christian Post*, April 4, 2024. https://www.christianpost.com/news/sbc-lost-over-1200-churches-in-2022-data-shows.html.

Guerrasio, Jason. "Seth Rogen Explains Why He and His Wife Are 'F—ing Psyched' to Not Have Kids." Business Insider, May 17, 2021. https://www.businessinsider.com/why-seth-rogen-and-wife-do-not-want-children-2021-5.

Habeshian, Sareen. "Distrust in Scientists Rises Among Both Republicans and Democrats: Poll." Axios, November 15, 2023. https://www.axios.com/2023/11/15/trust-scientists-declines-republicans-democrats.

Haelle, Tara. "A Massive 8-Year Effort Finds that Much Cancer Research Can't Be Replicated." Science News, December 7, 2021. https://www.sciencenews.org/article/cancer-biology-studies-research-replication-reproducibility.

Hansen, Melanie. "College Tuition Inflation Rate." Education Data Initiative, September 9, 2024. https://educationdata.org/college-tuition-inflation-rate.

Harper, Tyler Austin. "The Humanities Have Sown the Seeds of Their Own Destruction." *The Atlantic*, December 19, 2023. https://www.theatlantic.com/ideas/archive/2023/12/humanities-university-conservative-critics/676890/.

Harrington, Rebecca, and Paolo Rosa-Aquino. "11 Qualities in Men that Women Find Attractive, According to Science." Business Insider, January 17, 2023. https://www.businessinsider.com/science-backed-qualities-in-men-women-like-2016-6.

Harris, Leslie M. "I Helped Fact-Check the 1619 Project. *The Times* Ignored Me." *Politico*, March 6, 2020. https://www.politico.com/news/magazine/2020/03/06/1619-project-new-york-times-mistake-122248.

Hart, David Bentley. *Atheist Delusions: The Christian Revolution and Its Fashionable Enemies*. New Haven: Yale University Press, 2009.

———. *The Beauty of the Infinite: The Aesthetics of Christian Truth*. Kindle. Grand Rapids: Eerdmans, 2003.

———. "Believe It or Not." First Things, May 1, 2010. https://www.firstthings.com/article/2010/05/believe-it-or-not.

———. *The Experience of God: Being, Consciousness, Bliss*. New Haven, CT: Yale University Press, 2013.

———. "Richard Dawkins Discovers His Ideal Idiom and Audience." Church Life Journal, December 19, 2019. https://churchlifejournal.nd.edu/articles/richard-dawkins-discovers-his-ideal-idiom-and-audience/.

———. *You Are Gods: On Nature and Supernature*. Notre Dame, IN: University of Notre Dame Press, 2022. Kindle.

Harvard University. "New Data Show How the Pandemic Affected Learning Across Whole Communities." Harvard Graduate School of Education. May 11, 2023. https://www.gse.harvard.edu/ideas/news/23/05/new-data-show-how-pandemic-affected-learning-across-whole-communities.

Hausmann, Ricardo, and Francisco R. Rodríguez, eds. *Venezuela Before Chávez: Anatomy of an Economic Collapse*. University Park, PA: The Pennsylvania State University Press, 2014. Ebook. https://www.psupress.org/books/titles/978-70-271-5631-9.html.

Hayward, Steven. "UMass-Boston Faculty Says 'Enough!'" Power Line (blog), November 28, 2022. https://www.powerlineblog.com/archives/2022/11/umass-boston-faculty-says-enough.php.

Hedges, Larry. "'An Existential Crisis' for Science." Institute for Policy Research, February 28, 2024. https://www.ipr.northwestern.edu/news/2024/an-existential-crisis-for-science.html.

Heller, Nathan. "The End of the English Major." *The New Yorker*, February 27, 2023. https://www.newyorker.com/magazine/2023/03/06/the-end-of-the-english-major.

Hemingway, Mark. "News for the Elite." Law and Liberty, February 14, 2022. https://lawliberty.org/book-review/news-for-the-elite/.

Herszenhorn, Miles J., and Claire Yuan. "'I Am Sorry': Harvard President Gay Addresses Backlash over Congressional Testimony on Antisemitism." *The Harvard Crimson*, December 8, 2023. https://www.thecrimson.com/article/2023/12/8/gay-apology-congressional-remarks/.

Hitchens, Christopher. *God Is Not Great: How Religion Poisons Everything*. New York: Twelve, 2007.

Hobbes, Thomas. *Leviathan*. Rudram, 2016. Kindle.

Hodgson, Geoffrey M. "What Are Institutions?" *Journal of Economic Issues* 40.1 (2006) 1–25. https://doi.org/10.1080/00213624.2006.11506879.

House Judiciary. "The Weaponization of 'Disinformation' Pseudo-Experts and Bureaucrats: How the Federal Government Partnered with Universities to Censor Americans' Political Speech." November 6, 2023. https://judiciary.house.gov/sites/evo-subsites/republicans-judiciary.house.gov/files/evo-media-document/EIP_Jira-Ticket-Staff-Report-11-7-23-Clean.pdf.

Houston, Allen. "Social Rapidly Replacing TV as America's Primary News Source: YouGov's Media Report." Marketing Dive, January 25, 2024. https://www.marketingdive.com/press-release/20240125-social-rapidly-replacing-tv-as-americas-primary-news-source-yougovs-medi/.

Huleatt, Verry. "Progressive Seminary Students Offered a Confession to Plants. How Do We Think About Sins Against Nature?" The Washington Post, September 18, 2019. https://www.washingtonpost.com/religion/2019/09/18/progressive-seminary-students-offered-confession-plants-what-are-we-make-it/.

Hurley, Kendra. "The Decades-Long Travesty That Made Millions of Americans Mistrust Their Kids' Schools." Slate, October 15, 2023. https://slate.com/human-interest/2023/10/reading-phonics-literacy-calkins-curriculum-public-school.html.

Husock, Howard. "Hillary Clinton Still Owes Tammy Wynette an Apology." American Enterprise Institute, December 10, 2022. https://www.aei.org/op-eds/hillary-clinton-still-owes-tammy-wynette-an-apology/.

Hyer, Marjorie. "Newly Merged Presbyterian Church Elects First Moderator, Faces Future." The Washington Post, June 11, 1983. https://www.washingtonpost.com/archive/politics/1983/06/12/newly-merged-presbyterian-church-elects-first-moderator-faces-future/ccc8ba6f-afea-4b5b-9d06-6be25759f5e4/.

IMDb. "Dead Poets Society (1989)." http://www.imdb.com/title/tt0097165/characters/nm0000245.

International Labour Organization. "50 Million People Worldwide in Modern Slavery." September 12, 2022. https://www.ilo.org/resource/news/50-million-people-worldwide-modern-slavery-0.

Inside Higher Ed. "What Took the Place of Western Civ?" February 18, 2020. https://www.insidehighered.com/views/2020/02/19/how-revision-western-civ-curriculum-resulted-no-curriculum-all-opinion.

Irwin, Véronique, et al. "Report on the Condition of Education 2023." National Center for Education Statistics. https://nces.ed.gov/use-work/resource-library/report/compendium/condition-education-2023?pubid=2023144.

Jacobs, Rose. "The Downfall (and Possible Salvation) of Expertise." Chicago Booth Review, November 30, 2020. https://www.chicagobooth.edu/review/downfall-and-possible-salvation-expertise.

Jago, Arthur G. "Can It Really Be True that Half of Academic Papers Are Never Read?" The Chronicle of Higher Education, June 1, 2018. https://www.chronicle.com/article/can-it-really-be-true-that-half-of-academic-papers-are-never-read/.

Jamison, Peter, et al. "Home Schooling's Rise from Fringe to Fastest-Growing Form of Education." The Washington Post, October 31, 2023. https://www.washingtonpost.com/education/interactive/2023/homeschooling-growth-data-by-district/.

Jeglic, Elizabeth L. "Educator Sexual Misconduct Remains Prevalent in Schools," Psychology Today, May 17, 2023. https://www.psychologytoday.com/us/blog/protecting-children-from-sexual-abuse/202305/educator-sexual-misconduct-remains-prevalent-in.

Johnson, Keith. "How Venezuela Struck It Poor." Foreign Policy, July 16, 2018. https://foreignpolicy.com/2018/07/16/how-venezuela-struck-it-poor-oil-energy-chavez/.

Johnston, Bradley C., et al. "Unprocessed Red Meat and Processed Meat Consumption: Dietary Guideline Recommendations from the Nutritional Recommendations (NutriRECS) Consortium." Annals of Internal Medicine 171.10 (2019) 756–64. https://doi.org/10.7326/M19-1621.

Johnston, William Robert. "SBC Organization, Membership, Enrollment, Attendance Data." Johnston Archive, November 23, 2008. https://www.johnstonsarchive.net/baptist/sbcdata1.html.

Jones, Jeffrey M. "Congress' Job Approval Drops to 13%, Lowest Since 2017." Gallup, October 27, 2023. https://news.gallup.com/poll/513410/congress-job-approval-drops-lowest-2017.aspx.

Jones, Rick. "PC (USA) Church Membership Still in Decline." Presbyterian Church (USA), May 1, 2023. https://pcusa.org/news-storytelling/news/2023/5/1/pcusa-church-membership-still-decline.

Kamarck, Elaine. "The Iranian Hostage Crisis and Its Effect on American Politics." The Brookings Institution, November 4, 2019. https://www.brookings.edu/articles/the-iranian-hostage-crisis-and-its-effect-on-american-politics/.

Kant, Immanuel. Critique of Pure Reason. Translated by Norman Kemp Smith. New York: St. Martin's, 1965.

Kaiser, Jocelyn. "Potti Found Guilty of Research Misconduct." Science, November 9, 2015. https://www.science.org/content/article/potti-found-guilty-research-misconduct.

Kasperkevic, Jana. "Georgia Cheating Scandal: 11 Teachers Found Guilty of Racketeering." The Guardian, April 1, 2015. https://www.theguardian.com/us-news/2015/apr/01/atlanta-teachers-found-guilty-cheating.

Kearny, Melissa S. The Two-Parent Privilege: How Americans Stopped Getting Married and Started Falling Behind. Chicago: University of Chicago Press, 2023.

Keeports, Aaron. "Blog: The Slow Burn of Digital Transformation and the Downfall of Sears." Cleo. https://www.cleo.com/blog/downfall-of-sears.

Kelling, George L. "How New York Became Safe: The Full Story." City Journal, 2009. https://www.city-journal.org/article/how-new-york-became-safe-the-full-story/.

Kennedy, Brian, and Alec Tyson. "Americans' Trust in Scientists, Positive Views of Science Continue to Decline." Pew Research Center, November 14, 2023. https://www.pewresearch.org/science/2023/11/14/americans-trust-in-scientists-positive-views-of-science-continue-to-decline/.

Kerney, Melissa, et al. "The Mystery of the Declining U.S. Birth Rate." Econofact, February 15, 2022. https://econofact.org/the-mystery-of-the-declining-u-s-birth-rate.

Kim, Juliana. "Harvard Professor Who Studies Dishonesty Is Accused of Falsifying Data." NPR, June 26, 2023. https://www.npr.org/2023/06/26/1184289296/harvard-professor-dishonesty-francesca-gino.

King, Ryan. "Veterans Slam Pentagon's Reported Social Media Surveillance Push." New York Post, June 23, 2023. https://nypost.com/2023/06/23/veterans-slam-pentagons-social-media-surveillance-push/.

Kirby, Alan. "The Death of Postmodernism And Beyond," Philosophy Now 58 (2006). https://philosophynow.org/issues/58/The_Death_of_Postmodernism_And_Beyond.

Knight Foundation. "American Views 2022: Part 2, Trust, Media and Democracy." February 15, 2023. https://knightfoundation.org/reports/american-views-2023-part-2/.

Knowledge at Wharton Staff. "How Venezuela Fell Apart." Knowledge at Wharton, July 12, 2016. https://knowledge.wharton.upenn.edu/article/how-venezuela-fell-apart/.

Knox, Liam. "Can High Schoolers Save the Community College?" Inside Higher Ed, November 21, 2022. https://www.insidehighered.com/news/2022/11/22/community-colleges-struggle-dual-enrollment-grows.

———. "Shrinking Pains at West Virginia University." Inside Higher Ed, June 23, 2023. https://www.insidehighered.com/news/governance/executive-leadership/2023/06/23/distraught-west-virginia-u-faculty-push-back.

Koons, Robert C. Is St. Thomas's Aristotelian Philosophy of Nature Obsolete? South Bend, Indiana: St. Augustine's, 2022.

Kopp, Carol. "Anatomy Of A Mistake." CBS News, March 16, 2003. https://www.cbsnews.com/news/anatomy-of-a-mistake-16-03-2003/.

Kredo, Adam. "America's Missile Defense System Is in Tatters, Government Report Finds." The Washington Free Beacon, May 23, 2023. https://freebeacon.com/national-security/americas-missile-defense-system-is-in-tatters-government-report-finds/.

Krisher, Tom. "Auto Prices Are Starting to Cool After Nearly Three Years of Inflationary Hikes." WCNC Charlotte, February 28, 2024. https://www.wcnc.com/article/news/nation-world/car-prices-lowering-after-years-of-inflationary-increases/507-38c393bf-86a5-4e46-a0f0-ac87858e426a.

Kruse, Michael. "The TV Interview that Haunts Hillary Clinton." Politico, September 23, 2016. https://politi.co/2AdwRdw.

Lafree, Gary. "Social Institutions and the Crime 'Bust' of the 1990s." Journal of Criminal Law and Criminology 88.4 (1998) 1325–68. https://doi.org/10.2307/1144258.

Lahoud, Nelly. "Bin Laden's Catastrophic Success." Foreign Affairs, August 13, 2021. https://www.foreignaffairs.com/afghanistan/osama-bin-ladens-911-catastrophic-success

Lederman, Doug. "Citing Significant Budget Deficits, Several Colleges Face Cuts." Inside Higher Ed, October 2, 2023. https://www.insidehighered.com/news/business/cost-cutting/2023/10/02/several-colleges-plan-cuts-address-significant-financial-woes

Leonard, Bill. "The Nondenominationalizing of American Christianity." Baptist News Global, November 29, 2022. https://baptistnews.com/article/the-nondenominationalizing-of-american-christianity/.

Leonhardt, Megan. "When Women Make More, Couples Hide It." CNBC, July 18, 2018. https://www.cnbc.com/2018/07/17/when-women-make-more-couples-hide-it.html.

Lewis, Helen. "The Progressives Who Flunked the Hamas Test." The Atlantic, October 13, 2023. https://www.theatlantic.com/ideas/archive/2023/10/hamas-pop-intersectionality-leftism-israel/675625/.

Lewis, Ray. "Anti-Israel Columbia Students Call for 'Total Eradication of Western Civilization.'" Fox 45 News, August 8, 2024. https://www.foxbaltimore.com/station/share/anti-israel-columbia-students-call-for-total-eradication-of-western-civilization-divest-palestine-hamas-bangladesh-protests-demonstrations.

Lowe, Derek. "The Duke/Potti Scandal, From the Inside." Science, January 14, 2015. https://www.science.org/content/blog-post/duke-potti-scandal-inside.

Lu, Adrienne. "Should Colleges Make Anti-Racism Part of Their Mission? Proposal at UMass-Boston Alarms Critics." The Chronicle of Higher Education, March 11, 2022. https://www.chronicle.com/article/should-colleges-make-anti-racism-part-their-mission-proposal-at-umass-boston-alarms-critics.

Ma, Annie. "How the Presidents of Harvard, Penn and MIT Testified to Congress on Antisemitism." AP News, December 12, 2023. https://apnews.com/article/harvard-penn-mit-president-congress-intifada-193a1c81e9ebcc15c5dd68b71b4c6b71.

MacIntyre, Alasdair. *After Virtue: A Study in Moral Theory*. Notre Dame, IN: University of Notre Dame Press, 1984.

Maher, Katherine. "What Wikipedia Teaches Us About Balancing Truth and Beliefs." TED, August 2021. https://www.ted.com/talks/katherine_maher_what_wikipedia_teaches_us_about_balancing_truth_and_beliefs/transcript.

Mahnken, Kevin. "NAEP Scores 'Flashing Red' After a Lost Generation of Learning for 13-Year-Olds." The 74, June 21, 2023. https://www.the74million.org/article/naep-scores-flashing-red-after-a-lost-generation-of-learning-for-13-year-olds/.

Marketing Charts. "US Newspaper Ad Revenues Dropped by Almost 60% Over A Decade." December 12, 2023. https://www.marketingcharts.com/cross-media-and-traditional-231522.

Markovich, Ally. "Berkeley Schools Use a Discredited Reading Curriculum. Why Is It Still in Classrooms?" EdSource, January 24, 2024. https://edsource.org/2024/berkeley-schools-use-a-discredited-reading-curriculum-why-is-it-still-in-classrooms/704503.

Martin, Patricia Yancey. "Gender as Social Institution." *Social Forces* 82.4 (2004) 1249–73. https://doi.org/10.1353/sof.2004.0081.

Matos, Gregory. "Why So Many Young Males Are Single and Sexless." Psychology Today, February 24, 2023. https://www.psychologytoday.com/us/blog/the-state-of-our-unions/202302/why-are-so-many-young-men-single-and-sexless.

McCray, Vanessa. "Altered Test Scores Years Ago Altered Lives, Stained Atlanta Schools." *The Atlanta Journal-Constitution*, February 22, 2018. https://www.ajc.com/news/local-education/altered-test-scores-altered-lives-stained-atlanta-schools/nFHhI3jPSQ7MjIS9dRuCNM/.

McEntyre, Nicholas. "Former Washington High School Teacher Avoids Jail Time After Having Sex with Student, 17, While Husband Was on Hunting Trip." *New York Post*, March 30, 2024. https://nypost.com/2024/03/30/us-news/former-washington-state-high-school-teacher-mckenna-kindred-avoids-jail-time-after-having-sex-with-student/.

McGurran, Brianna. "College Tuition Inflation: Compare the Cost Of College over Time." Forbes, May 9, 2023. https://www.forbes.com/advisor/student-loans/college-tuition-inflation/.

Mead, Lauren B. *Transforming Congregations of the Future*. Once and Future Church Series. New York: Alban Institute, 1994.

Mehl, Gelsey. "Twenty Percent of Community College Students Are in High School. Now What?" New America, July 31, 2023. http://newamerica.org/education-policy/edcentral/dual-enrollment-growth/.

Mervosh, Sarah, et al. "What the Data Says About Pandemic School Closures, Four Years Later." *The New York Times*, March 18, 2024. https://www.nytimes.com/2024/03/18/upshot/pandemic-school-closures-data.html.

Meyer, Katharine. "The Case for College: Promising Solutions to Reverse College Enrollment Declines." Brookings. https://www.brookings.edu/articles/the-case-for-college-promising-solutions-to-reverse-college-enrollment-declines/.

Meyersohn, Nathaniel. "How It All Went Wrong at JCPenney." CNN, September 27, 2018. https://www.cnn.com/2018/09/27/business/jcpenney-history/index.html.

Mitchell, Anne Whisnant. "Another Small Liberal Arts College Has Closed, but This Time It Was Mine." Faith and Leadership, July 3, 2024. https://faithandleadership. com/another-small-liberal-arts-college-has-closed-time-it-was-mine.

Mintz, Steven. "The Humanities Are in the Midst of a Historic Paradigm Shift." Inside Higher Ed, March 4, 2023. https://www.insidehighered.com/blogs/higher-ed-gamma/humanities-are-midst-historic-paradigm-shift.

Missile Defense Project. "Ground-Based Midcourse Defense (GMD) System." Missile Threat, July 26, 2021. https://missilethreat.csis.org/system/gmd/.

Mitchell, Michael, et al. "A Lost Decade in Higher Education Funding." Center on Budget and Policy Priorities, August 23, 2017. https://www.cbpp.org/research/a-lost-decade-in-higher-education-funding.

Montanaro, Domenico. "Hillary Clinton's 'Basket Of Deplorables,' in Full Context of This Ugly Campaign." NPR, September 10, 2016. https://www.npr. org/2016/09/10/493427601/hillary-clintons-basket-of-deplorables-in-full-context-of-this-ugly-campaign.

Moody, Josh. "2024 Begins with Wave of Job Cuts." Inside Higher Ed, January 25, 2024. https://www.insidehighered.com/news/business/financial-health/2024/01/25/2024-begins-wave-job-and-program-cuts.

———. "University of Kansas Looks to Cut 42 Academic Programs." Inside Higher Ed, February 17, 2022. https://www.insidehighered.com/news/2022/02/18/university-kansas-plans-cut-42-academic-programs.

———. "What Do DePaul's Budget Woes Mean for Catholic Higher Ed?" Inside Higher Ed, May 05, 2023. https://www.insidehighered.com/news/business/financial-health/2023/05/05/what-do-depauls-budget-woes-mean-catholic-higher-ed.

———. "When Presidents Plagiarize." Inside Higher Ed, January 12, 2024. https:// www.insidehighered.com/news/governance/executive-leadership/2024/01/12/when-college-presidents-plagiarize.

Mooney, Taylor, and Justin Sherman. "How 'Cancel Culture' Changed These Three Lives Forever." CBS News, August 13, 2020. https://www.cbsnews.com/news/cancel-culture-changed-lives-forever-cbsn-originals/.

Moorpark College. "Do Philosophy Majors Get Jobs?" https://www.moorparkcollege. edu/departments/academic/philosophy/do-philosophy-majors-get-jobs.

Mostert, Christian, and Geoff, Thompson, eds. Karl Barth: A Future for Postmodern Theology? Hindmarsh: Australian Theological Forum, 2001.

Mousavizadeh, Philip. "A 'Proliferation of Administrators': Faculty Reflect on Two Decades of Rapid Expansion." Yale Daily News, November 10, 2021. https:// yaledailynews.com/blog/2021/11/10/reluctance-on-the-part-of-its-leadership-to-lead-yales-administration-increases-by-nearly-50-percent/.

National Academies of Sciences, Engineering, and Medicine, et al. "Detailed Case Histories." In Fostering Integrity in Research. Washington, DC: National Academies, 2017. https://www.ncbi.nlm.nih.gov/books/NBK475955/.

National Center for Educational Statistics. "Characteristics of Degree-Granting Postsecondary Institutions." Condition of Education, August 2023. https://nces. ed.gov/programs/coe/indicator/csa/postsecondary-institutions.

———. "Undergraduate Enrollment." Condition of Education, May 2023. https://nces. ed.gov/programs/coe/indicator/cha.

National Home Education Research Institute. "Research Facts." January 27, 2025. https://nheri.org/research-facts-on-homeschooling/.

NEA Today. "Sexual Violence in Schools." NEA Today, January 2021. https://www.nea.org/nea-today/all-news-articles/sexual-violence-schools.

Nelson, Libby. "Yale's Big Fight over Sensitivity and Free Speech, Explained." Vox, November 7, 2015. https://www.vox.com/2015/11/7/9689330/yale-halloween-email.

Nelson, Libby. "Inside UNC's Outrageous Academic Scandal: Athletes Took Fake Classes for 18 Years." Vox, October 22, 2014. https://www.vox.com/2014/10/22/7040107/unc-academic-scandal-explained.

NeuroLeadership Institute Staff. "How JFK Inspired the Term 'Groupthink.'" NeuroLeadership Institute, February 20, 2019. https://neuroleadership.com/your-brain-at-work/jfk-inspired-term-groupthink/.

Newsome, Teresa. "Little Self-Care Tips For A Happier Relationship." Bustle, May 17, 2016. https://www.bustle.com/articles/160468–11-little-self-care-tips-for-a-happier-relationship.

New York Post Editorial Board. "NYT Writer Blames the 'Partisan Politics' It Promoted for the Lab Leak Coverup." New York Post, June 4, 2024. https://nypost.com/2024/06/04/opinion/nyt-writer-blames-the-partisan-politics-it-promoted-for-the-lab-leak-coverup/.

Nichols, Thomas M. The Death of Expertise: The Campaign Against Established Knowledge and Why It Matters. New York: Oxford University Press, 2019.

Nietzel, Michael T. "Percentage Of U.S. Adults with College Degree or Postsecondary Credential Reaches New High, According to Lumina Report." Forbes, February 1, 2023. https://www.forbes.com/sites/michaeltnietzel/2023/02/01/percentage-of-us-adults-with-a-college-degree-postsecondary-credential-reaches-new-high-according-to-lumina/.

———. "State Support For Higher Education Tops $112 Billion, Up More than 6% Over Last Year." Forbes, February 3, 2023. https://www.forbes.com/sites/michaeltnietzel/2023/02/03/state-support-for-higher-education-tops-112-billion-up-more-than-6-over-last-year/.

Nietzsche, Friedrich. The Gay Science With a Prelude in Rhymes and an Appendix of Songs. Delhi: Grapevine India, 2002. Kindle.

Niskanen Center. "Elites Misperceive the Public." January 24, 2024. https://www.niskanencenter.org/elites-misperceive-the-public/.

Noel, Josh. "What Is the Average Monthly Car Payment?" Autolist, October 15, 2021. https://www.autolist.com/guides/average-car-payment.

North American Mission Board Staff. "A Brief History of Southern Baptist Missions in North America." North American Mission Board. https://www.namb.net/news/a-brief-history-of-southern-baptist-missions-in-north-america/.

Northwestern University. "Medill Report Shows Local News Deserts Expanding." Northwestern Medill, October 23, 2024. https://www.medill.northwestern.edu/news/2024/medill-report-shows-local-news-deserts-expanding.html.

Novelly, Thomas. "Even More Young Americans Are Unfit to Serve, a New Study Finds. Here's Why." Military.com, September 28, 2022. https://www.military.com/daily-news/2022/09/28/new-pentagon-study-shows-77-of-young-americans-are-ineligible-military-service.html.

Oberg, Ted, et al. "MPD Carjacking Task Force: 'We Need More' Officers as Crimes Soar." NBC4 Washington, February 23, 2023. https://www.nbcwashington.com/ investigations/mpd-carjacking-task-force-we-need-more-officers-as-crimes-soar/3285128/.

Ocasio, William, et al. "History, Society, and Institutions: The Role of Collective Memory in the Emergence and Evolution of Societal Logics." *Academy of Management Review* 41.4 (2016) 676–99. https://doi.org/10.5465/amr.2014.0183.

O'Dell, Hope. "1 in 5 Young People Around the World Are NEETs. What Are NEETs?" GlobalAffairs.org. Blue Marble, February 15, 2024. https://globalaffairs.org/ bluemarble/why-youth-neets-rise-worldwide-mental-health-cost-of-living.

Office of Student Life and Christian Mission. "Undergraduate Student Handbook 2024–2025." Campbell University, August 2024. https://assets.campbell.edu/wp-content/uploads/2024/08/student_handbook_20242025_final.pdf.

Olay, Matthew. "Kabul Airport Attack Review Reaffirms Initial Findings, Identifies Attacker." U.S. Department of Defense, April 15, 2024. https://www.defense. gov/News/News-Stories/Article/Article/3741245/kabul-airport-attack-review-reaffirms-initial-findings-identifies-attacker/.

Olohan, Mary Margaret. "PBS Fires Former Employee Following Project Veritas Video Exposing 'Hateful Rhetoric.'" The Daily Caller, January 12, 2021. https://dailycaller. com/2021/01/12/pbs-fires-former-employee-following-project-veritas-video-exposing-hateful-rhetoric/?utm_source=piano&utm_medium=email&utm_ campaign=2906&pnespid=i.I9_ehUFAaNObiPojKpoomfJmUUJjFxewHPsvlq.

Oransky, Ivan, and Adam Marcus. "There's Far More Scientific Fraud than Anyone Wants to Admit." *The Guardian*, August 9, 2023. https://www.theguardian.com/ commentisfree/2023/aug/09/scientific-misconduct-retraction-watch.

Orwell, George. *All Art Is Propaganda: Critical Essays*. New York: Mariner, 2009.

———."Notes on Nationalism." The Orwell Foundation. https://www. orwellfoundation.com/the-orwell-foundation/orwell/essays-and-other-works/ notes-on-nationalism/.

———. *Why I Write*. Great Ideas. New York: Penguin, 2005.

Padavic-Callaghan, Karmella. "Physicists Are Grappling with Their Own Reproducibility Crisis." New Scientist, May 21, 2024. https://www.newscientist. com/article/2431927-physicists-are-grappling-with-their-own-reproducibility-crisis/.

Parker, Kim, and Rachel Minkin. "5. What Makes for a Fulfilling Life?" Pew Research Center, September 14, 2023. https://www.pewresearch.org/social-trends/2023/09/14/what-makes-for-a-fulfilling-life/.

Parkih, Sudip. "Why We Must Rebuild Trust in Science." Pew Trusts, February 9, 2021. https://www.pewtrusts.org/en/trend/archive/winter-2021/why-we-must-rebuild-trust-in-science.

Pascal. "Napoleon: Personality, Routine, Life in Paris." Private Tour Guide in Paris (blog), March 20, 2022. https://www.tours-in-paris.com/post/napoleon-personality-routine-and-life-in-paris-and-fontainebleau.

Paul, Annie Murphy. "Atlanta Teachers Were Offered Bonuses for High Test Scores. Of Course They Cheated." *The Washington Post*, April 16, 2015. https://www. washingtonpost.com/posteverything/wp/2015/04/16/atlanta-teachers-were-offered-bonuses-for-high-test-scores-of-course-they-cheated/.

Pawlyk, Oriana. "One-Third of Youths Too Obese for Military Service, Study Finds." Military.com, October 10, 2018. https://www.military.com/daily-news/2018/10/10/one-third-youths-too-obese-military-service-study-finds.html.

Payne, Daniel. "As Home Schooling Soars in U.S., Catholic Schools Struggle to Recover from Pandemic." Catholic News Agency, November 18, 2023. https://www.catholicnewsagency.com/news/256048/as-homeschooling-soars-in-us-catholic-schools-struggle-to-recover-from-pandemic.

Perdomo, Williams. "At Least 33 Pro-Palestine Vandals Arrested for Causing Chaos at George Washington University." Voz Media, May 8, 2024. https://voz.us/en/society/240508/9961/at-least-33-pro-palestine-vandals-arrested-for-causing-chaos-at-george-washington-university.html.

Perry, John. "Are Drastic Swings in CRCT Scores Valid?" *The Atlanta Journal-Constitution*, July 5, 2011. https://dev.ajc.com/news/local/are-drastic-swings-crct-scores-valid/1uNxbbiLUZjvYQx6gMkyyN/

Peske, Heather. "Teaching Reading Is Brain Science." National Council on Teacher Quality, November 17, 2022. https://www.nctq.org/blog/Teaching-reading-is-brain-science.

Pew Research Center. "Newspapers Fact Sheet." November 10, 2023. https://www.pewresearch.org/journalism/fact-sheet/newspapers/.

———. "Public Trust in Government: 1958–2024." June 24, 2024. https://www.pewresearch.org/politics/2024/06/24/public-trust-in-government-1958-2024/.

———. "US Muslims Concerned About Their Place in Society but Still Believe in the American Dream." July 26, 2017. https://www.pewresearch.org/religion/2017/07/26/demographic-portrait-of-muslim-americans/.

Piper, Kelsey. "A Harvard Dishonesty Researcher Was Accused of Fraud. Her Defense Is Troubling." Vox, March 22, 2024. https://www.vox.com/future-perfect/24107889/francesca-gino-lawsuit-harvard-dishonesty-researcher-academic-fraud.

Podhoretz, John. "The Actual Pauline Kael Quote—Not As Bad, and Worse." Commentary, February 27, 2011. https://www.commentary.org/john-podhoretz/the-actual-pauline-kael-quote—not-as-bad-and-worse/.

Poleo, Germania Rodriguez. "Tufts University Students Are Ripped Apart for Praising the 'Creativity' of Hamas Terrorists Using Paragliders to 'Launch Historic Attack on Colonizers.'" *Daily Mail*, October 11, 2023. https://www.dailymail.co.uk/news/article-12620307/Tufts-University-students-palestine-statement.html.

Powell, Laura (@LauraPowellEsq). "March 10, 2020 Oakland High School in Oakland, California, a school with 85% of kids living in poverty The principal announces over the loudspeaker that school will close for three weeks, effective that day, joking, 'If you have any additional questions, don't ask them, because we don't have the answers.' A teacher tells students to let them know if they don't have internet access, but since many of them are tech savvy, "I know you're going to figure some way to get in touch with us." The school did not reopen for 17 months, and since then, around half of the students have been chronically absent. Never forget." X, post, June 29, 2024. https://x.com/LauraPowellEsq/status/1807179657860796850.

———. "@OXHarryH1 The Chronic Absentee Rate from the Most Recent Year Is 54.8%, According to the California Department of Education. I Don't Know How the Absentee Rate of Rural Districts in Florida Is Relevant. Https://T.Co/bnnf3RholQ." Tweet. Twitter, June 30, 2024. https://x.com/LauraPowellEsq/status/1807473381551513934.

Press TV. "US 'Vulnerable' to Foreign Attacks with Missile System in Tatters: Government Report." May 23, 2023. https://www.presstv.ir/Detail/2023/05/23/703978/US-patriot-air-defense-system-vulnerable-to-missiles-attacks-by-China-North-Korea-Iran.

Public Agenda. "America's Hidden Common Ground on Public Higher Education: What's Wrong and How to Fix It." July 11, 2022. https://publicagenda.org/resource/americas-hidden-common-ground-on-public-higher-education-whats-wrong-and-how-to-fix-it/.

The Pulitzer Prizes. "*The Boston Globe.*" https://www.pulitzer.org/winners/boston-globe-1.

Querolo, Nick. "Largest Catholic University in US Faces $56 Million Budget Gap," Bloomberg, April 14, 2023. https://www.bloomberg.com/news/articles/2023-04-14/depaul-university-faces-growing-budget-gap-as-enrollment-shrinks.

Quinn, Ryan. "Fired LSU Professor Accused of Student Affair, Illegal Anti-CRT Lobbying." Inside Higher Ed, December 8, 2023. https://www.insidehighered.com/news/faculty-issues/tenure/2023/12/08/ex-lsu-prof-accused-affair-illegal-anti-crt-lobbying.

Quoteresearch. "For There Is Nothing as Stupid as an Educated Man if You Get Off the Thing that He Was Educated In." Quote Investigator, April 25, 2019. https://quoteinvestigator.com/2019/04/25/educated/.

Rains, Taylor. "Boeing Whistleblower Said the Company Threatened Him and Other Engineers to Keep Quiet about Safety Concerns." Business Insider, April 17, 2024. https://www.businessinsider.com/boeing-whistleblower-said-was-threatened-to-keep-quiet-about-safety-2024-4.

Ray, Brian. "Research Facts." National Home Education Research Institute, January 27, 2025. https://www.nheri.org/research-facts-on-homeschooling/.

Read, Daniel, et al. "Balancing Mission Creep, Means, Effectiveness and Legitimacy at the World Anti-Doping Agency." *Performance Enhancement and Health* 8.2 (2020) 100175. https://doi.org/10.1016/j.peh.2020.100175.

Reinl, James. "Anti-Racism Scholar Accused of Copying from Asian-American Colleagues." *Daily Mail*, August 28, 2024. https://www.dailymail.co.uk/news/article-13788709/Robin-DiAngelo-white-fragility-racism-scholar-plagiarism-asian-american.html.

Religion News. "Majority of Americans Report Experience of God's Love Leads to Increased Benevolence." Religion News Service, December 18, 2012. https://religionnews.com/2012/12/18/majority-of-americans-report-experience-of-gods-love-leads-to-increased-benevolence.

Richardson, Bradford. "Religious People More Likely to Give to Charity, Study Shows." *The Washington Times*, October 30, 2017. https://www.washingtontimes.com/news/2017/oct/30/religious-people-more-likely-give-charity-study/.

Richburg, Keith B. "America Tried Nation-Building in Afghanistan—but Never Committed to It." The *Washington Post*, August 21, 2021. https://www.washingtonpost.com/outlook/2021/08/21/afghanistan-biden-obama-bush/.

Rizzo, Lillian. "Broadcast and Cable Make Up Less than Half of TV Usage for the First Time Ever." CNBC, August 15, 2023. https://www.cnbc.com/2023/08/15/traditional-tv-usage-drops-below-50percent-for-first-time-ever.html.

Robinson, Jenna A. "Did You Know? NC Subsidies for Colleges Top 5 Nationally." The James G. Martin Center for Academic Renewal, December 3, 2020. https://www.jamesgmartin.center/2020/12/did-you-know-nc-subsidies-for-colleges-top-5-nationally/.

Robinson, Linda. "Our Biggest Errors in Afghanistan and What We Should Learn from Them." Council on Foreign Relations, June 22, 2023. https://www.cfr.org/article/our-biggest-errors-afghanistan-and-what-we-should-learn-them.

Robinson, Matt. "*The New York Times* Just Destroyed Its Credibility—and Much More." Newsweek, October 19, 2023. https://www.newsweek.com/new-york-times-destroys-more-just-its-credibility-opinion-1836304.

Robinson, Tilly R., and Neil H. Shah. "Top Harvard Diversity Officer Sherri Charleston Faces Plagiarism Allegations." *The Harvard Crimson*, January 31, 2024. https://www.thecrimson.com/article/2024/1/31/sherri-charleston-plagiarism-allegations.

Robertson, Jo. "Telling It All?: Challenging Crisis Communications' Rules." *Public Relations Journal* 6.1 (2012) 1–16.

Rogers, Will. "There Is Nothing So Stupid as an Educated Man, if You Get Him Off the Thing He Was Educated In." Forbes. https://www.forbes.com/quotes/9722/#:~:text=There%20is%20nothing%20so%20stupid%20as%20an%20educated%20man%2C%20if,thing%20he%20was%20educated%20in.

Rosenthal, Linda J. "Mission Creep Faced by Detroit Nonprofit." For Purpose Law Group, February 13, 2020. https://www.fplglaw.com/insights/mission-creep-faced-detroit-nonprofit/.

Royston, Jack. "Jeffrey Epstein Hot Mic Scandal Goes Viral as Names Released." Newsweek, January 4, 2024. https://www.newsweek.com/jeffrey-epstein-hot-mic-amy-robach-prince-william-kate-middleton-1857802.

Rubio, Marco. "Marco Rubio: The Military Recruitment Crisis Is More Dangerous than We Know." The National Interest, January 22, 2024. https://nationalinterest.org/feature/marco-rubio-military-recruitment-crisis-more-dangerous-we-know-208758.

Rugaber, Christopher. "U.S. Inflation at 9.1 Percent, a Record High." PBS News, July 13, 2022. https://www.pbs.org/newshour/economy/u-s-inflation-at-9-1-percent-a-record-high.

Rufo, Christopher F. "Harvard's Plagiarism Problem Multiplies." City Journal, February 22, 2024. https://www.city-journal.org/article/harvards-plagiarism-problem-multiplies/.

Russell, Nichole. "COVID Guidelines Caused Millions to Suffer. Now Fauci Admits 'There Was No Science Behind It.'" *USA Today*, June 5, 2024. https://www.usatoday.com/story/opinion/columnist/2024/06/05/fauci-hearing-covid-social-distancing-wrong/73962967007/.

Rutgers Newark. "A Social Justice Champion." https://www.newark.rutgers.edu/meet-rutgers-newark/social-justice-champion.

Saad, Lydia. "Historically Low Faith in U.S. Institutions Continues." Gallup, July 6, 2023. https://news.gallup.com/poll/508169/historically-low-faith-institutions-continues.aspx.

Sadler, Kelly. "Top 10 Recent Examples of Cancel Culture." *The Washington Times*, February 16, 2021. https://www.washingtontimes.com/news/2021/feb/16/top-10-recent-examples-cancel-culture/.

Sagalov, Yuri (@yuris). "Slow evolution of a NYTimes headline. 'Israeli Strike'—> 'Strike'—> 'Blast.'" X, post, October 17, 2023. https://x.com/yuris/status/1714377474086506839.

Sánchez, Lily. "Why We Should Abolish the Family." Current Affairs, September 5, 2022. https://www.currentaffairs.org/news/2022/09/why-we-should-abolish-the-family.

Sandefur, Timothy. "The 1619 Project: An Autopsy." Cato Institute, October 27, 2020. https://www.cato.org/commentary/1619-project-autopsy.

Schermele, Zachary. "Public Trust in Higher Ed Has Plummeted. Yes, Again." The Chronicle of Higher Education, July 11, 2023. https://www.chronicle.com/article/public-trust-in-higher-ed-has-plummeted-yes-again.

Schiavenza, Matt. "Obama Will Focus on Wealth Inequality—Not Just Income." The Atlantic, January 18, 2015. https://www.theatlantic.com/politics/archive/2015/01/obama-to-shift-focus-from-income-to-wealth/384630/.

Schiffer, Zoë. "Google Fires Second AI Ethics Researcher Following Internal Investigation." The Verge, February 19, 2021. https://www.theverge.com/2021/2/19/22292011/google-second-ethical-ai-researcher-fired.

Schlott, Rikki. "Professor Fired for 'Faking Data to Prove Lynching Makes Whites Want Longer Sentences for Blacks,' 6 Studies Retracted." New York Post, August 4, 2023. https://nypost.com/2023/08/04/professor-fired-for-faking-data-to-prove-whites-want-longer-sentences-for-blacks/.

School of Public Health. "Examples of Racial Microaggressions." University of Minnesota. https://sph.umn.edu/site/docs/hewg/microaggressions.pdf.

Schneider, Howard. "The Fed's Stages of Inflation Grief, in Powell's Words." Reuters, June 14, 2023. https://www.reuters.com/markets/us/feds-stages-inflation-grief-powells-words-2023-06-14/#:~:text=By%20March%202022%2C%20the%20Fed,again%20surprised%20to%20the%20upside.

Schwantes, Marcel. "New Report: Only 12 Percent of Employees Are Fully Productive at Work (The Reason Why May Surprise You)." Inc., April 6, 2022. https://www.inc.com/marcel-schwantes/new-report-only-12-percent-of-employees-are-fully-productive-at-work-the-reasons-why-may-surprise-you.html.

Schwartz, Sarah. "Teachers College to 'Dissolve' Lucy Calkins' Reading and Writing Project." Education Week, September 5, 2023. https://www.edweek.org/teaching-learning/teachers-college-to-dissolve-lucy-calkins-reading-and-writing-project/2023/09.

Scruton, Roger. Beauty: A Very Short Introduction. Vol. 262 of Very Short Introductions. Oxford : Oxford University Press, 2011.

———. Fools, Frauds and Firebrands: Thinkers of the New Left. London: Bloomsbury, 2016.

———. Modern Philosophy: An Introduction and Survey. New York: Penguin, 1996.

Sedlak, A. J., et al. "Fourth National Incidence Study of Child Abuse and Neglect (NIS-4): Report to Congress." Office of Planning, Research and Evaluation, January 15, 2010. https://acf.gov/opre/report/fourth-national-incidence-study-child-abuse-and-neglect-nis-4-report-congress.

Sensoy, Özelm, and Robin DiAngelo. "Developing Social Justice Literacy: An Open Letter to Our Faculty Colleagues." Phi Delta Kappan 90.5 (2009) 345–52. https://doi.org/10.1177/003172170909000508.

Service, Robert F. "Physicist Fired for Falsified Data." Science, September 25, 2002. https://www.science.org/content/article/physicist-fired-falsified-data.

Shelley, Susan. "Mission Creep at the Department of Homeland Security Threatens Liberty and Free Speech." *Los Angeles Daily News*, November 6, 2022. https://www.dailynews.com/2022/11/06/mission-creep-at-dhs-threatens-your-liberty/.

Shellnutt, Kate. "1 in 10 Young Protestants Have Left a Church Over Abuse." Christianity Today, May 21, 2019. https://www.christianitytoday.com/news/2019/may/lifeway-protestant-abuse-survey-young-christians-leave-chur.html.

———. "SBC Membership Falls to 47-Year Low, But Church Involvement Is Up." Christianity Today, May 7, 2024. https://christianitytoday.com/news/2024/may/southern-baptist-church-decline-sbc-annual-church-profile.html.

Simón, Armando. "The Elites Hate Us—But We Outnumber Them." Issues and Insights, January 30, 2024. https://issuesinsights.com/2024/01/30/the-elites-hate-us-but-we-outnumber-them/.

Simons, Margaret. "'Trust the Science' Is the Mantra of the Covid Crisis—but What About Human Fallibility?" *The Guardian*, July 23, 2021. https://www.theguardian.com/commentisfree/2021/jul/24/trust-the-science-is-the-mantra-of-the-covid-crisis-but-what-about-human-fallibility/.

Sisk, Richard. "The Military Recruiting Outlook Is Grim Indeed. Loss of Public Confidence, Political Attacks and the Economy Are All Taking a Toll." Military.com, January 22, 2024. https://www.military.com/daily-news/2024/01/22/uphill-battle-boost-recruiting-military-faces-falling-public-confidence-political-attacks-economic.html.

Sitrin, Carly. "'How 'Reading Captains' Are Fueling Philadelphia's Push to Improve Early Literacy." Chalkbeat, January 16, 2024. https://www.chalkbeat.org/philadelphia/2024/01/16/reading-captains-fueling-early-literacy-movement/.

Slack, Donovan. "Clinton: I Regret Saying 'Half' Trump Support from 'Basket of Deplorables.'" *USA Today*, September 10, 2016. https://www.usatoday.com/story/news/politics/onpolitics/2016/09/10/clinton-trump-supporters-deplorable/90182922/.

Smith, Peter. "United Methodists Are Breaking Up in a Slow-Motion Schism." AP News October 10, 2022. https://apnews.com/article/religion-gay-rights-f3fc3ec9e1f39501495d227d5a0963f8.

Smith, Jesse, and Nicholas H. Wolfinger. "Testing Common Theories on the Relationship Between Premarital Sex and Marital Stability." Institute for Family Studies, March 6, 2023. https://ifstudies.org/blog/testing-common-theories-on-the-relationship-between-premarital-sex-and-marital-stability.

Smith, W. Thomas Jr. "'Here I Stand; I Can Do No Other': Commemorating the 500th Anniversary of Martin Luther's 95 Theses." Columbia Metropolitan, October 2017. https://columbiametro.com/article/here-i-stand-i-can-do-no-other/.

Smithsonian. "Our History." https://www.si.edu/about/history.

Soave, Robby. "Watch Students Tell Yale to Fire a Staffer Who Upset Their Safe Space." Reason, November 6, 2015. https://reason.com/2015/11/06/watch-students-tell-yale-to-fire-a-staff/.

Sokal, Alan, and Jean Bricmont. *Intellectual Impostures*. London: Profile, 2003.

Sopko, John F. "What We Need to Learn: Lessons From Twenty Years of Afghanistan Reconstruction." DataSpace. http://arks.princeton.edu/ark:/88435/dsp011j92gb6om.

Specia, Megan. "God Save the Cathedral? In England, Some Offer Mini Golf or Giant Slide." *The New York Times*, August 13, 2019. https://www.nytimes.com/2019/08/13/world/europe/uk-norwich-cathedral.html.

Special Operations Warrior Foundation. "Operation Eagle Claw." https://specialops.
    org/operation-eagle-claw/.

Spitzer, Robert. "Neil deGrasse Tyson's Cosmos: Filling in the Intellectual Gaps."
    The Catholic World Report, March 26, 2014. https://www.catholicworldreport.
    com/2014/03/26/neil-degrasse-tysons-filling-in-the-intellectual-gaps/.

Steig, Corey. "Men Get More Stressed When Their Wives Make More Money." CNBC,
    November 20, 2019. https://www.cnbc.com/2019/11/20/study-men-get-more-
    stressed-when-their-wives-make-more-money.html.

Steinke, Peter L. Congregational Leadership in Anxious Times: Being Calm and
    Courageous No Matter What. Lanham, MD: Alban Institute, 2006.

———. How Your Church Family Works: Understanding Congregations as Emotional
    Systems. Lanham, MD: Alban Institute, 1993.

Stetzer, Ed. "If It Doesn't Stem Its Decline, Mainline Protestantism Has Just 23 Easters
    Left." The Washington Post, April 28, 2017. https://www.washingtonpost.com/
    news/acts-of-faith/wp/2017/04/28/if-it-doesnt-stem-its-decline-mainline-
    protestantism-has-just-23-easters-left/.

———. "Pentecostals: How Do They Keep Growing While Other Groups Are
    Declining?" ChurchLeaders, June 27, 2023. https://churchleaders.com/
    voices/453879-pentecostals-how-do-they-keep-growing.html.

Stevens, R. Paul, and Phil Collins. The Equipping Pastor: A Systems Approach to
    Congregational Leadership. Lanham, MD: Alban Institute, 1993.

Stone, Mike. "Pentagon Fails Audit for Sixth Year in a Row." Reuters, November 15,
    2023. https://www.reuters.com/world/us/pentagon-fails-audit-sixth-year-
    row-2023-11-16/.

Strauss, Valerie. "How and Why Convicted Atlanta Teachers Cheated on Standardized
    Tests." The Washington Post, April 1, 2015. https://www.washingtonpost.com/
    news/answer-sheet/wp/2015/04/01/how-and-why-convicted-atlanta-teachers-
    cheated-on-standardized-tests/.

———. "Remember the Atlanta Schools' Cheating Scandal? It Isn't Over." The
    Washington Post, February 1, 2022. https://www.washingtonpost.com/
    education/2022/02/01/atlanta-cheating-schools-scandal-teachers/.

Stu (@thestustustudio). "At the George Washington University Gaza Solidarity
    Encampment today, the protesters held a 'People's Tribunal' where they put
    President Ellen Granberg, Provost Christopher Bracey, the Board of Trustees, @
    GWPolice, and many others on trial. Is it normal for students to want to hang their
    provost and chop the heads off of the Board of Trustees? 'Guillotine, Guillotine,
    Guillotine, Guillotine' 'Bracey, Bracey, we see you. You assault students too. Off to
    the motherfucking gallows with you.' 'As you already know where I am sending
    her [to the guillotine], her and her fuckass bob.' When will @GWtweets finally
    do something? If the students hurt any of these people in any way, the university
    will be completely at fault." X, post, May 3, 2024. https://x.com/thestustustudio/
    status/1786541753064931643.

Stump, Eleonore. Wandering in Darkness: Narrative and the Problem of Suffering.
    Oxford: Oxford University Press, 2010.

Sukheja, Bhavya. "Osama Bin Laden 'Miscalculated' US' Response To 9/11 Attacks,
    Show Navy SEAL Documents: Report." NDTV World, April 25, 2022. https://
    www.ndtv.com/world-news/osama-bin-laden-planned-a-second-terror-attack-
    against-us-after-9–11-navy-seals-documents-reveal-2917639.

Sweeden, Nell Becker. "Review of *After Virtue* by Alasdair MacIntyre." Center for Practical Theology. Baylor University. https://www.bu.edu/cpt/resources/book-reviews/after-virtue-by-alasdair-macintyre/.

Tanne, Janice Hopkins. "When Jesica Died." *British Medical Journal* 326.7391 (2003) 717. https://www.ncbi.nlm.nih.gov/pmc/articles/PMC1125622/.

Theis, Alexandra. "We Asked NEETs What They Do All Day." Vice, January 4, 2024. https://www.vice.com/en/article/y3weq5/neets-what-do-they-do.

The Times of India World Desk. "Iraq to Reduce Legal Marriage Age of Girls to 9 Years." *The Times of India*, August 9, 2024. https://timesofindia.indiatimes.com/world/middle-east/iraq-to-reduce-girls-legal-marriage-age-from-to-9/articleshow/112401138.cms.

Thomas, Lauren. "Sears Was the Amazon of Its Day. As Bezos' Behemoth Becomes the World's Most Valuable Company, It Teeters on the Brink of Closing." CNBC, January 9, 2019. https://www.cnbc.com/2019/01/09/sears-was-the-amazon-of-its-day-now-jeff-bezos-behemoth-reigns.html.

Tobey, John S. "The Federal Reserve's Folly: An Inflation Rate Of 20%." Forbes, March 26, 2024. https://www.forbes.com/sites/johntobey/2024/03/26/the-federal-reserves-folly-an-inflation-rate-of-20/.

Tones, Bianca Vázquez, and Sharon Lurye. "Thousands of Kids Are Missing from School: Where Did They Go?" Associated Press, February 9, 2023. https://projects.apnews.com/features/2023/missing-children/index.html.

Tracy, Ryan. "Facebook Bowed to White House Pressure, Removed Covid Posts." *The Wall Street Journal*, July 28, 2023. https://www.wsj.com/articles/facebook-bowed-to-white-house-pressure-removed-covid-posts-2df436b7.

Troderman, Jimmy. "Retail Gasoline Prices Rose Across the United States in 2021 as Driving Increased." U.S. Energy Information Administration, January 5, 2022. https://www.eia.gov/todayinenergy/detail.php?id=50758.

Trellis Law. "Motion-Secondary: Karen Dawn vs. Peter Singer." May 10, 2022. https://trellis.law/doc/163172995/brief-memorandum-points-authorities-filed.

Tupy, Marian L., and Ronald Bailey. "The End of Poverty." Human Progress, March 5, 2023. https://humanprogress.org/trends/the-end-of-poverty/.

Turley, Jonathan. "COVID Lab Leak Is a Scandal of Media and Government Censorship." *New York Post*, February 26, 2023. https://nypost.com/2023/02/26/covid-lab-leak-is-a-scandal-of-media-and-government-censorship/.

UNC School of Medicine. "Microaggressions/Microaffirmations." https://web.archive.org/web/20220630104134/https://www.med.unc.edu/ahs/about-us/diversity/jeditoolkit/microaggressions-microaffirmations/.

Union Theological Seminary. "About." https://utsnyc.edu/about/.

United Methodist Communications. "United Methodists At-A-Glance." The People of the United Methodist Church, April 16, 2024.https://www.umc.org/en/content/united-methodists-at-a-glance.

University of Alberta. "Researchers Show Parents Give Unattractive Children Less Attention." ScienceDaily, April 13, 2005. https://www.sciencedaily.com/releases/2005/04/050412213412.htm.

University of North Carolina at Chapel Hill. "History and Traditions." https://www.unc.edu/about/history-and-traditions/.

University of Minnesota. "Mission, Vision and Social Justice Statements." Gender and Sexuality Center for Queer and Trans Life. https://gsc.umn.edu/about-us/mission-vision-social-justice-statements.

US Bureau of Labor Statistics. "Postsecondary Education Administrators." https://www.bls.gov/ooh/management/postsecondary-education-administrators.htm.

USA Facts Team. "How Many People Are in the US Military? A Demographic Overview." USA Facts, February 21, 2024. https://usafacts.org/articles/how-many-people-are-in-the-us-military-a-demographic-overview/.

Valentine, Katherine A., et al. "Judging a Man by the Width of His Face: The Role of Facial Ratios and Dominance in Mate Choice at Speed-Dating Events." *Psychological Science* 25.3 (2014) 806–11. https://doi.org/10.1177/0956797613511823.

Van Noorden, Richard. "More than 10,000 Research Papers Were Retracted in 2023—a New Record." Nature, December 12, 2023. https://www.nature.com/articles/d41586-023-03974-8.

Vergun, David. "Nation Observes Anniversary of Operation Desert Storm." U.S. Department of Defense, January 15, 2022. https://www.defense.gov/News/News-Stories/Article/article/2879147/nation-observes-anniversary-of-operation-desert-storm/.

Venugopal, Arun. "'1619 Project' Journalist Says Black People Shouldn't Be an Asterisk in U.S. History." NPR, November 17, 2021. https://www.npr.org/2021/11/17/1056404654/nikole-hannah-jones-1619-project.

Viswanathan, Giri. "Americans' Trust in Science Declining, Pew Survey Says." CNN, November 14, 2023. https://www.cnn.com/2023/11/14/health/trust-in-science-pew-survey/index.html.

Volf, Miroslav. *Exclusion and Embrace: A Theological Exploration of Identity, Otherness, and Reconciliation*. Nashville: Abingdon, 1996.

Waldman, Katy. "A Sociologist Examines the 'White Fragility' That Prevents White Americans from Confronting Racism." *The New Yorker*, July 23, 2018. https://www.newyorker.com/books/page-turner/a-sociologist-examines-the-white-fragility-that-prevents-white-americans-from-confronting-racism.

Walker, Jackson. "Professor Argues Marriage 'Fundamentalism' Helps Bolster White Supremacy." NBC Montana, March 18, 2024. https://nbcmontana.com/news/nation-world/marriage-enforces-white-heteropatriarchal-supremacy-george-mason-professor-claims-bethany-letiecq-black-lives-matter-conservative-christian-and-right-wing-organizations-such-as-the-heritage-foundation-the-american-enterprise-institute-white.

———. "Taliban Parade US Military Vehicles, Weapons to Celebrate 3 Years in Power, AP Reports." NBC 15 News, August 14, 2024. https://mynbc15.com/news/nation-world/taliban-parade-us-military-vehicles-weapons-to-celebrate-3-years-in-power-ap-reports-afghanistan-war-united-states-withdrawal-bagram-airfield.

Warta, Ashlynn. "Administrative Bloat Harms Teaching and Learning." The James G. Martin Center for Academic Renewal, August 22, 2022. https://www.jamesgmartin.center/2022/08/administrative-bloat-harms-teaching-and-learning/.

Washington Literacy Center. "Left Behind: DC's Literacy Divide." May 12, 2020. https://www.washlit.org/single-post/2020/05/04/left-behind-dcs-literacy-divide.

Watson, Michael. "On the Elites and Counter-Elites: Polling the Elites." Capitol Research Center, June 19, 2024. https://capitalresearch.org/article/on-the-elites-and-counter-elites-part-2/.

WBRC Digital Staff. "Birmingham-Southern College to Close May 31." WBRC 6 News, March 26, 2024. https://www.wbrc.com/2024/03/26/birmingham-southern-college-close-may-31/.

Webb, Merryn Somerset. "Central Banks Need to Stop the Mission Creep." Financial Times, August 27, 2021. https://www.ft.com/content/55faaeae-b1b3-428e-9214-5c565bacd9c0.

Weir, Margaret. "The American Middle Class and the Politics of Education." In *Social Contracts Under Stress: The Middle Classes of America, Europe, and Japan at the Turn of the Century*, edited by Olivier Zunz et al., 178–203. New York: Russell Sage, 2004.

Wexler, Natalie. "Problems With Lucy Calkins' Curriculum Go Beyond Reading—To Writing." Forbes, November 21, 2021. https://www.forbes.com/sites/nataliewexler/2021/11/21/problems-with-lucy-calkins-curriculum-go-beyond-reading-to-writing/.

Wiener-Bronner, Danielle. "Cracker Barrel Is in a Battle for Relevancy. One of Its Solutions Is Surprising." CNN, June 1, 2024. https://www.cnn.com/2024/06/01/business/cracker-barrel-relevant-early-bird/index.html.

Wikipedia. "COVID-19 Lab Leak Theory." July 27, 2024. https://en.wikipedia.org/w/index.php?title=COVID-19_lab_leak_theory&oldid=1236972684.

Wilcox, Brad. *Get Married: Why Americans Must Defy the Elites, Forge Strong Families, and Save Civilization*. Kindle. New York: Broadside, 2024.

Willard, Dallas. *The Divine Conspiracy*. San Francisco: HarperSanFrancisco, 1997.

Wilson, Claire. "The Replication Crisis Has Spread Through Science—Can It Be Fixed?" New Scientist, April 6, 2022. https://www.newscientist.com/article/mg25433810-400-the-replication-crisis-has-spread-through-science-can-it-be-fixed/.

Wimpfheimer, Barry Scott. "What Is Happening in the Humanities? Theory, Politics, and Protest." Sources Journal. https://www.sourcesjournal.org/articles/what-is-happening-in-the-humanities-theory-politics-and-protest.

Winfield, Nichole. "A Global Look at the Catholic Church's Sex Abuse Problem." AP News, February 21, 2019. https://apnews.com/general-news-8cb4daf509464bad8c13ef35d44a0fc5.

Wingfield, Mark. "BSK and Wake Forest Divinity Announce Master's Degree Changes." Baptist News Global, January 26, 2024. https://baptistnews.com/article/bsk-and-wake-forest-divinity-announce-masters-degree-changes/.

———. "SBC Executive Committee Financials Missing from Online Report for Third Year, While 2022 Audit Shows Trajectory That Is 'Not Sustainable.'" Baptist News Global, February 16, 2024. https://baptistnews.com/article/sbc-executive-committee-financials-missing-from-online-report-for-third-year-while-2022-audit-shows-trajectory-that-is-not-sustainable/.

Winter, Jessica. "The Rise and Fall of Vibes-Based Literacy." *The New Yorker*, September 1, 2022. https://www.newyorker.com/news/annals-of-education/the-rise-and-fall-of-vibes-based-literacy.

Wiseman, Kathleen K. "Emotional Process in Organizations." In *Understanding Organizations: Applications of Bowen Family Systems Theory*, edited by Ruth Riley Sagar and Kathleen Klaus Wiseman, locs. 803–1002. Washington, DC: Georgetown University Family Center, 1982. Kindle.

Withe, Aaron. "Oregon Just Dropped All Graduation Standards, Failing All of Its Students in the Name of 'Equity.'" *The Hill*, November 2, 2023. https://thehill.com/opinion/education/4288044-oregon-just-dropped-all-graduation-standards-failing-all-of-its-students-in-the-name-of-equity/.

Witkowski, Rachel. "Average U.S. Mortgage Payment Skyrockets 46% in One Year." Forbes, September 29, 2023. https://www.forbes.com/advisor/mortgages/average-u-s-mortgage-payment-skyrockets-46-in-one-year/.

The Wall Street Journal. "Salary Increase by Major." WSJ.com. https://www.wsj.com/public/resources/documents/info-Degrees_that_Pay_you_Back-sort.html.

Woldehanna, Tassew, and Chanie Ejigu Berhie. "Beyond Academic Learning Loss: The Effect of School Closures on Students' Socio-Emotional Skills." RISE Programme, October 24, 2023. https://riseprogramme.org/blog/beyond-academic-learning-loss-SEL-dropout.

Wosen, Jonathan, and Angus Chen. "Dana-Farber Expands Studies to Be Retracted to 6, Plus 31 to Be Corrected over Mishandled Data." STAT, January 22, 2024. https://www.statnews.com/2024/01/22/dana-farber-research-retractions-corrections/.

YCharts. "US Retail Gas Price (I:USRGP)." https://ycharts.com/indicators/us_gas_price.

Younis, Mohamed. "Confidence in U.S. Military Lowest in Over Two Decades." Gallup, July 31, 2023. https://news.gallup.com/poll/509189/confidence-military-lowest-twodecades.aspx.

Zelizer, Julian. "Bill Clinton's Nearly Forgotten 1992 Sex Scandal." CNN, April 6, 2016. https://www.cnn.com/2016/04/06/opinions/zelizer-presidential-election-campaign-scandals-bill-clinton/index.html.

Zuckerman, Diana, and Sarah Pedersen. "Child Abuse and Father Figures: Which Kind of Families Are Safest to Grow Up In?" National Center for Health Research. https://www.center4research.org/child-abuse-father-figures-kind-families-safest-grow/.

www.ingramcontent.com/pod-product-compliance
Lightning Source LLC
Chambersburg PA
CBHW071842270326
41929CB00013B/2073